MENOPAUSE NATURALLY

MENOPAUSE NATURALLY

Kitty Campion

Newleaf

Newleaf

an imprint of

Gill & Macmillan Ltd

Goldenbridge

Dublin 8

with associated companies throughout the world

www.gillmacmillan.ie

© Kitty Campion 1998

0 7171 2716 8

Index compiled by Helen Litton

Print origination by

O'K Graphic Design, Dublin

Printed by ColourBooks Ltd, Dublin

A catalogue record is available for this book from the British Library.

3 5 4

CONTENTS

WARNING

While the herbal remedies and preparations given in this book are considered suitable for self-help, the author stresses that it is advisable to consult a professional for individual advice before embarking on any self-help treatment.

The publishers of this book cannot be held liable for any errors, omissions or actions that may be taken as a consequence of using it.

FOREWORD

It is a great pleasure to write the foreword for a book which I believe is desperately needed by many women in today's society. Once again Kitty has excelled herself in producing a book in which she shares some of her vast knowledge of women's problems.

Over the past ten years I have often asked myself why ever more women are consulting me about menopausal problems. The question is quickly answered by the fact that the three major influences on our wellbeing — food, water and air — are continually deteriorating in quality, and because these have a very marked effect on hormonal changes, problems associated with hormonal imbalance have become a daily subject in the doctor's or practitioner's consulting room.

When we consider that our diet consists of foods containing ever more additives and sugar, that the use of herbicides and pesticides is increasing and that much of our food is now grown by artificial means, it is hardly surprising that the direct result is a steady increase in hormonal problems. Stress — very much the 'in' word of the moment — is another factor; we must not forget that every negative influence causes not only skeletal problems but also emotional imbalance, which can in turn threaten and disrupt the hormonal balance.

Kitty Campion is a very experienced practitioner who has a special interest in women's problems and she has conducted extensive research into the menopause. In particular, I am very impressed by the depth of her research into hormone replacement therapy. As a practitioner with over forty years' experience, I would be delighted if I could say that I have never come across a woman suffering side-effects as a result of taking HRT. Unfortunately this is not so. I have seen cases of thrombosis and phlebitis, as well as possible cancers, fibroids and many negative effects on the liver and pancreas, that have resulted from this treatment. If there were no alternatives to HRT, I could understand why a woman would subject her body to it. However, there are many natural alternatives which not only relieve the menopausal symptoms but also have a much more positive effect on the body as a whole.

Kitty has answered many questions on this subject. She has suggested alternative methods for easing the situation, whether it be through diet, dietary supplementation such as vitamins, minerals and trace elements, herbal preparations or exercise. In addition, she has covered many other ways in which women can help themselves through the menopause naturally.

It is with great interest and respect that I have read this book. And I would have no hesitation whatsoever in advising any woman approaching or going through the menopause to read it. Not only will she find a wealth of information on how to come through the menopause as naturally and as trouble free as possible, but she will find advice on how to protect herself from the many symptoms that can make this very natural time of life unpleasant.

I often come across queries relating to menopausal problems when I give lectures in the United States. Many vain American women have attacked me by saying that taking HRT is the only way to help them avoid getting a wrinkled and dried-out prune face! This is not at all true, for there are many other, more natural ways to maintain a beautiful skin, as this book shows. Many American women also moan that once they turn fifty they will no longer be attractive to men. What absolute nonsense! Let me say that once a woman turns fifty, she has many years of experience behind her and, drawing from this fund of wisdom and self-knowledge, should take the opportunity to live her life as joyfully and healthily as she possibly can.

This book is essential reading for every woman approaching the menopause, and I am sure it will become an invaluable addition to the bookshelf of many bedside cabinets.

Jan de Vries
D.Ho.med.D.O.M.R.O., N.D.M.R.N., D.Ac., M.B.Ac.A.

INTRODUCTION

I began to study herbal medicine in my early thirties, spurred on by a chronic and seemingly intractable bowel problem. I originally trained as a professional chef and spent much of my youth in private houses and hotels in Europe and America happily filling myself with gallons of cream and alcohol in true old-fashioned *haute cuisine* style. My passionate interest in whole foods, vegetarianism and finally veganism did not come as a Saul-on-the-road-to-Damascus experience. It began gently enough when I first went into practice as a medical herbalist fifteen years ago and started to rage, full flood, as I was confronted by a burgeoning number of patients who, through sheer ignorance, were quite literally digging their own graves with their cutlery. These then are the mainstays of my practice — diet and herbal medicine — though I am trained in iridology and five different types of body work including colonic irrigation, a topic guaranteed to bring any dinner party to a grinding halt.

I chose to stay and practise in Stoke-on-Trent partly because I studied for my PhD at a university nearby but mainly because it is a disadvantaged and highly polluted area which cries out for good practitioners to re-educate and make a real difference to the community. I ardently believe that 'there is nothing in the world that is so transitory and fragile as a snowflake and nothing so irresistible as an avalanche, which is simply millions of snowflakes. So that if each one of us, little snowflakes, just does our part, we will be an irresistible force.' [1]

I like to think I have helped to make a difference to the community in which I have lived, and I'm now moving on to London. It seems an appropriate time for change as I enter my fiftieth year and begin to notice and welcome tiny signs of the Change in myself. The majority of my patients are women and many of these have grown with me and are entering the menopause or are out the other side and enjoying their Wise Women years.

That I am a woman to whom other women gravitate doesn't surprise me. Centuries ago throughout Europe it was indeed the 'wise women' who gathered roots and herbs for medicinal use. When women lost this control and were condemned to being burned for knowing too much or demoted to the subordinate role of nurse, men began to rule the medical profession and much of it they designed for their own convenience. Men who have neither vagina nor uterus still dominate gynaecology and until recently labour wards were constructed for the convenience of the doctor, not the labouring mother. I practise so successfully because I can see women the way they are, not as men or even women would like them to be, and I teach them to view themselves in a new light — to live heroically rather than traditionally, to honour their innate beauty and power.

The baby boom at the end of the Second World War has ensured more women are entering the Change now than at any other time in history. I tell my patients the good news: that 80 per cent of women achieve menopause without any assistance or any difficulty; that it is not a deficiency state that needs to be medicalised; that many of my patients report stronger orgasms after menopause and more enjoyable, liberated sex; that bone mass can be easily increased by diet and exercise; that there are many reliable herbal allies that can be used, without harmful side-effects, should they be needed. Above all, I tell them that menopause is a time to be celebrated, and this surprises many of them, duped as they are by the flawed studies relentlessly publicised by the pharmaceutical industry, shored up by allopathic doctors (of which more in Chapter Two).

The first chapter of this book gives the basic outline of what the menopause is; it explains female anatomy and how a woman's health, mental, physical and spiritual, is so intimately bound up with this, as well as the role of oestrogen and progesterone. Chapter Two exposes all the medical myths surrounding HRT and osteoporosis. Chapter Three explains why specific eliminative channels need special care during this period of transition and how to achieve this naturally, and Chapter Four presents diet as the bedrock of all good health and outlines special foods which are specifically helpful during the menopause. Chapter Five details the problems which may occur during the menopause; it explains how to assist yourself herbally and enlarges on the mind–body link. Chapter Six tells you how to put all of this into practice practically, preparing your own herbal formulations, for internal and external use. Chapter Seven, meanwhile, gives a list of herbs that are specifically helpful to women in the menopause, explaining in detail their effects and applications. The botanical index at the back of the book will help you to cross-check the Latin names of herbs if you are confused as to what to order (many herbs have several 'common' names) and the Resources Directory will, I hope, prove invaluable as a reference section for where to buy your herbs from, along with various associations and workshops which may prove useful.

If making up your own preparations seems too daunting or your health problem is not easily solved or has been inaccurately diagnosed, I would encourage you to seek the help of a professional medical herbalist (see Resources Directory). My advice is to go initially by personal recommendation if you can. I have never had need to advertise. I have a clinic overflowing with referrals from other enthusiastic and satisfied patients and this must surely be the best recommendation of all. True healing, I often think, is a joining of the heart, an indelible linking between yourself and your practitioner which involves dedication, commitment, a sense of adventure and, above all, love. When I reach out to a person I am working with and offer them my love and understanding, I find them eager to know the truth I can reveal, and their openness to this love, understanding and truth makes them somehow more than they were before, while at the same time I myself become more. That is why I am here.

Kitty Campion

ONE

Back to Basics

LET'S TAKE AN INVENTORY

There is an inherent bliss in being female in which I revel. Yet it is something which a distressing number of the women I meet have lost sight of. Some because they are bogged down in wifely duties or worn out trying to be Superwoman, others because they find it impossible to live up to a sex symbol image and others because they are crippled with the horrifying conviction that anatomy is destiny.

And so it is, but only partly. It is true that women walk differently from men, they throw differently, bulge in different places and have a few different internal organs, but not all of the differences are apparent in monthly centrefolds. When I was a teenager a woman could be defined more easily by what she could not do as by what she could. Now centuries of women's self-abnegation are being atoned for. Integrity, delight, commitment, bravery and intelligence are winning through and this recent acknowledgement of female competence is intoxicating. It embraces taking responsibility for our own healthcare, appreciating, evaluating and treasuring our wonderful bodies in a totally new way.

Aristotle thought that women's bodies were entirely inferior to men's, even that their mouths contained fewer teeth! Similarly absurd notions about women's bodies persist today. It is thought that women's hair grows faster. False. They cannot get erections. Untrue. (There are in fact three places on a woman's body that become erect with arousal.) Their skin is softer. Erroneous. They have fewer muscles. Again untrue.

How you think of your body depends on your upbringing, the

things you have heard that men do or do not like, and the endless comparisons you may have made between your own and others' bodies. The same is true of men, of course, but when you look at yourself you do not see a sexual object, simply a mirror image of what other women see when they look at themselves. Yet you know that when a man looks at you he sees something different. It is unfortunate because a woman's body is, of course, more than just erect nipples and pouting lips.

As we will see, the overall health of a woman, emotional, physical and spiritual, is intimately bound up with the health of her reproductive organs, which are mostly hidden from external inspection.

OUTER FEMALE REPRODUCTIVE ORGANS

The first and most obvious feature of a mature woman is the pubic hair. This grows out of the pubis and the outer lips of the vulva (labia majora). The pubis (mons veneris) is the rounded fatty area covered in hair that lies in front of the pubic symphysis, the area at which the pubic bone meets the hip girdle. Pubic hair on the vulva is there to protect the outside of the vagina and the clitoris. The vulva sweats more than any other part of the body and its secretions respond to emotional as well as physical stimuli.

The clitoris, which varies in length from a quarter to one inch (0.5–2.5 cm), is a small piece of erectile tissue that is essential to every female orgasm. Just like its male counterpart, the penis, it comes complete with shaft and glans. The shaft is hidden under a hood and the glans sticks out. The clitoris has hollow areas which fill with blood during sexual arousal causing it to become erect.

The hood, which covers the shaft of the clitoris (just like the uncircumcised hood of a penis), is attached to the labia minora, the inner lips of the vulva, which also swell during sexual arousal, and are hairless and shiny and are often a darker colour than the outer lips. After the menopause the hair covering the labia majora tends to become sparser and can turn grey. Both labial lips usually lose some of their tissue and become thinner, exuding less moisture and so becoming friable and less elastic.

Both the urinary and vaginal openings are cupped by the vulval lips. The urinary opening is just between the vagina and the clitoris, which is why it can become sore after prolonged intercourse. The vaginal opening is situated between the perineum and the urinary opening. The perineum is the whole area lying between the vagina and the anus.

The hymen is a thin fold of membrane at the entrance to the vagina and comes in many shapes and thicknesses. Little folds of tissue remain even after it has been stretched, and it may be entirely absent even in a virgin. That you only lose your hymen with intercourse is a myth; it can just as easily be lost through the stretching involved in exercise.

INNER FEMALE REPRODUCTIVE ORGANS

Just inside the vagina are the two Batholin's glands, which lie under the surface on either side of the entrance and are therefore not easy to see. They produce mucus but do not provide much vaginal lubrication during intercourse, contrary to what was commonly believed.

The vagina lies between the bladder and the rectum at a 45 degree angle when the body is upright. A 4 in. (10 cm) tube made extremely elastic by many folds of skin within, it is capable of considerable expansion during childbirth and to a lesser degree during intercourse. It may be fractionally longer in taller than in smaller women but in every woman it balloons to within a millimetre or two of the same diameter during arousal. The outer third of the vagina is sensitive to touch while the rest has almost no nerve endings at all, which is why penis size is largely irrelevant.

The vagina is lined with a special covering of cells known as squamous epithelium. These are thin, scaly, pink and shiny, quite unlike our outer skin. The walls are kept flexible by being constantly bathed in fluid that seeps through them, a fluid that is composed of glycogen, discarded cells from the upper layer of tissue and Doederlein's basilis. These useful organisms convert glycogen to lactic acid which inhibits the growth of many infections and therefore renders washing or douching of the vagina quite unnecessary.

You will have noticed that vaginal secretion changes both in amount and appearance during your menstrual cycle and over the years. Before puberty the vagina does not produce a discharge and the first appearance of one is often a sign that the first period is about to take place.

Vaginal lubrication will accelerate during sexual excitement, physical exertion or nervousness. Before a period it can look a bit like semolina, the result of the increased shedding of epithelial cells. All vaginal secretions have a fairly noticeable smell which is perfectly pleasant and slightly musky in odour when fresh, becoming fishy only when one has not washed recently. Most men find the musky smell quite exciting. After menopause the secretion will lessen and the walls of the vagina can become thinner, paler, less flexible and more fragile.

The pelvic floor muscles surround the vagina, urethra and anus and support the lower organs. If they are weak, stretched or cut during a poorly executed episiotomy following childbirth, it can result in a prolapsed uterus or bladder, or in incontinence. However, the pelvic floor muscles can be strengthened by Kegel exercises (see Chapter Five, 'Bladder Problems'), particularly if you concentrate on the pubococcygeus muscle, the one you use to control the flow of urine.

The uterus, when not pregnant, is about the size of a balled fist. This thick-walled muscular organ rests between the bladder and the rectum. The bladder is beneath the abdominal wall, the uterus stands behind it and the rectum is nearest the backbone. The narrower part of the uterus, the cervix, protrudes into the top part of the vaginal canal. The cervix is sensitive to pressure and you can touch it with your fingers. If you have never had a baby, it feels like the end of your nose with a small dimple in it, which is the entrance to the uterus. If you have had a baby, it may feel more like a rounded chin. The uterus shifts during the course of the menstrual cycle so some days you may find it difficult to reach the cervix. The entrance into the uterus through the cervix is about the size of a very thin straw and is called the os.

The two Fallopian tubes, which look like backward-facing ram's horns, run back and out from the top of the uterus and each end in a fringed funnel shape which partially embraces but does not touch the ovaries. The tubes themselves are so small that only a very thin needle can penetrate them and some of the cells inside the mucous membrane lining are ciliated (hairlike), moving and waving like the arms of a sea anemone. This induces a current in the fluids circulating in the pelvic cavity running all the way down from the ovaries through the Fallopian tubes and into the uterus.

The ovaries hang from the ligaments near the open end of the Fallopian tubes like two unshelled almonds, surrounded by a protective mass of fat. During girlhood they are shiny and smooth, roughening and puckering during the reproductive years till, during menopause, they shrink, harden and turn whitish blue. Ovaries produce eggs, hence the small gap between the ovary and the corresponding Fallopian tube which allows the egg to float freely after it bursts from the ovary. The ciliated cells at the end of Fallopian tube waft the egg into it and down into the uterus. In rare cases, if the egg misses the Fallopian tube and is fertilised, it can result in an abdominal pregnancy — that is, outside the uterus. The ovaries also produce the hormones oestrogen and progesterone, whose function we will explore later in this chapter.

For women having difficulty visualising their reproductive anatomy, I ask them to think of the vagina as a flattened toilet roll supporting an inverted pear, the tip of which sticks into the top of the roll as the cervix. From either side of the pear are two electrical wires which end in unshelled almonds (the Fallopian tubes and ovaries respectively). That seems to do the trick.

ENERGY AND A WOMAN'S ANATOMY

More interesting to me than the fine anatomical detail is the energy associated with a woman's reproductive anatomy.

There is an energy field that surrounds every living thing and all of this energy is laden with information. That this electromagnetic field exists has been indisputably proven by Kirlian photography (a method evolved in the 1950s by the Russia engineer Semyou Kirlian), which shows up the changing pattern of colours that constitutes the outline of living beings. This technique is now used by the Russians to diagnose disease which cannot be discovered by any other means. Through it they are finding that in most illnesses there is a pre-clinical phase where physical symptoms have yet to manifest and they have proved that it is possible to predict a disease by photographing this phase.

This electromagnetic field has been found to carry our emotional as well as physical energy. The emotions from our life's experience — our personal relationships, belief patterns and attitudes, reactions to events, whether disturbing or uplifting — stamp themselves on our biological systems and partially contribute to the formation of our cell tissue, which in turn generates a quality of energy that reflects these emotions.

It is thus no surprise to me that physical ailments of the reproductive organs seem to occur as a result of troubles in a woman's personal life or job. A woman with a problem in the vagina, vulva or cervix, for instance, may be feeling forced to do something that is abhorrent to her. The source of this abhorrence may lie far back in memories of incest, childhood violation, confusion about sexual identity or guilt about sexuality in general. She may be trading sexual favours in return for financial, physical or emotional security. Or she may be feeling corralled and controlled by a manipulative partner or work colleague. Whatever the situation, she feels trapped, unable to change the negative aspects of what has become an unhealthy relationship or to get out altogether. If she is afraid to leave, for whatever reason, she is portraying what is known psychoanalytically as a 'prostitute archetype', and her physical symptoms (chronic vulvitis and vaginitis, cervical dysphasia and even cancer) are diseases commonly documented in prostitutes.

A study conducted back in the 1950s showed that women with cervical cancer were much more likely to have a history of poor sexual adjustment, lower incidence of orgasm during sexual intercourse, and even an active dislike of intercourse. Characteristically such women have experienced an early rejection, growing up in a home lacking a guiding male figure.[1]

Similarly, the good health of the ovaries, Fallopian tubes and uterus depend upon a woman feeling in control, powerful, stable and able to express herself creatively. If she stays trapped in a relationship because she feels she cannot survive alone, emotionally or economically, or she feels frustrated by various competing needs, this can manifest itself in her reproductive organs in the form of cysts and fibroids, chronic pelvic pain or endometriosis.

Visualise the uterus as your innermost sense of self, the sacred vessel in which you house your dreams and all the many creations to which you would like to give birth. Its health will be endangered if you do not believe in yourself or if you are excessively critical of yourself.

The ovaries also react to threats, whether emotional or physical, from the outside world. They are the female equivalent of a man's testicles. A man is said to have 'balls' when he faces the challenges of a dangerous world with acts of derring-do. A woman needs to understand how to use her 'balls' in less gung-ho, more life-enhancing and creative ways. Nurturing babies, tending gardens, writing, painting, sculpting, all spring from our special ovarian wisdom which needs special cultivation to yield creative results. If a woman's creative wisdom is suffocated because of fears and insecurities about the outside world, ovarian problems can arise, from benign cysts to cancer.

As we have seen, all disease begins in the energy field and finally manifests itself physically. For our bodies to be truly well we must transform our consciousness first and hence our energy fields. I see far too many women licking their wounds from the past without ever healing them, or worrying about a future which may never happen. We cannot heal anything unless we live mindfully in the now. One of my teachers used to urge us to be present to our feelings and, when an emotion surfaces from the subconscious, to be willing to stop at once, experience the present moment and breathe freely and deeply. It's invaluable advice for true healing.

THE BALANCING ACT

Fundamental to a woman's health on both an emotional and physical plane is a well-balanced hormonal system. As Leslie Kenton affirms in her excellent book *Passage to Power*, 'so central are hormonal events to how women think and feel that it would be no exaggeration to say that the female endocrine system is an interface between body and spirit'.[2]

SO WHAT ARE HORMONES?

These are chemicals, present in minute amounts, that transport messages from one part of the body to the other. Produced in specialised glands, the endocrine glands, they are circulated in the blood to specific body cells where they make their presence felt.

Imagine the endocrine glands as an orchestra. The pituitary gland is the conductor, the thyroid gland is the first violin — the leader — the pancreas the woodwind section, the adrenal glands the brass and the ovaries the percussion. Governing what would otherwise degenerate into chaos is the pineal gland as composer and the thymus gland as the score. So the endocrine system is all melody and counterpoint, tone and volume; it speeds up, slows down, changes key, producing the individual music of homeostatis, the finely tuned balance of activity within the body.

Hormones are so potent that a millionth of an ounce of one hormone is enough to produce an effect. Individual hormonal molecules are too minute to be seen even under the most powerful microscope. They are like chemical keys that access metabolic locks in the cells. The pituitary gland produces follicle-stimulating hormone and luteinising hormone, both of which control the ovaries, growth hormones which regulate the growth of the body, and prolactin which is responsible for milk production. The thyroid gland produces thyroid hormone which keeps all the body systems active, and parathyroid hormone which maintains blood calcium levels. The adrenal glands produce adrenalin which primes the body for action, and cortisone which helps manage stress levels. Insulin, made in the pancreas, maintains blood-sugar levels. Meanwhile, oestrogen and progesterone, produced in the ovaries, control menstruation and maintain pregnancy.

We all march to different hormonal drumbeats and every woman has her adrenal trumpet blasts now and again. The pituitary gland sets the pace, determining how other hormones will be made and distributed. Maybe the adrenal brass will predominate or perhaps the thyroid will lead the way. If discord results, harmony is difficult to restore, for hormonal imbalance is one of the most difficult patterns of disease to correct quickly.

Once hormones have completed their tasks, they are either broken down by the cells in which they have acted or are sent to the liver for breakdown. The resulting compounds are either excreted or used again to manufacture new hormone molecules. Overall endocrine balance can contribute more to your whole health and wellbeing than any other body system.

HORMONES AND THEIR CHEMICAL INTERRELATIONSHIP

Pituitary

The pituitary gland is profoundly affected by light, the amount of which varies according to the time of year; hence the lowering of spirits during the shorter days of winter. Other endocrine glands respond similarly to changes in the environment: thus it is not unusual to skip a period when travelling for several weeks or more (thyroid), to pile on weight or drop it when anxious (adrenal glands) or to vomit with travel sickness (pancreas). Theoretically the pituitary controls all this, but the thyroid can speed up to such a degree that pituitary participation is lessened, causing hormone signalling control to devolve temporarily to the other glands. Several plants, particularly sage and ginseng, stimulate pituitary function directly.

Thyroid

The twin lobes of the thyroid govern the state of your hair, skin and nervous system, including your metabolism, and the tiny twinned parathyroid glands are responsible for how calcium is absorbed (of which more in Chapter Two). Periods of intense hormonal activity, like puberty, pregnancy, childbirth and the menopause, are notorious for sudden swings in weight when thyroid hormones can become unpredictable. Skullcap, mugwort, blue flag, poke root, pulsatilla, sarsaparilla and sea vegetables all help to relieve the symptoms of thyroid imbalance but they take time and, because the thyroid is so delicately balanced, should not be prescribed by an amateur. Bach Flower Remedies, which treat the spiritual/emotional aspects of illness, work particularly well on the thyroid (see Chapter Six).

Pancreas

The pancreas is an extremely complex organ, second only to the liver in its complexity. The stabilising of blood-sugar levels is the most important of its endocrine functions. Pancreatic enzymes of all sorts behave better when sweet is balanced by sour in food tastes during a meal. Fennel, dandelion, alfalfa, fenugreek, horseradish, papaya and cider vinegar are all useful here.

Adrenal Glands

Worry wears out the adrenal glands. Keep your adrenal hormones stable and you will have superabundant energy and the ability to fend off viral, bacterial, environmental and even circumstantial attack with ease. Any trauma, emotional or physical, conjures adrenal response. Hence the frequent application of cortisone in allopathic (conventional) medicine because it combats pain so quickly. The problem is that the administering of cortisone jet-propels the adrenal glands at the expense of the thyroid and in particular control of calcium distribution by the parathyroid glands. Bones can become porous and fragile, the skin mottled and thin, and the hair dank and lack-lustre. The emotions governed by the thyroid may be adversely affected, and long-term application of synthetic cortisone can cause depression and emotional distress. Foods rich in vitamin C can help here, such as rose hips, parsley, all the berries, citrus fruit and leafy green vegetables.

Several of the adrenal glands are involved in sexual and reproductive orchestration. Progesterone is fairly close in molecular structure to aldosterone, the fluid-retaining hormone. I have observed that menopausal women are very susceptible to oedema simply because this is a vulnerable changeover time when the aldosterone signal can become confused.

Adrenal hormones work closely with those in the ovaries. The sexual urge is determined by the adrenal hormone levels, the act itself by the ovarian ones. Aggression and sex should be like the balancing pans on a weighing scale, drive and enthusiasm leading to peace and pleasure. An abundance of adrenal hormones will stimulate their endocrine partners, the ovaries, into action.

Androgens

During the menopause the ovarian hormones dwindle. Because menopausal women's ovaries produce less androgen, it has been postulated that this is why libido levels may decrease in certain menopausal women. But you need to remember that androgenic hormones are also manufactured by the adrenal glands, the skin, muscle, brain, pineal gland, hair follicles and body fat. These hormones, as well as being associated with creating a sense of wellbeing, are responsible for sexual response and libido. During the menopause these other organs normally take over from the ovaries in the production of androgen, but chronic stress over a long period of time leads to adrenal depletion which may result in various menopausal difficulties. I have observed that the stronger a woman's adrenal glands and the better her nutrition, the easier she flies through the menopause (see Chapter Three, 'Adrenal Support').

Thymus
The thymus gland, housed just behind the sternum in the chest, though largely ignored by the allopathic medical profession because in humans it begins to shrink in childhood and is therefore regarded as useless, is partially responsible for optimising the general immune process of the whole body which is vital to the basic function of life.

Pineal Gland
Practitioners of conventional medicine tend also to condemn the pineal gland as useless too, but this is where we house our animal instincts. Have you ever taken an immediate liking or dislike to someone? Some people call it 'chemistry' but it is actually the use of that deeper inner instinct surfacing in your not-so-primitive pineal gland informing you what is good or bad for you. Women, I've noticed, trust their pineals more than men do!

HORMONAL CONTROL OF THE FEMALE MONTHLY CYCLE
The female monthly cycle is controlled by various reproductive hormones including oestrogen, progesterone, follicle-stimulating hormone (FSH) and luteinising hormone (LH). When oestrogen and progesterone levels are low at the beginning of each menstrual cycle, the pituitary gland excretes FSH which stimulates an ovarian follicle to grow. As the oestrogen level rises, it inhibits FSH and stimulates the pituitary to release another hormone, LH, which triggers ovulation generally midway through the menstrual cycle. The ovum — that is, the egg — is released from the follicle in the ovary at ovulation and passes down the Fallopian tube. Then the ovaries secrete progesterone

which prevents any further ovulation taking place, at least during that cycle, and if the egg is not fertilised the lining of the womb breaks down and is passed out of the body in the monthly bleed or period. During this time levels oestrogen and progesterone plunge and the cycle begins all over again. By the time the menopause is reached only a few eggs remain in the ovaries.

Without the rising levels of the oestrogen in the first half of the menstrual cycle sending a message back to the ovaries to produce smaller amounts of FSH, the levels of FSH in the bloodstream keep rising. So a period can take place without ovulation occurring but with escalating levels of FSH and LH. A blood test can be taken to determine the levels of FSH and LH. During the menopause the pituitary gland and the ovaries begin subtly to change — ovulation decreases and the FSH and LH levels gradually increase. This is because when the ovaries are no longer producing eggs, the pituitary gland continues to send out FSH and LH simply because it is not getting the normal hormonal messages from the developing egg to tell it to slow down. Quite why this happens is not clearly understood.

When these hormones reach a specifically high level in the blood, they are pronounced in the menopausal range. This may not stay steady but may flow back and forth for a while and it is possible to get pregnant during this time.

Oestrogen and Progesterone and Their Effects on the Female Body

Oestrogen

- is responsible for our curvy shape, development of the breasts and pubic hair
- causes the womb lining to thicken
- acts as a cervical softener and prepares vaginal secretions of the right texture and moisture to lubricate the vagina during intercourse and encourage sperm to ascend the vagina
- stimulates cell growth in both the uterus and breast so increasing the risk of cancer of the breast and womb
- encourages water retention

- lays down fat stores
- exacerbates blood clotting
- depresses libido and can make you more prone to headaches and depression.

Progesterone
- maintains pregnancy
- actively protects against the worst effects of oestrogen (cancer, fibrocystic diseases of the breast, blood clotting, lowered libido and depression)
- aids diuresis naturally
- helps burn fat.

As levels of these hormones gently dwindle during the menopause, the pattern of periods change and, in a healthy body, such changes are experienced as relatively smooth and comfortable. The problem with modern gynaecology is that it treats these delicate, carefully interwoven patterns of change as if they were the individual symptoms of a disease rather than part of complex whole. As one shift happens in the body, so everything follows. Fire hormone replacement therapy into a woman's body and the result is highly damaging because it upsets everything else. You cannot cast a stone into water without causing ripples to spread right to the very edge of the pool.

We will be examining this topic in greater detail in the following chapter, but let us first take a look at what shapes our attitudes towards the menopause, and at the 'ageist' culture responsible for creating HRT.

WHAT IS THE MENOPAUSE?

The menopause — literally, a 'stop' in a woman's 'menses' — is a very important rite of passage. No comparable phenomenon takes place in a man's body. Men can remain fertile throughout their lives, and although testosterone levels drop with age, they continue to produce viable new sperm. The menopause is a good time to pause — literally; to rest for a moment and re-examine your values, to enjoy your accomplishments and, most of all, to love and appreciate your female processes and the changes in these. It is a beginning not an ending; a time for looking forward, not one of sadness or regret; a time for a renewal, not for a fear of ageing. Paavo Airola puts it beautifully: 'Menopause is a divinely designed phase in a woman's life, with the purpose of liberating her from duties as pro-creator with God and giving her time for self-improvement, for the perfection of her human and divine characteristics, and her spiritual growth.'[3]

The ancient Greeks used to call the menopause the climacteric meantime, regarding it simply as one of the seven-year periods forming the life cycle — 'a step in the ladder'. They understood it as a time when gradually, gently and gracefully a woman is relieved of the burden of being able to have children. Indeed, it is true that nature has designed the menopause to be a slow downward shift in the process of producing oestrogen by the ovaries, with minimal side-effects. The problem is, hypnotised as we are by our ageist culture, many women expect their minds and bodies to deteriorate as they age, instead of remaining strong, vital and sexually attractive. One of my simplest but most powerful affirmations is 'If you think so, it *is* so'. So really it is up to you. What are your beliefs on the subject, who are your role models? Do you trust your body to remain strong and healthy during the menopause and beyond? If you have to, would you change your family script about the menopause? I have observed many of my patients who have watched mothers, sisters, grandmothers or aunts going through a difficult time in the menopause and unconsciously following suit. It seems their expectations of menopausal problems lead to them experiencing precisely the same ailments. This does not surprise me. In the words of Louise Hayes, the famous metaphysical teacher who healed herself of various gynaecological cancers by first 'healing' her head and her heart: 'Every thought you think is creating your future.'[4]

WHEN DOES THE MENOPAUSE BEGIN?
Interestingly most women go through the menopause during the same span of time as their mothers did. Some have worked conscientiously to alter the genetic and unconscious 'tapes' that bind them to their mothers, but these are the exception. On average women in the West enter the menopause aged about fifty-one — forty-eight in the USA,

fifty-two in the UK. The whole rite of passage may take 6–13 years, and during this time periods may stop for a few months and then re-start. Some women joke that there are many pauses in their blood flow before it stops, hence the nomenclature 'menopause'.

Smokers usually have an earlier menopause by about two years because smoking has an effect on the secretion of oestrogen from the ovaries, causing a decrease in levels of this hormone. Women who have suffered with pre-menstrual syndrome (PMS) often begin the menopause a year later on average. A hysterectomy where the ovaries are left intact can accelerate the onset of the menopause by five years. Women with fibroids are known to have higher levels of oestrogen and therefore may postpone their menopause. Plump women do the same because extra oestrogen is manufactured in their fat cells. Conversely, malnourished women and women who have never had children often have an earlier menopause.

But the wonderful, positive news is that, regardless of when they start, 80 per cent of women have a normal menopause and experience only minor symptoms, if any.

AGEIST CULTURE
The medical profession would have us believe that menopause is a deficiency disease, not one of life's natural processes. In our culture women are regarded primarily as baby-producing machines and when they can no longer fulfil this biological function they are seen to be withering, atrophying and drying out. As a culture we worship the freshness and ebullience of youth and preach that ageing people become depressed, tired, forgetful, incontinent, creaky and slow.

Applied to menopausal women, this picture is far from accurate and has come about as the result of a relatively small group of women who consult the medical profession with menopausal problems. Those neither seeking nor needing medical advice, that is the *majority* of women, find the menopause far from the negative event it is typified to be. In a study conducted on such a group of healthy menopausal women, only 3 per cent expressed any regret of moving out of their reproductive years.[5]

Most menopausal women in the West expect to have to endure hot flushes, yet very few Japanese women appear to suffer from them, and the ! Kung culture in Africa simply do not have a word for them. In both cultures is this just because they do not get them or, more likely, is a hot flush thought about in an entirely different context and therefore not viewed as a problem?

Hot flushes are a natural phenomenon which I, as a medical herbalist, have to go to considerable trouble to induce as a means of treating viral and bacterial infections. This involves artificially raising the temperature of a patient with hot herbal drinks and baths, after which the temperature is lowered by wrapping the body in a cold, wet sheet. For every degree the body temperature is raised, the speed of the white blood cells which gobble up invading infection is accelerated by 10 per cent. So at a body temperature of 104 degrees, these blood cells are roaring through the body at 64 mph. Could it be that hot flushes are in fact designed to kill off viral and bacterial infections, thereby accelerating a woman's immune system as she enters the menopause?

AGEING
Contrary to popular belief, ageing does not begin with the menopause. The first signs happen long before a child is even born. For example, a twenty-week-old female foetus has more eggs in her ovaries than at any other time in her life and these begin to decay before she is even born. The lens of the eye, which enables it to focus on objects at varying distances, begins to lose some of its elasticity and is less able to focus from age ten onwards. Hearing loss, in the upper frequencies of sound, also begins around the age of ten.

On the other hand and according to the latest evidence on ageing, IQ and memory can remain pretty much intact throughout most of life; the picture of the brain as an ever-expanding sieve through which recent events and memories leak away is being revised in the light of new research on gerontology.

But ageing is still regarded by the orthodox medical profession as a condition that needs treating, and HRT as its way of 'treating' the menopause.

TWO

MISGUIDED MEDICINE

HORMONE REPLACEMENT THERAPY

What angers me about the modern medicalisation of the menopause is that it is treated as a disease, not a natural rite of passage. Why are we not allowing ourselves the gift of ageing naturally, of awakening to the wisdom of the elders? Our best ally, as we enter the menopause, is the Old One, the Wise Woman. Where is she in our culture? Discarded by a society which worships youth above all else. Discarded by modern medicine too, for it is only women over seventy who, together with pre-pubescent girls, are not hounded by a medical profession which insists on controlling every stage of a woman's hormonal processes. Why are women not badgered then? Because these are the two stages in a woman's life when she is, if anything, even more devalued culturally.

In a patriarchal society, as ours has been for thousands of years, which equates our sexuality with our ability to have children, there is something horrible about the medical profession's paternalistic pressure on women that they forever have pink, juicy genitals, firm breasts and peachy skin. The entrenched sexism of modern medicine reveals itself in all its obvious bias more clearly in the menopause than at any other time of a woman's passage through life. Frances McCrea has identified four themes that underlie the medical definition of menopause.

- Women's potential and function are biologically destined.
- Women's worth is determined by fecundity and attractiveness.
- Rejection of the female role will bring physical and emotional havoc to a woman.
- Ageing women are useless and repulsive.[1]

So are women to be defined merely as baby-producing machines who become worthless when they can no longer give birth? Is a natural bodily state — the menopause — a disease to be cured? It certainly seems so if it is deemed to have commercial potential by drugs companies as well as being seen as a means of social control designed to rob women of their power by exploiting their worries about ageing.

How did this state of medically inspired mass hypnosis come about? It began with the discovery of the contraceptive pill which in turn blossomed into a pharmaceutical search for ever wider applications of synthetic oestrogen. Sandra Coney, in her well-researched and hard-hitting book *The Menopause Industry*, explains:

> Medicine can create diseases to provide a market for new products developed by the pharmaceutical industry. There are two alternate scenarios in the development of drugs: biomedical scientists can go for a cure for a known illness, such as cancer; but new compounds are sometimes synthesised in the laboratory without anyone being initially clear what purpose they can be put to. The end result is a drug in need of a disease. The more broadly the disease can then be defined, the greater the treated population and the greater the potential sales. Well people and others experiencing social problems are obvious targets.[2]

Until the 1960s the menopausal woman remained unmolested by the pharmaceutical industry, but she was an obvious sitting duck for an all-out assault. Initially she was subjected to psychotropic drugs (for controlling depression), and hard on their heels came oestrogen, until by the 1990s the idea of menopause as a disease of oestrogen deficiency (just as diabetes is a disease of insulin deficiency) was firmly entrenched. And who would not be seduced by all the hyped-up marketing depicting hormone replacement therapy (HRT) — notice the word 'replacement' — as the fountain of youth, the protector against heart disease, osteoporosis, stroke, senile dementia and even inflammatory bowel disease?

THE ORIGINS OF HRT
Oestrogen therapy has been around since the 1930s. Originally called

oestrogen replacement therapy, because oestrogen only was used, its popularity plummeted when it was found to increase the risk of cancer of the womb and breast sevenfold. Progestogen, the synthetic version of progesterone, was added for 10–14 days every month and a new treatment was born — HRT. Progestogen was added to protect the endometrium from too much cell growth, and consequently cancer, and to cause a regular 'break-through' bleed.

HRT is a combination of steroids, the same steroids that make up the Pill. The difference between the Pill and HRT is that the Pill is now made up of synthetic steroids, whereas those that comprise HRT are natural, extracted from a pig's ovaries or a pregnant mare's urine (of which more on the subject later in the chapter). The progestogens used in the Pill and HRT are the same and because both medicines have so much in common they can induce the same catalogue of side-effects — headaches, weight gain, oedema (water retention) and depression.

A SUMMARY OF THE SIDE-EFFECTS OF HRT

Apart from the inconvenience of monthly breakthrough bleeding similar to a period, the effects of progesterone therapy, from ten to fourteen days a month, can include headaches, loss of energy, depression, lack of sexual interest and other emotional problems similar to those experienced by sufferers of pre-menstrual syndrome. *The Physician's Desk Reference*, an American publication which is obliged to list risks in much more depth than our watered-down British version, *MIMS (Monthly Index of Medical Specialities)*, lists the following side-effects of HRT:

- breast tenderness or enlargement
- mental depression
- weight gain or loss
- bloating
- thrombophlebitis (inflammation of the veins of the legs thereby increasing the danger of blood clots)
- increased blood pressure
- reduced carbohydrate tolerance
- reduced glucose tolerance

- abdominal cramps
- skin rashes
- hair loss
- vaginal thrush
- jaundice
- vomiting
- cystitis-like syndrome (caused by thinning of vaginal and urethral tissue rather than by bacteria)
- endometrial cancer.

All this besides the even more serious risks to health outlined below.

CONTRAINDICATIONS FOR HRT

In addition to these side-effects, certain women would do best to avoid taking HRT. Those who have had breast cancer or endometrial cancer or a history of liver disease or of thrombosis should definitely avoid HRT. Individuals who are heavy smokers, those with fibroids, endometriosis, otosclerosis, heart disease, hyperlipidaemia (a genetic predisposition to high cholesterol), high blood pressure or who suffer from migraines should all think twice before considering HRT.

MEDICAL MYTHS

We have looked at the medically acknowledged side-effects and contraindications for HRT. But what about the benefits of taking it? In my view, far from being the elixir of youth, HRT is in fact the biggest medical bungle of this century and every single claim made for it can be contested and disproved.

- HRT does not prevent osteoporosis. As soon as a woman stops taking it, even after ten years of use, bone mineral density catches up fast so that the bone mass of a 75-year-old woman who has never taken HRT matches that of one who has.[3] (The whole issue of osteoporosis and its treatment is covered in much greater detail later in this chapter.)
- HRT does not protect against heart disease, and studies suggesting that this is the case have been flawed in terms of selection, bias and assumptions made. Professor Jan Vandenbroucke, working at

Leidan University Hospital in Holland, concluded his vast review of all the individual studies concerning HRT and heart disease specifically with the sour observation: 'We should demand some colossal well-controlled trials before we let the genie of universal preventive prescription escape from the bottle.'[4]

- HRT does not protect against strokes and actually may induce them. It has a similar effect on the circulatory system as the Pill and can exacerbate high blood pressure, migraines and thrombosis.[5]

- HRT does not protect against senile dementia and Alzheimer's disease. Reduction in cognitive function of women on or off HRT is precisely the same.[6]

- HRT is psychologically addictive to about 15 per cent of women taking it. 'Oestrogens are psychoactive. They lift mood, can be given by injection and their use has powerful effects,' concluded Dr Susan Bewley, a gynaecologist at the University College Hospital, London, and her partner, Dr Thomas Bewley, one-time president of the Royal College of Psychiatrists.[7]

- Oestrogen replacement therapy can increase the risk of breast cancer by 60 per cent. (Remember oestrogen increases cell growth so it directly affects the most receptive parts of a woman to oestrogen — the womb and the breasts.) Combined HRT may even increase that risk, according to a huge study carried out on 23,244 women in 1989.[8]

- A study conducted in 1995 proved that women on oestrogen had a seven times greater risk of endometrial cancer.[9] With combined HRT the risk of endometrial cancer is three times greater than that. Worse still, hyperplasia (increased cell growth) does not stop once HRT itself is halted. Progesterone by itself needs to be taken for at least two years afterwards to keep the womb lining under control.[10]

- HRT, if taken for ten years, increases the risk of ovarian cancer by a stunning 70 per cent, according to a study carried out by the American Cancer Society on 200,000 women and reported in 1995.[11]

- Oestrogen replacement therapy doubles the risk of gall bladder disease, elevates blood pressure, exacerbates breast tenderness, depression and is even capable of changing the shape of the eyes.[12]

- Progesterone alters glucose and insulin levels, elevates calcium in the blood beyond normal levels, increases the risk of hepatitis, jaundice and liver cancer, urinary tract infections, excessive fluid in the body, worsens endometriosis and encourages virilisation (increased facial hair and a deeper voice).[13]

Reviewing so much research that proves hormone replacement therapy to be so deeply flawed, I am driven to the conclusion that HRT is actively dangerous and has no health benefits at all. What concerns me even more is that the highly profitable and slickly marketed menopause industry would have us believe that taking potent steroids is a normal way of life, that such mass intervention is acceptable (30 per cent of post-menopausal American women use HRT, as do 10 per cent of British and Australian women). If this trend continues, a quarter of post-menopausal women, two million in all, will be using it by the year 2000. The reason why this figure is so large is because the height of the post-war baby boom was 1948, which means that 1997–2000 are the unofficial 'years of menopause'.

In addition to concerns about the threat of HRT to personal health, there are moral issues at stake too.

DOWN ON THE FARM

Prempak-C and Premarin, two of the better-known brands of HRT, are both marketed by Wyeth-Ayerst and touted as 'natural' (which is undoubtedly true because they are manufactured from pregnant mares' urine). Although the company states that Premarin is unique because it contains a blend of ten biologically active components whereas alternative products contain just one or two, by no means all of the oestrogen in the mixture is natural to humans — and why would it be, coming as it does from horses? Some of these components behave like the synthetic ethanol oestradiol, present in the Pill, which affects liver metabolism by producing changes in blood clotting and blood-fat levels.

Most women, if they investigated exactly how this urine is farmed and collected, would refuse to take it on grounds of conscience. Every year of their fertile lives, 45,000 mares are deliberately put in foal to produce the raw material. For six months of the year, they are tethered in such small stalls that they are unable to walk backwards, forwards or even lie down. This, unsurprisingly, causes psychological frustration as well as oedema and swollen legs. The horses are kept permanently thirsty and limited to 6–8 gallons (29–38 litres) of water a day so the urine they produce is more concentrated with oestrogen, and they while away endless hours by licking hopefully round the water-tank lid. Enforced thirst is also a good financial move if you want to cut down transportation costs.

Then there is the medieval-looking urine-collecting device itself. A rubber urine bag and harness are strapped over the mare's vagina with elasticated hoses, fastenings are secured around her front and then run over a pulley attached to the ceiling in order to keep her immobilised. The urine runs down a tube into a plastic container or a pipe leading to the central collection tank where it is chilled, stored and sold at a profitable £10 a gallon.

Once the mare can no longer get pregnant, she is killed for horse meat, as are the majority of her foals.[14] There are many organisations concerned about this cruelty and they need your support. (See Resources Directory for addresses.)

IS 'NATURAL' PROGESTERONE THE ANSWER?

'Natural' progesterone has become the buzz menopausal product of the 1990s. Its proponents claim that it can help with a whole range of problems, from oedema and lack of libido, to fibroids and sciatica. When it first came to my attention, I had a strong sense of déjà-vu: most of these claims echoed those made in the 1960s when oestrogen was the miracle cure-all.

Then I investigated how it is made and found that, far from being natural, it is in fact synthesised from the rhizomes of wild yams by several chemical processes, in the same way as digitalis was once synthesised from foxgloves. The diosgenin in wild yam can only be extracted by alcohol and must then be synthesised to produce progesterone because progesterone itself is not naturally present in wild yam. In other words, if you eat yams your digestive system cannot extract progesterone from them because we lack the necessary enzymatic processes. So the term 'natural' progesterone is really one which identifies it as being an extract equivalent to the progesterone produced by humans and thereby differentiates it from the synthetic progestogen used in HRT.

During the menopause production of both progesterone and oestrogen declines *naturally*, so why should we be adding these back into our bodies by whatever means? As progesterone is needed to ensure pregnancy, why in any case would we need it during the menopause? Surely by rubbing it into our skins we are contradicting our body's inner wisdom to take care of us naturally?

Some would argue that during a lifetime we become overloaded with xenoestrogens — largely petrochemically produced and present in plastic packaging and in pesticides — which have an oestrogenic effect. While this environmental overload is certainly real, can it be wise to bombard the body with yet more synthetic hormones to counterbalance such oestrogen dominance?

Besides this, 'natural' progesterone has its problems, including initially exacerbating PMS or menopausal symptoms in some women. Nor do we as yet know if it is addictive. Used in this form, it has not been around long enough, or tested with sufficient rigour, to confirm the beliefs of its advocates, and again I emphasise that the menopause is *not* a hormone deficiency disease. The administering of progesterone, like oestrogen, would treat it as if it were.

For several decades we have been subjected to experiments en masse by the Pill and have only recently woken up to its long-term drawbacks. The insidious experiment with HRT is just beginning and progesterone therapy is jostling for space beside it. Are you willing to be a human rat for experimentation purposes?

OSTEOPOROSIS: LIES AND TRUTHS

One of the biggest claims made by advocates of HRT is that is helps fend off the onset of osteoporosis — abnormal porosity of bones — in ageing women. Perhaps women are right to be fearful, for statistics about osteoporosis show that in the UK it has increased six times in the last thirty years. One in eight men get it and one in three women.

But osteoporosis is not directly linked to bone breakage. In a study of women aged sixty and older, low bone mass did not correlate with higher rates of fracture.[15] In fact, as the American College of Physicians has opined: 'The majority of women with hip fracture have a density of the hip that is within normal range.' In other words, osteoporosis does not necessarily lead to broken bones. The number of hip fractures in women soar between the ages of forty and forty-four, well *before* the menopause begins.

Bone loss begins well before the menopause and up to 50 per cent of the bone you will lose in your lifetime is lost before you ever reach the menopause. Indeed 16–18 per cent of women between the ages of eighteen and twenty-four have been found to have an abnormally low bone density. During the menopause there is a 2–5 per cent bone loss over a five-year period, after which it tends to level off.

Osteoporosis is not an oestrogen deficiency disease as doctors so commonly preach, nor is it a normal part of ageing. While it regularly occurs in men deficient in testosterone and women deficient in progesterone, it shows itself in surprising places. In Singapore more men than women get osteoporosis, while in Hong Kong it is the reverse. Black women are less osteoporotic than white women, Asian women come somewhere in between. Vegetarians are at less risk of osteoporosis than meat eaters, as are heavy-boned, fat women. Skinny female athletes with erratic menstrual cycles suffer more bone loss, and stress makes the problem worse, as does lack of sunlight, a high-protein diet, smoking, caffeine and heavy alcoholic intake.

REPLENISHING BONES
Our bones are constantly renewing themselves just like every other part of our body. Osteoclasts dissolve and resorb old bone, leaving behind empty spaces which osteoblasts obligingly fill with new bone. The dense outer bone, the cortical layer, shields the inner, spongy trabecular layer. Trabecular bone renews itself every two to three years, while cortical bone takes about twelve years. Wrists, thighs and vertebrae (the most commonly fractured parts) are made up mainly of trabecular layers. As we age, bone renewal naturally slows down; where osteoporosis is present, the process slows at a much greater rate, or stops altogether.

EARLY SIGNS OF OSTEOPOROSIS

- Persistent backache, especially the lower back.
- Severe periodontal disease (gum infections, loose teeth).
- Severe or sudden insomnia.
- Twitching legs, restlessness, foot cramping.
- Gradual loss of sight.

Should you experience any of these symptoms, please do not panic; they could just as easily be minor complaints totally unconnected with osteoporosis. If you are at all worried, though, consult your doctor.

SELF-SCREENING FOR BONE DENSITY

Once you have reached the age of thirty-five, your arm span and height should be equal, give or take an inch. Measure your armspan with arms outstretched from the tip of one middle finger to the tip of the other. Then measure your height. Do this once yearly and keep a record. Detecting a decrease in height, however, is not an immediate reason to panic. It may be the result of years of ongoing bad posture and my advice would be to get yourself checked by a therapist in the Alexander technique (see Resources Directory).

I am not keen on bone density measurements, which I consider invasive diagnostic techniques. Indeed, as the Canadian Task Force on Periodic Health Exams has observed: 'There are no studies of the effectiveness of early detection in achieving incidence of fracture or of bone demineralisation.'[16] As I stated at the beginning of this section, density of bone is *not* an accurate prediction of resistance to fracture. Besides which, the rate of bone loss cannot be estimated accurately as it is not constant or predictable in any one person.

If you wonder if you have broken a bone and do not want to be subjected to x-rays, place a vibrating tuning fork at one end of the bone causing concern and another at the other end. If the bone is fine, the vibration will be pleasant, if broken it will feel painful and uncomfortable. If you do not feel confident about trying this, please consult your doctor for a diagnosis.

I try and encourage patients with bone breaks to have them put in a splint rather than a plaster cast if at all possible. This way herbal poultices and massage, including reiki, which is particularly beneficial, can be applied to accelerate healing.

OSTEOPOROSIS RISK FACTORS IN WOMEN

- Being light-boned, white-skinned and with a fair complexion.
- Subjecting yourself to a lifetime of punishing diets.
- Smoking (see below).
- Insufficient exercise.
- Those who have had a total hysterectomy, including the removal of their ovaries.
- Drinking excessively, as this acidifies the bloodstream forcing the body to rob alkalinising minerals from the bones to keep blood pH from becoming so acidic that it damages cells. (See also below.)
- Certain drugs increase the risk of osteoporosis, including cortisone, thyroxin, tamoxifen, diuretics, heparin, barbiturate anticonvulsants and antacids.
- Taking only small amounts of absorbable calcium and other essential micro-nutrients into your diet. Note that caffeine and alcohol encourage the excretion of calcium as does excessive salt, which not only makes our bodies excrete more calcium but also encourages excretion of phosphorus, an important constituent of bone, so speeding up bone loss. Sugar also alters the calcium/phosphorus ratio in the bloodstream by making the phosphorus level drop. Malabsorption can also occur as the result of using antibiotics or of insufficient levels of hydrochloric acid in the stomach.
- A high-protein diet (see below).

Smoking, Alcohol and Caffeine

Smoking reduces bone mass by 25 per cent. Smoking poisons the ovaries and hinders the production of all the ovarian hormones. Smokers, together with those who take more than two alcoholic drinks a day, are at the highest risk of osteoporosis. The liver produces a special protein designed to combat the harmful dissolving effects of adrenalin. Burden your liver with the task of detoxifying your body from the effects of drinking alcohol and it will not be able to produce this protein effectively so that adrenalin is liberated to attack your bones. The same is true of coffee, which provokes the release of excessive adrenalin, besides causing an acid reaction in the body which in turn rallies calcium in its role as neutraliser. Two cups of coffee or four cups of tea daily thereby greatly increase the risk of hip fracture. Three cups of coffee daily increases the risk of osteoporosis by an astonishing 82 per cent! In addition, the tannin present in tea stops you absorbing other essential micro-nutrients in your food. If you must drink it, do not combine it with meals.

Fluoride

Fluoride actually decreases bone strength so do not use it in toothpaste (some of which gets swallowed) and try not to drink it in water (see Chapter Four).

The Dangers of a High-Protein Diet

Milk is touted as a great natural source of calcium, and we are frequently told to eat plenty of calcium to prevent osteoporosis. In fact, some evidence suggests that eating dairy products can actually increase the rate at which calcium is lost from the body and so hasten osteoporosis.[17] As well as being high in calcium, dairy products are also high in protein. If you have too much protein in the diet, in milk products or from any other source such as meat, fish or eggs, the body has to get rid of the excess. As the kidneys cleanse the blood of excess protein, calcium is lost in the process.

People in the United States and Scandinavian countries consume more dairy products than anywhere else in the world, yet they have the highest rate of osteoporosis. This fact emphasises the threat of excessive protein in the diet and supports the claim that ingestion of dairy products offer no protection against osteoporosis.

Far from taking a diet rich in dairy products, it is best to cut right down on your protein intake and preferably to become a vegan. The body's ability to absorb and utilise calcium depends on the amount of phosphorus in the diet. When there is not enough phosphorus in the body, calcium cannot be absorbed. The higher the calcium/

phosphorus ratio, the less bone loss takes place and the stronger the skeleton, provided the intake of protein is not excessive. Fruit and vegetables contain high calcium/phosphorus levels and are therefore highly beneficial. Dairy products, on the other hand, actually upset the balance of phosphorus in the body so that large amounts of calcium are unabsorbable.

THE ROLE OF MINERALS AND VITAMINS IN COMBATING OSTEOPOROSIS

Calcium

The Importance of Bioavailable Calcium

Ninety-nine per cent of the body's calcium is stored in our skeleton. Ingesting calcium-rich foods in our mouths does not automatically guarantee they will slip into our bones. Stomach acid (hydrochloric acid) and vitamin D are needed to absorb calcium effectively. Only about 20–40 per cent of the calcium we eat is absorbed and this percentage tends to decrease with age.

Calcium is incorporated into our bones in response to the hormone calcitonin. If blood levels of calcium drop, the parathyroid hormone steps in to reabsorb calcium from our bones, circulating it back into the blood to ensure balance. So the two hormones act like the opposing ends of a seesaw. Oestrogen stops parathyroid hormone executing its natural business which is why the oestrogen in HRT is said to protect against osteoporosis. The problem is, as we have seen, the administering of unopposed oestrogen carries with it a myriad of health problems. In addition, once HRT is stopped bone loss quickly resumes, which is not surprising because it is progesterone (present in only a relatively small amount in HRT) which is the bone trophic (bone-building) hormone, *not* oestrogen. The way HRT actually works is by slowing down bone cell degeneration, not actively nourishing bone cell growth. In 1988 a study was conducted in Italy in which women with fibroids placed on drugs to lower oestrogen were all tested for bone mineral content, bone density and bone width. Despite the lower levels of oestrogen present, no significant changes were seen in their bones, so I would conclude that less oestrogen does not automatically result in brittle bones.

The key to healthy bones is to maintain the delicate balance between the bone hormones calcitonin and parathyroid. This may be achieved by adhering to a healthy diet containing highly absorbable calcium (see Chapter Four, 'Dairy Products — Other Sources of Calcium') that is distributed through the bloodstream into the bones by weight-bearing exercise (see 'Calcium and Exercise' below).

Acid/Alkaline Balance and Calcium Absorption
Calcium acts a neutraliser in our digestive process. As we have seen, if we eat too many acid-forming foods (meat, dairy products, fish, eggs), take chemical drugs such as laxatives or antacids, or drink tea, coffee or alcohol, we continually burn up our stores of calcium as well as other minerals. The worst culprit here is animal protein. For every extra 10 g of protein ingested, 100 mg of calcium is excreted in our urine. This is one of the reasons why vegetarians, with a much lower intake of protein, have only 18 per cent bone mass loss compared to the 35 per cent of meat eaters.

Sources of Assimilable Calcium
It is vital to get calcium from sources which are easily absorbed. Take in too much inassimilable calcium and you will get calcareous deposits in the body such as kidney and gallstones as well as calcification of the arteries (arteriosclerosis) and eventually loss of appetite, abdominal cramps and even internal bleeding. The recommended dose of calcium is 1000–1500 mg daily for those on a high-protein diet, but Asian women, who eat far less meat and almost no dairy products compared to their Western cousins and have far less osteoporosis, require only 400 mg of calcium daily. A low-protein diet — 40 g daily — can easily be met by good sources of bioavailable calcium (see Chapter Four). As we have seen, dairy produce is not the best source of calcium. Besides being one of the most common food allergens, the galactose in the milk sugar lactose is toxic to the ovaries and interferes with fertility. A host of other reasons why you should avoid dairy products are outlined in Chapter Four.

Of all the calcium-rich herbs (see Chapter Four), horsetail is the most effective bone-density restorer. By working synergistically it actively thickens and stabilises bones.

BONE-STRENGTHENING COMBINATION

Equal parts of:

comfrey

horsetail

lobelia.

One teaspoon of the herbs, dried and powdered,

administered daily in juice.

I used this combination on a patient who had been run over by a rubbish-collecting truck and who was consequently in hospital with a ruptured spleen, many broken ribs and a broken arm. Admittedly for such severe injuries I trebled the dose and practically bathed her (internally) in carrot juice. However, she was out of hospital in five weeks, fully mobile.

Calcium and Exercise
Calcium can only be transported into the bones by vigorous weight-bearing exercise, which actively strengthens bones. Thirty to 45 minutes three times a week is ideal to stimulate piezoelectric activity (vibrations beneficial to the bones) in them. Even fifty jumps a day with a skipping rope will make them denser.

Yoga is very helpful because it keeps the spaces between the vertebral discs more open and supple and expands the protective auric field around the body.

Magnesium
Magnesium is essential for the proper metabolism of calcium. Without it joints and soft tissues calcify, leaving the body highly susceptible to the inroads of osteoporosis. Richly present in organic whole grains, beans, lentils and peas, it is woefully inadequate in the average highly processed Western diet. Dr Guy Abraham demonstrated that 600 mg of magnesium taken daily over a period of nine months radically increased the bone mass of women.[18]

Boran

Boran reduces urinary calcium loss and accelerates serum levels of 17 oestradiol (the oestrogen which is most biologically active). A trace element richly present in nuts, fruits and vegetables, the minimum dose of 2 mg daily can easily be met by a wholefood vegetarian diet.

Zinc

Zinc acts in synergy with vitamin D (see below), encouraging calcium absorption. Good sources are pumpkin and sunflower seeds.

Vitamin C

Ensure 2000 mg per day for collagen synthesis and repair. Collagen makes up 90 per cent of our bone matrix. Oranges and dark-green leafy vegetables are particularly rich in vitamin C.

Beta-carotene

This is a pro-vitamin which converts into vitamin A and promotes a healthy intestinal epithelium, essential for the optimal absorption of nutrients, and encourages strong joints. It is superabundant in any vegetables which are yellow and orange, especially carrot juice, and in dark-green leafy vegetables, especially broccoli.

Vitamin D

This helps to absorb calcium and phosphorus from the digestive process and incorporate them into the bones. You need 350 iu's daily, which 30 minutes of natural light will provide, so get outside when you exercise and try and expose your arms and face.

Vitamin B$_6$

B$_6$ increases the strength of connective tissue in bone and is richly present in organic whole grains, nuts, bananas and avocados. A deficiency in this vitamin caused osteoporosis in experimental rats.[19]

Vitamin K

Frequent resorting to antibiotics can result in vitamin K deficiency and this vitamin, available in green leafy vegetables, helps synthesise osteocalcin, a unique protein found in bone which helps to harden calcium.

How to Adopt an Osteoporosis-Protective Lifestyle

Become a vegan, or if you simply cannot do this, cut down your intake of animal protein and dairy produce.

- Cut out caffeine and cut right back on alcohol.
- Stop smoking.
- Ensure easily assimilable sources of calcium in the diet.
- Eat plenty of raw fruits and vegetables, whole organic grains, nuts and seeds. The more variety you have, the better your chances of obtaining the correct amount of vitamins and minerals and, as you can see, osteoporosis has much more to do with nutritional deficiencies than hormonal changes.
- Expose your skin to the healing rays of the sun for a short period each day — the actual length of time you spend in the sun will depend on your own skin type, but 30 minutes a day is optimal.
- Exercise regularly for 40 minutes 3–4 times a week, ensuring that it is weight-bearing exercise.
- Cut down on salt and eat a diet specifically rich in the superfoods indicated for the menopause (see Chapter Four).

THREE

TOWARDS A BETTER LIFESTYLE

For those of you dreading the process of ageing and the menopause let me give you the good news. Biologically, psychologically and emotionally women have the advantage throughout their lives. Intellectually, creatively, in fact in everything except physical strength, women are, if not actually superior, at least equal to men. Differing diets, ways of life, cultures abound throughout the world but one thing remains unwaveringly the same — women outlive men. The frailty of women is more myth than reality. Five out of six people widowed in the West are women. Overall the death rate for men is 73 per cent higher than it is for women of retirement age. In the final analysis, women's strength lies in their hormones and genes on account of the second X chromosome that men do not have. The oestrogen that bathes all of a woman's tissues protects her body from the cholesterol deposits that plague men, and female chromosome make-up guards against inherited diseases like haemophilia, colour blindness and even one type of muscular dystrophy.

THE IMPORTANCE OF EXERCISE

Many of the bodily changes we dread as we get older have absolutely nothing to do with the ageing process. The decreased muscle mass and increased fat are not an inevitable part of growing older but the result of inactivity and cultural hypnosis. The Tara Humara Indians in Mexico, renowned for their endurance running, some of whom complete the equivalent of a marathon each day, honour runners in their sixties as having better stamina than their younger counterparts.

Researchers have found that those with the best cardiovascular fitness and lung capacity are in fact found in this age group.[1]

So cultural belief matters. If we believe that our minds and bodies deteriorate with age, they will. I am not asking the impossible, that collectively we change our cultural negativity about ageing with immediate effect. But should we not show the way forward by acting individually as a shining role model to others?

Aerobic Activity

Exercise matters even more as you grow older. Extensive research going back to the 1950s shows that exercise does encourage longevity. A Harvard University study suggested that people who expended 2,000 calories a week exercising lived 1–2 years longer than their sedentary counterparts.[2] But in order to work off 2,000 calories a week, you have to spend roughly one and a half years exercising during your lifetime, about the same amount of time gained lengthening your life. So it is best to make it enjoyable. I am large and heavy-breasted and when I finally gritted my teeth and tried jogging, unsurprisingly I came to grief. Then I discovered the joys of walking and realised, to my infinite relief, that I did not have to make an embarrassing spectacle of myself, sweaty, red faced and on public display, to get the same benefits walking as jogging. In fact I discovered walking would produce beneficial results equal to those of *any* other aerobic exercise, as well as being easier on the joints and bones, particularly as one grows older.

The importance of aerobic activity in regard to health is that it oxygenates the blood, which in turn floods every cell with oxygen. I am fond of pointing out to my patients that the first prerequisite of life is air. We can live without water for days, without food for many weeks, but without air for only a few minutes.

When you walk, or take any form of aerobic exercise, you use your body's large muscles, which allow the entire aerobic mechanism to work harder than when you are at rest. Keeping up a programme of brisk walking throughout your life has been proved to be the best possible means of reducing the risk of cardiovascular disease. Added to this, walking will stimulate the activity of your lymphatic system. What is so heartening is that even if you currently lead a sedentary lifestyle, by exercising regularly for a year you can restore your ability to take up and use oxygen to that of a much younger person.

Even the most moderate, unstructured walking programme will reap substantial benefits, although up to a point the more vigorously you exercise the more benefits to health you will enjoy. But for those who detest the thought of exercise the exciting news is that even low levels of activity are beneficial. Taking regular, hour-long strolls will reduce a woman's risk of heart disease, and walking four miles will burn more fat than running the same distance in less time. A mere ten minutes of extra activity daily can reduce the risk of heart disease by 80 per cent.

You can keep your walking programme down to as little as 40 minutes three or four times a week and still protect yourself against circulatory problems and osteoporosis. In addition, walking has the advantage of greatly reducing the risk of injury or sudden death due to cardiac arrest following extreme or sudden over-exertion. While our capacity to utilise oxygen diminishes with increasing age, it has been shown that a sixty-year-old who exercises regularly can use oxygen as efficiently as a sedentary forty-year-old. The mere act of pumping extra blood through the arteries helps to dislodge plaque from artery walls, and regular exercise helps regulate the levels of different types of fatty acid in the blood. Exercise also activates fibrinolysis, the body's natural anticlogging system of rapidly acting enzymes that immediately dissolve small abnormal clots in the blood before they are able to block the arteries.

Among its many other miraculous abilities, the body is able to build new arteries which travel around any blockage in an existing artery and so protect the section in jeopardy. The *only* factor that will actually accelerate such development is exercise. During the menopause it is very common for the percentage of body fat to increase by as much as 11 lb (5.95 kg). Very gradually the total body weight tends to follow suit. Exercise can actually help to reverse this process. I should emphasise that there is no reason why there should automatically be an increase in body weight except through inactivity. Being inactive makes your lean body mass (LBM)-to-fat ratio shrink as does yo-yo crash dieting, which is why, as their metabolic rate slows down, so many women truthfully say they eat very little yet cannot lose weight.

WEIGHT TRAINING

Aerobic exercise is not the only type of activity necessary to gain optimum fitness, health and longevity. The best combination of exercise is some kind of resistance training, such as light weight-lifting, coupled with aerobic activity because such weight training increases LBM more effectively than aerobic exercise alone. This is important because one pound of muscle needs to burn up 30–50 calories a day for maintenance, whereas one pound of fat requires fewer calories. Women with more muscle have higher metabolic rates and, providing they continue to exercise, burn off more calories and remain slimmer than their more sedentary counterparts. However, weight training should be conducted on machinery incorporating removable weights that can be added or taken off according to the level of strength of the individual and the type of exercise undertaken. Machines incorporating fixed weights, by their very nature, limit the range of movements possible for each exercise. When using free weights, it is vital to keep the body centred with each movement, concentrating on the specific muscle group you are working on, and to remember that resisting the return movement, as you lower the weights, is just as important as the up-lift. Indeed it is the stress placed on muscles as they lengthen under resistance that contributes most to both gains in strength and LBM.

PREPARING THE BODY FOR EXERCISE

Whatever the form of exercise you take, dehydration can be a real problem. You need to drink plenty of water to replenish all your body processes. Remember your body is approximately 70 per cent water and generally you lose about 2–2.5 quarts (2.4–3 litres) a day. This increases to 4 quarts with vigorous exercise. Drink a glass of water before you exercise and when you have finished exercising. Naturally drink more if you feel the need. Far better to have a little more than not enough while exercising. Indeed studies conducted in the US at Harvard and Loma Linda universities have proved that drinking extra water reduces fatigue and stress while increasing stamina and energy to an extraordinary degree.[3] To maintain excellent health it is better to drink *more* water than you think you need just to quench your thirst. Athletes who were forced to do this found they were able to continue indefinitely without fatigue or overheating.

If you are taking a walk, it is best to do so early in the morning on an empty stomach, having consumed only a glass of water. If you walk in the heat of the day, you absorb heat not only from the sun but also from the pavement and this will tire you out faster. In addition, it has been shown that when exercise is performed in the morning, 75 per cent of participants stick to the programme compared with 75 per cent who drop out when exercise is scheduled for any other time of the day.[4]

It is always best to exercise on an empty stomach because digesting demands energy and detracts from your ability to exercise well. This is particularly important if you are trying to lose weight. The exception to the rule is eating fruit, which requires very little energy to digest.

Stretching is necessary before and after any exercise because it prepares the muscles for strenuous activity and relieves stiffness, so increasing the range of motion of your muscles and preventing injury. Stretching should be performed very slowly and should never go to the point of causing pain.

A SUMMARY OF THE BENEFITS OF EXERCISE

- It increases both the strength and efficiency of the heart and muscles.
- It increases energy levels and stamina.
- It improves overall strength, flexibility, balance and mental agility.
- It encourages more restful sleep and greater relaxation as well as allaying anxiety and depression.
- It normalises blood pressure and helps diabetics by increasing insulin sensitivity.
- It encourages a better LBM-to-fat ratio.
- It improves the elimination of wastes and alleviates symptoms of PMS.
- Exercise after eating, providing it is gentle, causes food to move quickly through the stomach, helping to relieve minor indigestion.
- It boosts the immune system, enhancing immune function by

increasing the levels of lymphocytes, interleukin 2, neutrophils and other disease-fighting chemicals in the immune system. It specifically lowers cancer rates in women, particularly cancer of the colon. By stimulating the lymph system it helps to prevent breast cancer.

- It builds strong bones.
- It increases life expectancy, on average by seven years.
- Walking in particular actually lowers levels of cholesterol in the body as well as helping to strengthen the back.
- A study at Appalachian State University showed that women who walk 45 minutes a day recovered twice as fast from colds than those who took no exercise at all.[5]
- The good news for women is that healthy men aged 35–65 who start a regular exercise programme kiss their wives more often, have more intercourse and more orgasms than those who neglect their exercise.[6]

DETOXIFICATION THROUGH FASTING

In addition to taking exercise, the body requires other forms of revitalisation and of all the healing tools available to me as a naturopath fasting is the one I consider the finest. When I raise the subject with a patient, as inevitably I do sooner rather than later, I am usually met by dismayed looks of prejudice and incomprehension; but those who bracket fasting with starvation are guilty of the most unforgivable ignorance of the workings of the human body. Almost as bad as equating swimming with drowning!

Fasting is especially helpful during the transitional upheaval of the menopausal years because it helps to rebalance the body mentally, spiritually, physically and emotionally. A juice fast instigates regeneration and rejuvenation, supplying the body with a good quantity of minerals, vitamins and micro-nutrients which support enzyme reaction and hormonal balance. Fasting is a key element in preventing disease and far from making you feel tired it accelerates energy and stamina levels. The process of digestion uses 30 per cent of your energy, which is unsurprising when you take into account the full extent of the digestive activities involved in ingesting food, processing it and extracting nutrients before delivering them to the cells. This is in addition to the activity involved in the elimination of waste and all the interactions of the organs, including the stomach, intestines, pancreas, liver, kidney and spleen, as well as the metabolic processes that take place to turn food into blood, muscle and bones.

Have you ever eaten a big meal and then volunteered to run a marathon? I expect a gentle horizontal snooze was more in order!

Prolonged fasting heals all sorts of problems. Ironically some of those who survived starvation in concentration camps during the Second World War found their customary aches and pains disappeared during their ordeal only to return, sometimes even more forcibly, after the war was over and 'normal' eating was resumed. There is the famous case of villagers in Austria who were forced to live off little but grass during the war and who found such a monodiet obliterated, among other ailments, dental problems and arthritis.

Fasting also extends longevity. Dr Roy Walford, one of the world's most eminent gerontologists, conducts numerous experiments on ageing by using mice and making them fast for two days a week. Most mice live for about two years but the fasting mice lived twice as long and showed significantly lower rates of heart disease and cancer. Such diseases as do develop do so at a much later age.[7]

HOW DOES FASTING WORK?

One-quarter of your body cells are growing, half are at the height of their working powers and the remaining quarter are dying and being replaced. Only by speedy and efficient elimination of these dead cells can the building of fresh cells be stimulated. Fasting accelerates the elimination of dead cells and speeds up production of new healthy cells. You may think this impossible, as so little nourishment is taken (in a water fast none at all), but it is a proven physiological fact.[8] Meanwhile protein levels in the blood remain constant and normal because proteins are constantly decomposed and resynthesised for alternative use. The building blocks of protein — amino acids — are released and reused in the process of building new cells, while the cleansing capacity of every eliminative organ in the body is enhanced. Discarded toxic waste in the urine has been measured as increasing up to ten times during a fast and an over-burdened liver can deposit its waste six times more quickly than usual, especially when the fast is enhanced by hydrotherapy. Fluids in the lymphatic system become measurably cleaner and flow more easily, particularly if aerobic exercise is taken and skin brushing is carried out (see later in the chapter).

How to Fast

A fast can last from four hours to many days. It is possible to fast daily, overnight from 5 o'clock in the evening to 8 o'clock the following morning, for one or more days or for one or more weeks. By fasting from 6 p.m. to 8 a.m., the body has enough time to cleanse the waste products of metabolism, facilitating the release of the hormones that stimulate the immune system which are released both by fasting and during sleep. Practised regularly, short fasting prevents any great build-up of metabolic debris in the body, so reducing the possibility of any serious illness and minimising the necessity for really long fasts.

Some purists consider water fasting — taking nothing but water — the only true way to fast. My feeling is that a water fast has distinct drawbacks in our polluted, industrialised world (see following chapter). We are all laden with internal stores of insecticides, pesticides, strontium-90 and other forms of radiation. Unhappily no creature on earth has escaped the poisoning of the planet. DDT, for instance, has been found in the breast milk of mothers in the Gobi desert as well as in the livers of penguins in the Antarctic. Such toxins are usually stored in the places which pose the least hazard, that is the body's fat. A fast that breaks down fat stores also releases these poisons into the bloodstream. A water fast, if prolonged, is unable to buffer internally released toxic waste and provides none of the minerals needed for proper nerve function. If you really insist on a water fast, it should be done in the cleanest possible countryside environment for a short time only and under proper supervision.

A juicer is the first of two items anybody working with me purchases because fasting with freshly pressed fruits and vegetables can alter the quality of the bloodstream more rapidly than any other method available. Juices bought from healthfood stores and supermarkets tend to be boiled and so leached of many of their digestive enzymes or they have preservatives added to them. Anything that is labelled organic is generally acceptable, although there are juices that are organic but that contain whey (see below). Fasting on these is better than not fasting at all, but I prefer my patients to find a source of organic fruit and vegetables and juice them freshly as needed.

Whey
Whey is a by-product of cheese production. It looks like pus, tastes appalling and stinks. Only 10 per cent of the milk used to make cheese actually ends up as cheese. The rest is separated out into unlovely whey and the cheese industry has to dispose of it somehow. Whey is so toxic that it cannot be poured into sewers as very few ordinary sewage works are capable of treating it. Dumping it into streams merely leaches out all the oxygen and kills the fish. Putting it into land fills may mean it seeps into water supplies. Nevertheless whey is found not only in some bottled juices but in baked goods, ice cream, luncheon meat, substitute chocolate, soup mixes and chocolate beverages.

GETTING THE ACID/ALKALINE BALANCE RIGHT
A juice fast coupled with potassium broth (see Chapter Four, 'Salt') is alkalinising because of the minerals in the juice or broth. It therefore helps balance the acidifying effects of a diet that has been high in protein, flour and sugar. It is most effective when combined with vigorous exercise. I have, however, observed that prolonged fasting on cold juices can overtax the kidneys of susceptible individuals because of the excessive liquid intake. In this instance pain may manifest itself in the kidneys because they are overworked and I would instead recommend a macrobiotic or grain fast mixed with alkalinising seaweed, miso (available from healthfood shops) and a touch of sea salt. This is a particularly effective type of fast for those addicted to sugar or weaning themselves off recreational drugs. It should be followed for no more than ten days because beyond this it can become overly acidifying.

THE BENEFITS OF JUICE
Freshly pressed homemade juice is particularly beneficial because it contains more vitamins, trace elements, minerals and digestive

enzymes than purchased juices. While ingesting water alone over a period of time has the dangerous capacity to distort circulation, drinking fruit juice helps to maintain a stable blood-electrolyte balance so ensuring that the circulation remains constant. Above all, juices are easily digested. Within twelve minutes of being swallowed they are absorbed into the bloodstream. They do not stimulate the secretion of hydrochloric acid in the stomach, a particularly important point for those with ulcers or tender stomach linings. In addition, they contain an unidentified factor which stimulates the micro-electric tension in the body which is responsible for a cell's capacity to absorb nutrients from the bloodstream and so promote the effective excretion of metabolic waste. This is very exciting news for cellulite sufferers. Cellulite arises partly as a result of the colon failing to dispose of waste as efficiently as it should and partly as a result of poor lymphatic drainage whereby waste becomes trapped in spaces between the cells. A juice's ability to cleanse the lymph and bloodstream rapidly helps to disperse cellulite. For those with heart and circulatory problems the concentrated sugars present in juice actually strengthen the heart.

How Much Juice Should I Take?

My main problem when supervising patients through juice fasting is to get them to drink enough juice. Aim to drink one fluid ounce (30 ml) of juice for every pound (450 g) of your body weight every day. Depending on your weight, you may well be drinking up to a gallon (4.8 litres) of liquid a day. The more liquid you ingest, the quicker you flush out all those accumulated toxins and the less possibility there is of retaining water, because mineral water or purified water and juices are natural diuretics.

How to Juice

All juices should be served at room temperature and, if at all possible, pressed freshly as needed (to minimise oxidation and the loss of essential nutrients) and they should be well 'chewed' before swallowing. You do not actually have to move your jaw to do this. Just swish them around your mouth to ensure they are mixed with plenty of saliva before swallowing.

The skins of oranges and grapefruits contain toxic substances and should not be consumed in large quantities if they are included in the juicing process. However, the white pithy part of the peel should be included because it contains valuable bioflavonoids (see Chapter Four, 'The Special Protective Superfoods'). Tropical fruits such as kiwi and papaya should be thick peeled before being juiced because they are grown in countries where carcinogenic sprays are still legal and still used. The skins of all other fruits and vegetables, including lemons and limes, can be left on, but if the fruit has been waxed remove the peel. All stones should be removed before juicing but seeds can be placed in the juicer with the fruit. Those fruits and vegetables that contain little water, for example bananas and avocados, cannot be juiced but can be used as an ingredient in a delicious fruit 'smoothy' — fresh fruit juice liquidised with fresh and frozen fruit. My favourite recipe is 8 fl. oz (240 ml) of apple juice liquidised with a fresh banana and a cupful of frozen berries (I particularly favour blueberries) at high speed until the whole mixture is thick and creamy.

Before juicing wash all your produce well and remove any mouldy or bruised parts. Throw the excess pulp on to your compost heap, if you have one. If you have to prepare juice in advance, store it in a Thermos flask and fill it up to as near to the top as possible so that there is no air left in the flask, adding the juice of a lemon to stop oxidation. Try to make juice only from locally grown produce in its proper season. Juice will keep adequately in a Thermos flask without fermenting for up to eight hours.

Potassium broth is a very useful addition to a fast. Do not mix fruit and vegetable juices together as the enzymes in them are incompatible. The only exception to this rule is carrot and apple juice. Various types of juice will help to heal specific conditions. Watermelon juice, for instance, is excellent for treating oedema; the juice of whole lemons and oranges strengthens the heart; and carrot juice will help maintain a healthy liver — of vital importance during the menopause (see below).

STARTING AND FINISHING A FAST
Ease into and out of a fast by eating only fresh fruits and vegetables for one, two or even three days beforehand and afterwards. Never shock

the body by changing from a heavy diet, particularly one containing meat and dairy products, to fasting or vice versa unless you are fasting for emergency, first-aid purposes.

Breaking a fast is as important as the fast itself. It was George Bernard Shaw who observed that any fool can fast but it takes a wise man to break a fast properly. You can undo most of the good gained by a fast by breaking it improperly or unwisely. It is best to break a fast by eating a homemade vegetable soup containing some well-cooked grains or made from uncooked vegetables, such as a gaspacho, or by eating fresh fruit followed later by a large raw salad lightly dressed with olive oil, garlic herbs and lemon juice. Spend as long breaking the fast as you did taking the fast itself. So if the fast took three days, introduce solid foods gradually over a three-day period.

If you have never fasted before, fast for between one and three days only. Fasting for longer than a week needs supervision from a professional experienced in the techniques.

Do not be too rigid about how long you fast. I have started three-day fasts and gone on for ten days because I was feeling so fabulous; but I have also set out to do seven-day fasts and finished after only thirty-six hours because I had simply had enough. Fasting has the advantage in that it requires less time spent on menu preparation than normal eating patterns (providing, that is, you have not bought dirty carrots and had to spend all day at the sink scrubbing them) and eliminates the amount of choice and hence temptation.

Fasting for more than a day actually lowers the metabolic rate and the spectacular amount of weight that is lost during the initial days of the fast is merely the result of the liver disposing of glycogen and of water levels readjusting in the body. A substantial percentage of the weight lost during a long fast is rapidly regained after normal eating has been resumed, which is reassuring news for very thin people, but not good for overweight ones.

Fasting for those who want to lose weight is a wonderful introduction to *controlled* eating because it shores up willpower and shrinks the stomach so that smaller helpings suffice, and because digestion of any food eaten after a fast is greatly enhanced and hormonal secretions are stimulated.

WHAT TO EXPECT DURING THE FIRST THREE DAYS OF A FAST

It is common to experience symptoms such as dizziness, mild heart palpitations, weakness, light-headedness, tiredness, forgetfulness, slight nausea, a nasty taste in the mouth, a furred tongue and a gnawing or empty feeling in the stomach and abdomen. If you experience any of these, just take extra rest, detach yourself from anything negative that floats through your mind, inspire yourself and shore up your willpower by reading books on fasting (see Select Bibliography). *Never try to pep yourself up with stimulants during the course of a fast.*

All the unpleasant physical symptoms that may be experienced during the first three days of a fast are merely the result of toxins flowing out of the body. The more fasts you undertake, the less likely it is that you will experience such symptoms as the build-up of toxins will be less. During a prolonged fast it is very common to experience a 'healing crisis' in which the body rids itself of toxins at a high rate. This usually begins on the tenth or eleventh day and may show itself in a variety of ways ranging from flu-like symptoms to skin eruptions and other interesting eliminative processes. It can last for a day or for up to a month, its length determined by the constitutional strength or weakness of an individual — the stronger you are, the shorter it will be. A healing crisis is to be welcomed with joy, although I have noticed a lot of my patients do not feel like this when they are in the middle of one, which is understandable.

SUPPLEMENTATION OF DRUGS DURING FASTING

If you are taking drugs prescribed by a doctor, do not begin a fast without taking your doctor's advice. If you are taking any natural medicines under the supervision of a naturopath, medical herbalist or homeopath, do not start a fast without consulting them. In either case, your fast might need supervision by a naturopathic professional.

Any vitamin and mineral supplementation during the fast is strictly forbidden. The exceptions to these are the superfoods listed at the end of the following chapter. These are easily ingested as juices themselves, so place no extra burden on the digestive system. I have found spirulena, chlorella and nutritional yeast particularly helpful for stopping swings in blood-sugar levels during the first three days of the fast and for appeasing the appetite. Use them in copious quantities if desired. You can take up to six or seven heaped teaspoons a day of spirulena and chlorella, liquidised into your juices. Nutritional yeast is delicious as an addition in potassium broth.

FASTING AIDS
Skin brushing regularly (see below) every morning and evening, and wearing only natural fabrics as well as sleeping in cotton sheets will allow your skin to breathe properly. Walk barefoot on grass for 5–10 minutes every day. 'Air bathe' for a few minutes daily, if possible exposing the whole body naked to the air while lying in the shade. If it is icy or snowing outside, air bathe by standing naked in front of your open window. Fresh air accelerates wound healing and encourages the skin to breathe properly. Obviously if you live in a heavily built-up area and are worried about shocking the neighbours, you may have to compromise and stand further back from the open window. Take time to breathe properly and deeply.

Follow the natural rhythm of the day, getting up when the sun rises and taking a rest shortly after it sets. You will probably find you need extra sleep during a fast, at least in the initial stages. Try and fit in some extra rest before midday when the liver is still very active. The liver bears the brunt of cleansing during a fast and is at its most active between 4 a.m. and midday. Sometime between these hours apply a castor oil poultice to the area of the abdomen above the liver and lie down. By lying down you will increase the blood flow to the liver by 40 per cent and the castor oil pack boosts this flow by a further 20 per cent. For instructions on how to apply a castor oil poultice, see Chapter Six.

Before you go to bed, take an enema each day of your fast. This is by far the quickest and most efficient way to cleanse the colon (see again Chapter Six). Alternatively, if you are on a long fast and know a good colonic therapist, have a colonic irrigation 2–3 times a week. I am one of the few colonic therapists in Britain who offer Dr Bernard Jensen's deep tissue cleansing management programme, which involves a colonic every day, together with an enema morning and evening. You would be surprised at the amount of waste that is disposed of on this programme. A lot of people fasting on juices get complacent and think the colon will have nothing to excrete, but one of its functions is to act in much the same way as the skin does, drawing waste from the blood and the lymph through the semipermeable intestinal wall.

Do not watch television and be selective about the things you read, concentrating on your favourite poetry, inspirational books about health, healing and fasting or books that make you laugh. Fasting is also a form of spiritual cleansing and if you stuff yourself with mental rubbish it will leach your emotional energy and may even give you bad dreams. I have found that one of the major benefits of fasting is that my senses become heightened as my body cleanses itself. My taste buds pick up every tiny nuance of flavour and my sense of smell becomes very acute. Colours get brighter, sounds more distinct and my sense of touch becomes much more sensitive.

Exercise daily, preferably by taking long brisk walks well wrapped, unburdened and breathing deeply as you move along. During a fast you will find your metabolic rate drops and your lymphatic system slows down, but skin brushing and vigorous walking will speed it up again and help to gather up waste and dispose of it more efficiently from both the lymphatic system and the colon.

A THREE-DAY FAST

Having been on a light diet of only raw foods the day before, on your first morning of the fast and every morning thereafter do half an hour's deep breathing and stretching and then take a liver flush (see below). Do not eat or drink anything for one hour after your liver flush. If possible use the time to lie down with a castor oil poultice over the area of your abdomen above liver. When the hour is up, drink 8 fl. oz (240 ml) of prune juice (see below, 'The Liver').

Half an hour after taking the prune juice, have a further 8 fl. oz of another juice, diluted half and half with still mineral or purified water. Continue taking this mixture at half-hourly intervals throughout the day.

Choose one juice for each day of the three-day period, alternating between fruit and vegetable juices, so that you maintain a balance between cleansing and regeneration. If you are pushed for time, there are some excellent organic bottled juices, both fruit and vegetable, on the market. However, because they are not freshly pressed, they will lack the digestive enzymes present in fresh ones.

If your body temperature plummets and you feel cold, take potassium broth with extra nutritional yeast stirred into it. Herbal teas may be taken freely throughout the day. In addition, detox tea (see below, 'The Liver') may be drunk as often as you like during the course of the day. Take an enema before bed and do not forget to use all your other aids during fasting. I would remind you once again to break your fast wisely.

OPENING UP THE ELIMINATIVE CHANNELS

The first step of natural healing is to open up the eliminative channels and get rid of any congestion or waste. In my experience an iridology test — in which the presence of tissue inflammation in the body is detected via analysis of the iris of the eye — is perhaps the most valuable way of finding out exactly how your eliminative organs are functioning. I can safely say that nearly 80 per cent of the women who consult me are in some way drowning in their own poisons, a condition that we naturopaths term auto-intoxication, meaning literally self-poisoning.

THE BOWEL
The Importance of Bowel Cleansing During the Menopause
After fifteen years in practice I am still amazed about how little many women know about their internal anatomy. The ovaries, even if the bowel is perfectly shaped (which is rare in the Western world for reasons noted below), practically rest on the lower colon, which is semipermeable and designed to flush minerals out into the surrounding blood and lymph as one of the last stages of the digestive process. If the bowel is congested, what gets flushed out are toxins which then bathe the ovaries, flooding down through the Fallopian tubes into the uterus and creating mayhem. Ninety per cent of the gynaecological problems women bring to me are cleared up simply by altering the diet and cleansing the bowel.

Constipation and indigestion tend to increase during the

menopause due to the slowing of the gastrointestinal tract, as oestrogen is a gastrointestinal stimulant. So it is not uncommon for bowel patterns to change during the menopause, which means it is of paramount importance to keep the colon functioning healthily.

Disorders of the Bowel

Most people think that what they see in the toilet is what they ate a couple of meals back, but in truth a normal twentieth-century diet ensures that a lot gets left behind in the colon that does not come out at all. Colon rectal cancer, in both men and women, is the most widespread cancer in the Western world. Even the notoriously conservative American Medical Association has admitted that the main reason for this is dietary. Hundreds of thousands of people suffer from other colon disorders and everyone at some time in their lives has experienced some type of bowel disorder, generally constipation or diarrhoea. The fact that thousands of tons of laxatives and anti-diarrhoea medicines are sold all over the Western world confirms this.

In an average bowel movement there may be starches that have not been digested properly by pancreatic secretions. Drugs and barium meals as well as catarrh-forming foods like dairy products, sugar and eggs get pasted on to the sides of the colon turning into encrusted mucus the weight of which forces the wall of the colon outwards to form diverticular pockets. It is now estimated that more than 80 per cent of men and women over the age of sixty have diverticular pockets in their colon. In some people this encrusted waste can cause the colon to weigh as much as 40 lb (18 kg) and to balloon out from the customary 4 in. (10 cm) to as much as 9 in. (23 cm).

The fact is that our modern lifestyles have wrecked havoc with our colons. You should have a bowel movement for every meal you eat; therefore if you eat three meals a day, you should have three reasonably copious bowel movements a day. Constipation is therefore the hub of the mechanism in the disease process. The heart of the problem lies in the passage of toxins and micro-organisms through the intestinal wall into the body, in general causing an endless array of disturbances. When the body absorbs poison from the decaying waste in the colon, every other organ has to bathe in this poison. Meat, fish and eggs provide the most harmful metabolites which, on entering the bloodstream, create a toxic blow for the cells throughout the body, in particular the liver and kidneys. Auto-intoxication causes fatigue, poor concentration, irritability, insomnia, muscular aches, headaches, poor skin and bad breath and can lead to all the degenerative diseases including cancer. It has been observed that the populations with a high incidence of colon rectal cancer consume diets containing less fibre, fewer grains, vegetables, fruits, nuts and seeds and more animal and protein fat and refined carbohydrates than populations with a low incidence of the disease. It should be remembered that diarrhoea is often the sister face of constipation because its cause is a substance which irritates the colon so badly that peristalsis — the wavelike movement of muscular contraction and relaxation whereby waste matter is propelled through the intestine — goes into overdrive in an attempt to expel it. The build up of faecal matter trapped in the colon becomes so great that this induces a state of continuous peristalsis resulting in chronic diarrhoea.

Constipation

Factor	Causes of Constipation	Promotes Good Colon Elimination
Food	Meat and all animal products, eggs, dairy products and any highly refined food.	Fruits, vegetables, grains, seeds, nuts. Live food creates life. When you start to eat it you will actually feel new activity in your bowel.
Liquid	Not enough liquid, dehydrated foods.	Drink 1 gallon (4.8 litres) of liquid every day, in the form of water, herbal teas and fruit and vegetable juices.

Factor	Causes of Constipation	Promotes Good Colon Elimination
Movement	Sedentary lifestyle with a lot of sitting or lying down.	All movement, especially deep breathing and abdominal exercise. Even walking can work wonders.
Emotional	Fear, or negativity, holding on to problems, holding on to old, useless material possessions.	Courage, letting go of people and things, opening up your mind, being an open, aware and loving person.
Drugs	Any drugs which sedate or are narcotic with opiate derivatives such as codeine.	Digestive-stimulating and cathartic herbs.
Intestinal Flora	Antibiotic drugs, extremely hot food, essential oils, loud noises over 72 decibels, x-rays, sudden violent changes in the weather, bottlefeeding as a baby.	Fermented nuts, seeds, grains and vegetables such as sauerkraut, positive ions, breastfeeding from birth, garlic.
Toilet	Sitting upright on a Western-type of toilet necessitates pushing down against the rectum and positively encourages haemorrhoids.	Squatting with your feet elevated on a box or pile of magazines ideally raised to within 6 in. (15 cm) of the toilet seat with your knees spread and your elbows resting on them is the ideal way to take a bowel movement, and this position relieves the bearing down on rectal muscles.

A Good Bowel Movement

Many of my patients have libraries in their bathroom, but if you have time to read while sitting on the toilet, it is a sure sign of constipation.

Having a bowel movement should be easy, comfortable and quick. When you feel the urge you should be able to evacuate your bowels in less than two minutes and be finished, without straining, squeezing or grunting. Every bowel movement should be soft and mushy like cottage cheese, slightly gaseous and should crumble and break up as it reaches the water on the surface of the toilet. If it is well formed or any harder or dryer than this, you are definitely constipated. Remember, ideally you should be having a bowel movement for every meal you eat, but in no case, even when fasting, should you have less than two a day.

A properly functioning bowel means better food assimilation, increased vitality and better absorption of nutritents and it often reduces the desire to eat as much food. With chronic constipation only 10 per cent of the food eaten is utilised. Do remember that most laxatives are poisonous and merely serve to irritate the bowel, doing nothing to remove the encrusted mucus. If laxatives are used regularly the colon becomes addicted to them and in time grows weaker from over-stimulation and irritation so that the dosage has to be increased.

The triangle of environmental, emotional and biological or physical stress that is the basis of many illnesses apply particularly to the bowel. People are often reluctant to let go of faecal matter simply because they are so uptight by nature. In this case simple relaxants such as skullcap or valerian are often very helpful, serving to relax the bowel enough to allow it to do its work naturally.

Exercise

Exercise is a vital factor in good bowel health. In order to encourage peristalsis, use your legs. Their movement improves circulation and lung capacity, and strengthens the abdominal muscles, thereby stimulating the peristaltic action of the bowel.

Friendly Bacteria

Every colon holds 3–4 lb (1.4–1.8 kg) of resident bacteria as indigenous flora. It is made up of 300–400 different species of bacteria whose activities affect our metabolism, physiology and biochemistry in ways that are both beneficial and harmful. So vital is this intestinal metabolic activity that it surpasses that of the liver in its wide range of metabolic processes.

These micro-organisms are both indigenous and transient. The former colonise particular ecological niches in the intestinal tract by adhering to the muscosal epithelium; the latter are ingested in food and drink and are constantly in transit from the mouth to the anus. Together they make up nearly 40 per cent of the whole weight of our faecal matter.

The bacterioids, together with coliform bacilli and *E. coli*, are the putrefactive bacteria responsible for the decaying matter in the colon. They enjoy a diet full of protein and fat which accelerates the output of undesirable metabolites like bile salts, urea, phenols, ammonia and other dietary degradation products which are all potentially harmful substances, doubly so if there is already constipation or a malfunctioning liver present. A high population of harmful bacteria is one of the main contributory factors to the development of all sorts of degenerative diseases like ulcerative colitis, diverticulosis, haemorrhoids and colonic cancer. Unfortunately most people have a ratio of 85 per cent of these potentially harmful bacteria to only 15 per cent beneficial bacteria.

The beneficial bacteria produce acetic, lactic and formic acid which lowers the pH of the intestine, so preventing the colonisation of fungus like *Candida albicans*. When the percentage is better balanced, with 75 per cent of the good bacteria, peristalsis is stimulated, flushing out toxic bacterial metabolites and waste products in the faeces and so checking putrefactive bacteria.

Intestinal Flora

Certain foods are known to promote benign intestinal flora such as natural, raw, unsalted sauerkraut, miso soup and fermented grains (which can be obtained from healthfood shops and made into rejuvelac, for instance), as well as some herbs, especially garlic. Garlic is capable of destroying bacteria that are harmful to us while actually increasing the number of good bacteria.

The most vicious destroyers of beneficial intestinal flora are antibiotics. Whether we consume them as by-products of the meat or dairy industry or take them for infections, all antibiotics cause enormous quantitative as well as qualitative changes in the intestinal flora, creating a perfect seedbed for pathogenic micro-organisms and actively encouraging the growth of *Candida albicans*. The radiation of the abdomen with gamma rays or x-rays upsets the normal microbial balance of the colon, as do sudden violent changes in the weather and prolonged loud music (above 72 decibels).

Stress

The profound effect that stress has on intestinal ecology is interesting. It does not matter what the source of the stress is; the stress response stimulates the release of adrenalin and cortisol as the body alerts itself for 'fight or flight'. These hormones then induce a number of physiological changes, including the drying up of oral and gastric secretions, the retention of sodium chloride and the acceleration of potassium excretion and raised blood sugar. All these reactions cumulatively alter the intestinal habitat, decreasing the micro-organic goodies and increasing the baddies. When you consider how much routine stress you are exposed to, ranging from bright lights, atmospheric pressure, noise, crowds, long journeys, and how much more is self-generated from fatigue, anger, anxiety, pain and fear, it really makes you appreciate just how hard it is to generate the right sort of balance.

Corrective Formulae

The following formulae are designed to help proper bowel function and aid elimination.

Intestinal Corrective Formula No. 1

This is a unique and unbeatable formula for treating bowel problems and is also helpful as part of a treatment for haemorrhoids. Its aim is to restore normal bowel function, not to create dependence like so many laxatives do. The combination of herbs in this formulation cleanses the

---

liver and gall bladder, starts the bile flowing and stimulates peristalsis so that the layers of encrusted ancient mucus can gradually slough off as the bowel is rebuilt, resulting in the perfect assimilation of food. It also clears up diverticular pockets in the bowel, healing any inflamed areas and relaxing any areas of tension. It was originally designed by Dr Christopher, the world-famous American herbalist.

Two parts of:
cascara sagrada
One part of:
bayberry bark
cayenne
fennel
goldenseal
lobelia (available only from qualified herbalists)
red raspberry leaves
Turkey rhubarb root.

Combine all the herbs, which should be finely powdered, sieve them well together and fill size 0 gelatine capsules (see Chapter Six) with them.

DOSAGE
The dosage of this formulation produces widely differing results in different people and therefore must be monitored and adjusted according to individual response. As there are no two persons alike in age, size or physical condition (and people's bowels are as different as their fingerprints), you will need to regulate the dose of this formula according to your own needs.

Begin by taking 2 capsules three times a day with meals, or if you do not eat three times a day, take 2 capsules with every meal that you do eat in order to achieve a bowel movement for every meal ingested. If you get diarrhoea cut down the dosage. If you cannot get a movement then raise the dosage until you can.

The bits of mucus that emerge over time may look very odd. You may see nuts and seeds that have been lodged in the colon for months or even years; traces of barium meal (if you have ever had one); bits of what may look like rubber tyre, tree bark or coloured Vaseline jelly. Alternatively, bowel movements may emerge smelling particularly foul or may come out accompanied by a great deal of rumbling or flatulence. Do not be alarmed by any of this and do not taper off the formulation so much that you lose momentum and so the continuity of this remedy.

The formulation must, of course, be coupled with correct diet (see following chapter), a positive attitude and a good exercise programme in order to be effective. As the colon cleanses, heals and rebuilds itself, you will find you will naturally be able to taper off and finally finish the formulation altogether.

The following two formulations were designed by Richard Schulze, principal of the College of Herbs and Natural Healing in the UK and an internationally recognised authority on herbal medicine.

Intestinal Corrective Formula No. 2

This highly effective tonic — affectionately labelled 'TNT' by its creator because it certainly gets patients off to a flying start if they are chronically congested — is both cleansing and healing to all parts of the gastrointestinal system. It disinfects, halts putrefaction, stimulates peristalsis, soothes and heals the mucous membrane lining of the digestive tract, relieves flatulence and cramping, improves digestion, increases the flow of bile — which is cleansing to the gall bladder, bile ducts and liver — promotes healthy intestinal flora, acts as an antibacterial, antiviral and antifungal agent, destroys intestinal parasites and increases gastrointestinal circulation. It is 3–4 times stronger than the Intestinal Corrective Formula No. 1.

Two parts of:
cascara sagrada

---

senna leaves and pods
One part of:
bayberry root
Cape aloes
cayenne
Curaçao aloes
garlic
ginger root.

Combine all the herbs, which should be finely powdered, sieve them well together and fill size 0 gelatine capsules with them.

DOSAGE

Start by taking one capsule of this formula during or just after supper as it works best when mixed with food. The next morning you should notice an increase in your bowel movements and in the amount of faecal matter that you eliminate. The consistency should also be softer. If you do not notice any difference or the difference was not dramatic, double up the dosage the next day. Continue to increase your dosage every evening by one capsule each time at supper until you notice a pronounced difference in the way your bowel works. There is no limit to the number of capsules you should take. I find most of my patients need only 2–3 capsules but a few have needed up to 30. Remember it takes most of us years to create a sluggish and ineffective bowel, so be patient with yourself and do not expect an immediate result.

Note: *do not use this formulation during pregnancy.*

INTESTINAL CORRECTIVE FORMULA NO. 3

This soothing and cleansing formula is to be used alongside Intestinal Corrective Formula No. 2 or 1 as a strong purifier of the intestinal tract. It will remove old, hardened faecal debris from the wall of the colon and from any bowel pockets. It will also draw out toxins, poisons, heavy metals such as mercury and lead, and radioactive elements like strontium-90. The charcoal in the formulation has the ability to draw out 3,000 different kinds of chemical drug from the bowel and through the bowel wall from the bloodstream and the lymphatic system. In addition, the natural mucilaginous properties of the formulation make it an excellent remedy for inflammation of the stomach and intestines. This property is also valuable for softening hardened, dried faecal matter for easy removal. Many of my patients have discovered that this formulation has also removed colon polyps. It is also an antidote for food and other types of poisoning.

Two parts of:
charcoal, powdered
ground flax seeds
psyllium seeds
One part of:
benetonite clay
carob pod, powdered
fruit pectin
liquorice root
slippery elm bark.

DOSAGE
Take one rounded teaspoon 2–5 times daily, mixing each dose in a blender with 4–6 fl. oz (120–180 ml) of fruit juice. It is essential to drink an additional 16 fl. oz (480 ml) of any type of liquid after every dose of this formulation and you may need to increase your dose of Intestinal Corrective Formula No. 1 or 2 while taking this.
Linusit Gold (organically grown flax seed), available from most healthfood shops, is a useful addition to this formulation but not a substitute. Add 2 teaspoons to each dose of the formula.

THE LIVER
The demands on the liver during the menopause are particularly heavy. Among its many complex functions, the liver is a recycling centre. The hormones manufactured daily are broken down by the liver once they

are no longer needed and their parts become available for the production of other hormones. Of necessity during the menopause hormones like LH and FSH (see Chapter One) are produced in such huge quantities that the poor liver struggles to keep up with its invaluable recycling work and so neglects one of its other duties, the digestive process — yet another reason why indigestion can become more common in the menopause. Add to this the fact that our livers have a particularly hard task today because they are inundated with so many chemicals, the result of environmental poisoning or ingesting totally synthetic food. Indeed we eat substances which are so heavily processed that they can no longer be recognised as food. Even in some brands of wholemeal bread I have observed as many as eight additives, including the ubiquitous whey (see above).

The main function of the liver is to maintain the body's dynamic balance by preparing fats, carbohydrates and protein for its use, by storing some nutrients, by manufacturing enzymes, bile, antibodies, and the specific proteins needed for blood clotting and by maintaining the proper blood levels of glycogen, amino acids, hormones and vitamins, as well as neutralising any poisons which enter the bloodstream. In short, the liver is an amazingly sophisticated chemical factory.

If your liver is ailing, you may have feelings of heaviness or discomfort in the area of the lower margin of the ribs on your right side, coupled with a feeling of general sluggishness and tiredness for no reason. Indigestion with flatulence may go on for years as well as alternating constipation and diarrhoea. The tongue is often thickly coated, white or yellow, and bad breath may be a problem.

Eating only natural healthy foods and living in an environmentally clear atmosphere will delight your long-suffering liver. Any kind of exercise, particularly walking, is beneficial, relieving digestive gas and improving transit time in the liver and intestine. Stressed livers particularly hate all processed, fried and fatty foods, especially dairy products and deep-fried food. They need plenty of vitamins A and D and calcium to assist them in maintaining healthy internal mucosa. Alcohol should be taken in moderation: leave at least three days a week alcohol free. Livers particularly benefit from a daily ingestion of lecithin granules (available in healthfood stores) which can be sprinkled into soup or porridge. They also like plenty of garlic, ginger, onions, lemons and vegetables from the mustard family. In addition, I actively encourage liver cleansing during the menopause.

A Spring Clean for the Liver

Spring is a particularly appropriate time to do a liver cleanse because the body is just emerging from a winter of heavy fatty congestive foods and not enough exercise. Liver flushes are an excellent way of stimulating the elimination of waste from the body by opening and cooling the liver and increasing the bile flow, so improving overall liver function. They also help to purify the blood and the lymph. My favourite liver flush is as follows:

LIVER FLUSH

Take one (building up to three) cloves of garlic and 1 in. (2.5 cm) of peeled fresh ginger. Liquidise them at high speed in 8 fl. oz (240 ml) of juice, with a thinly pared and sliced fresh lemon. As you liquidise, add 1–4 tablespoons (15–60 ml) of flax seed or organic olive oil. The juice you choose can be a combination of freshly squeezed citrus juices, apple, carrot, or carrot mixed with beetroot. Garlic and ginger have excellent liver-protective qualities and garlic in particular provides important sulphur compounds that the liver needs to build enzymes.

LIVER TONIC

Equal parts of:
black walnut
dandelion
fennel
garlic
gentian
ginger
milk thistle

Oregon grape
wormwood
in tincture form.

Add 70 drops of this to the liver flush while liquidising and take a further 70 drops in water four more times for a week after eating.

The herbs in this tincture are famous for their ability to stimulate, cleanse and protect the liver and gall bladder and rid the body of parasites. Milk thistle has certain chemicals that bind and coat liver cells, not only healing previous damage but also protecting the liver from any future damage. The Oregon grape, gentian, wormwood and dandelion stimulate digestion, helping the liver to excrete more bile which, in turn, cleans both the liver and gall bladder. This is a particularly useful formulation for anyone who has had constipation, eaten large amounts of animal foods, including dairy products, throughout their life or drunk alcohol, tea or coffee or eaten chocolate in large quantities. It is also particularly recommended for those with high cholesterol or a family history of liver or gall bladder problems.

This formation works best if taken simultaneously with a bowel cleanse. You may keep it up for between one and four weeks in the spring, while adhering to a light diet and fasting on the seventh day on carrot and beetroot juice, or carrot and apple juice. You may notice your faeces will produce a little green colouring during the cleanse or, better still, you may notice some parasites coming out of your bowel movements because there are a number of anti-parasitic herbs in the formulation. Remember a 1 in. (2.5 cm) cube of beef can contain over 1,000 parasite larvae just waiting to hatch in your body, and as much as 65 per cent of fresh fish may contain toxic levels of bacteria and parasites.

Follow any liver flush with 1–2 cups (240–480 ml) of piping hot detox tea.

DETOX TEA

Equal parts of:
black peppercorns
carob pods
cinnamon sticks
clove buds
coriander seeds
fennel seeds
ginger
hawthorn berries
horsetail
juniper
liquorice root
orange peel
parsley
roasted chicory
roasted dandelion root
uva ursi.

To make this tea as effective as possible, put 2 tablespoons of the herbs into 1 pint (600 ml) of pure water, allowing the tea to steep in cold water overnight. In the morning heat up to a boil while tightly covered, reducing to simmer for 15 minutes. Strain out the herbs but do not discard them. Drink two cups of the liquid as hot as possible and then put the herbs back into the pot. Add a tablespoon of fresh herbs and a further pint (600 ml) of pure water. Let it sit overnight and repeat the whole process again. Keep adding new herbs to the old ones for three days, then discard all the herbs and start again.

This tea is based on an old East Indian digestive tea formulation known as yogi spiced tea. It is stimulating to the digestion and soothes the stomach, and is mildly cleansing for the blood, skin, liver and gall bladder. It also flushes out the bile and fats that the liver flush has purged out of the liver and gall bladder, and is a mild diuretic and disinfectant to the kidneys and bladder — it may make you urinate a little more within an hour after ingestion. Best of all it is an excellent coffee replacement and tastes very nice. It increases the circulation but has no caffeine and will help wean you off coffee and tea.

Do not eat or drink anything for one hour after your liver flush. If possible use the time to lie down with a castor oil poultice over the area of your abdomen above the liver. When the hour is over, drink 8 fl. oz (240 ml) of prune juice. If you make it yourself, soak ten organic prunes in two glasses of water overnight. Liquidise this in the morning but remember to take the pits out first. Prune juice has an extraordinary ability to draw toxins from every part of the body and eliminate them through the bowel, which is why bowel movements after prune juice often smell so strange and strong.

Major Gall Bladder Flush

As we saw in Chapter Two, HRT has been found to accelerate the risk of cancer of the gall bladder. If you have been on HRT and have decided to stop and use natural alternatives instead, I would encourage a major gall bladder flush preceded by a month of diligent liver cleansing, which will help you to ease your way into it.

This gall bladder flush is recommended only for those who are already experienced with fasting and cleansing and want to remove even more old wastes stored in liver cells and other tissues. It is an extremely strong cleanse but during the hundreds of gall bladder flushes I have supervised in my time I have never seen patients become anything more than nauseated at the very worst. It should not be undertaken without the supervision of a medical herbalist.

This flush activates the liver and gall bladder even more strongly than the liver flush. By combining it with a three-day juice fast, toxic waste released during fasting will be effectively eliminated during the strong bile flush and enema. People very often eliminate lots of green putty-textured stones and, while I have heard them called gall stones manufactured from cholesterol, I have my doubts and feel they may well be saponified oil.

I have also observed a lot of anger, negativity and frustration purged during the course of a gall bladder flush. In addition, people who take gall bladder flushes in groups can behave as if they were drunk. Whether this is due to old drug residues being re-experienced as they are eliminated from the body or the result of a systemic hormonal reaction to all the oil in the flush, does not really matter. Either way the gall bladder flush is an extremely powerful and effective cleanse for the liver and gall bladder.

At 7 o'clock in the evening of the third day of your juice fast, liquidise 1 pint (600 ml) of organic olive oil with the juice of nine freshly squeezed lemons and take 5 tablespoons (75 ml) every 15 minutes. If you find yourself vomiting up any olive oil, continue to take the remainder but do not go back to the beginning. Sucking an ice cube or sipping a little decocted ginger tea in between doses of oil and lemon juice often helps with nausea.

If you find drinking olive oil in such large quantities truly horrendous, try sipping it through a straw so that it does not contact the lips but goes right down the back of the tongue and throat easily. Once you have finished drinking the oil, lie on your right side with your knees tucked up and your hips elevated and stay in this position for at least two hours, unless you are actually sitting up to drink the olive oil and lemon juice. Meanwhile distract yourself with some of your favourite music or a good television video if you can see it from this angle.

Once the oil is finished go to bed with a warm castor oil compress over the liver and a hot-water bottle, and if you need anything else to drink, sip only ginger tea or water.

The next morning take a chicory enema or a warm-water enema with the juice of half a lemon squeezed into it. Both will help to stimulate elimination, but the chicory one is more effective. People bring me gifts of what they consequently produce in jars, and the 'gall stones' range in size from gravel to beans and seeds to lumps the size of golf balls. If stored in a jar they will dissolve within a couple of days. In order to retrieve them (and naturally this is for your own interest only, and possibly that of your practitioner), you will need to wash the bowel movements with running water through a sieve so it is best to defecate in a potty.

Please note that this cleanse should be done only once a year and should *always* be preceded by at least ten days of the liver flush.

THE KIDNEYS

Another major organ of the body that needs special care during the menopause is the kidneys, as oedema can be a problem at this time. Bloating, swelling of the fingers, ankles and legs, breast tenderness and emotional outbursts can all be the result of water retention. Oestrogen helps to regulate fluid balance, and while it fluctuates considerably during the menopause, it can cause the body's sodium level to escalate which has a knock-on effect of making the cells retain more water. Only a few ounces of excess water can cause breast tenderness, swelling and mood fluctuations. If we get dried out as the result of too little water in the body, it can make us feel hot and bad-tempered. If our cells are too waterlogged, we can feel weepy, overly emotional and depressed.

It is not a good idea to resort to chemical diuretics (see below); nor should you cut down on your fluid intake, for water is actually nature's best diuretic (see Chapter Four).

While the liver acts internally to neutralise and eliminate poisons, the kidneys' role in elimination is all too obvious. Any job which ought to be done by the kidneys but which is not will result in impure blood returning to the heart. This is one of the main reasons why diuretics are often prescribed for heart problems by allopathic doctors, but remember that all chemical diuretics work by irritating the delicate tubules in the kidneys, forcing them to pass water and, in doing so, leaching out potassium from the body, so much so that synthetic potassium has to be given in its place.

Herbal diuretics are inherently safe because they contain potassium and the various complex nutrients needed to maintain an efficient input and output. They raise both potassium and sodium levels so that the cellular pump-action improves both ways. For example, celery is high in sodium with a touch of potassium, while dandelion is high in potassium with a little sodium.

Healthy kidneys need to be constantly flushed out, so drink lots of pure water and potassium-rich broth made from tough outer green leaves of vegetables and potato skins (see Chapter Four, 'Salt', for the recipe). Try to cut out tea, coffee, cocoa, salt and alcohol completely and drink plenty of fruit and vegetable juices. Follow a diet which is high in fresh fruit and vegetables and keep it free as far as possible from processed foods. Strawberries are especially useful for dispelling uric acid.

Never ignore a full bladder. I am amazed how seldom many of my patients urinate, often only two or three times a day. By holding on, the lining of the bladder gets intensely irritable as its contents are subjected to chemical change if harboured too long. A full bladder will press down on all the pelvic organs, especially the lower bowel and reproductive organs and aggravate the possibility of prolapse. If we are eliminating efficiently we should lose at least one gallon (4.8 litres) of water every day through the skin, the kidneys and other eliminative organs. Evidence of water retention if your kidneys are malfunctioning includes puffy angles, swollen fingers and feet which spill over the sides of your shoes. Waterlogged kidneys are evidenced by dark circles and bagginess under the eyes.

Barley water is an idea drink to soothe and cleanse the kidneys and maintain them in peak condition. It has the added bonus of strengthening the nails and improving the quality and quantity of milk of lactating mothers as well as helping to relieve asthma because of the hordein it contains.

BARLEY WATER

Pour 1.5 pints (900 ml) of water over 1 oz (30 g) of whole-grain barley (pot barley will not do) and boil until the quantity is reduced by half. Add the zest of the rind of one lemon (excluding the white pith) and sweeten with a little organic maple syrup, organic honey or apple juice if desired. Drink freely at room temperature. It tastes very pleasant.

KIDNEY FLUSH

On rising, add to 16–32 fl. oz (480–960 ml) of pure water (it can be warmed) the juice of a freshly squeezed lime and a lemon (or two lemons if limes are not available). Add a generous pinch of cayenne pepper and, if desired, organic maple syrup to sweeten. To this add the mixture that follows.

KIDNEY/BLADDER TONIC

Equal parts of:
burdock
cornsilk
goldenrod
juniper berries
parsley
uva ursi leaves
in tincture form.

Add 60 drops to the morning drink. This tonic is both diuretic and disinfectant. It works best if you take a further 60 drops four more times during the course of the day in extra liquid, and should be used alongside kidney bladder tea.

KIDNEY/BLADDER TEA

Equal parts of:
cornsilk
dandelion
goldenrod
gravel root
horsetail
hydrangea root
juniper berries
marshmallow root
orange peel
parsley
peppermint
uva ursi.

> *Use leaves or berries in every instance except for the roots and orange*
> *peel. Make as a decoction and drink 2 cups (480 ml) three times a day.*
> *You can keep on this kidney cleanse for a month.*

If in the summer you want to do some further cleansing, fast for three days on water melon juice, including some of the seeds and 1 sq. in. (6.5 sq. cm) of the rind juiced into every 8 fl. oz (240 ml) of juice. Known as a water melon flush, this is an extremely effective diuretic. You can also include potassium broth on your three fasting days in copious amounts.

Adrenal Support

During the menopause the ovaries produce fewer hormones, including androgens. As we saw in Chapter One, these are also made by the adrenal glands, muscle, skin, brain, pineal gland, hair follicles and body fat, all of which normally take over from the ovaries during the menopause. Since androgens can themselves act as weak oestogens and their production is increased twofold during the menopause, most healthy women can get through the menopause unaided because their bodies are fully equipped for coping with the hormonal changes the ovaries are going through.

In addition, the metabolism of androgens does not appear to be affected by age. The liver remains the major site of androgen metabolism both during and after the menopause (hence the need for liver maintenance; see above). If the adrenal glands are functioning well, and androgens are being metabolised effectively, it will result in superabundant energy and a well-charged immune system able to fight off disease quickly and efficiently. Women also have better vaginal lubrication when they are adrenally well stocked since androgenic hormones are also associated with sexual response and libido.

However, prolonged stress can lead to adrenal depletion, the symptoms of which include nervous disorders, severe depression, irritability, fatigue and unpredictable mood swings — all remarkably similar to menopausal symptoms. Hence some otherwise healthy women require hormonal, nutritional and emotional support simply because they may arrive at the menopause in such a state of adrenal depletion due to stress.

ADRENAL TONIC

The following formulation is designed to restore hormonal function, support the adrenal glands, regulate blood sugar and increase the body's resistance to disease, so helping to counteract stress. As an added bonus it is also a rather good remedy for jet lag if taken a week before the flight and for a week after.

Two parts of:
Siberian ginseng root
One part of:
bladderwrack
echinacea
gotu kola
in tincture form.

The normal adult dosage is 15 drops taken three times a day.

FORMULA FOR CHRONIC ADRENAL EXHAUSTION

The following formulation will help the adrenal glands by nourishing and supporting them in the long term and is particularly useful when stress has become chronic.

Equal parts of:
liquorice
prickly ash
Siberian ginseng
in tincture form.

The normal adult dosage is 20 drops three times a day.

The Skin

The skin has to work very hard during the menopause if you suffer from hot sweats and flushes. It can become much more sensitive, often feeling prickly or itchy and, of course, it is the ever-present barometer of the ageing process. It becomes drier due to dwindling supplies of oestrogen and shifting levels of nutrients. I am often complimented on my excellent skin and I put it down to a good vegan diet, the flax seed oil I put into my daily liver flush, diligent skin brushing and regular hydrotherapy.

If your skin is spotty or has a poor texture, it may be evidence of a chronically congested bloodstream or bowel. Dr Christopher has designed an excellent blood-purifying formulation which contains not only blood rebuilders but cleansers and astringent herbs which increase the range and power of the circulation, particularly to those parts of the body which have been deficient (usually the extremities like the hands, head and feet). This formulation also removes cholesterol, kills infection and makes the veins more elastic while strengthening the arterial walls so that the herbal nutrients in it will travel efficiently through the blood and lymph and be effectively utilised.

Dr Christopher's Blood-Purifying Formula

Equal parts of:
buckthorn bark
burdock root
chaparral
liquorice root
Oregon grape root
peach bark
poke root
prickly ash bark
red clover blossom
stillingia.

All herbs should be finely powdered and put into size 0 gelatine capsules.

> *Take 3 capsules with each meal. If you get diarrhoea, it means that the formulation is working too hard and may also indicate the urgent necessity for bowel and liver purification. Attend to these two and then try and reduce the dose of the blood-purifying formula to a comfortable level.*

Regular exercise involving profuse sweating will help the skin. The sweat excreted from such exercise contains more toxic waste than the sweat you flush out during the course of a Turkish bath or sauna. However, these do help too, so do not reject them, although neither treatment should be taken if you have high blood pressure or are pregnant.

Too many people suffocate their sins with synthetic fibres. Wear only natural fabrics next to the skin. The healthiest fabric is cotton or, failing that, linen, silk or wool. Remember the palms of the hands and soles of the feet are particularly richly endowed with sweat glands so never suffocate these areas with non-leather shoes or nylon socks.

I do not recommend the routine use of synthetic soap all over the body. Choose an organic not a detergent soap (see Resources Directory) and use this only areas that are particularly sweaty or dirty. Skin brushing will do the rest (see below).

The skin is a two-way street, flushing outwards and ingesting inwards, so never put anything on your skin that you would not be prepared to eat. A few drops of a herbal essential oil mixed in a carrier base of almond or olive oil and added to bath water will act therapeutically on the skin as well as moisturising it. Never use mineral oil (sometimes sold as baby oil) or products containing it (as many commercial cleansing creams do).

Try to avoid using synthetic antiperspirants or deodorants because they block the skin's natural cleansing action and destroy the natural bacteria on the skin, upsetting its delicate protective pH balance. In addition, many of them contain aluminium, which is poisonous. If you smell particularly obnoxious it is because your body is off-loading toxins through your skin and you need to look at the inside not the outside to remedy the problem. Washing twice daily should keep you smelling sweet. If it does not use a natural deodorant (for a supplier see

Resources Directory). Alternatively wash more often until your body's purification is complete.

Do not wash your clothes with detergents that contain enzymes. In some people the body's defence mechanism responds to enzymes by launching an assault as if it were attacking an infection and sooner or later you may end up developing a serious form of skin irritation.

Skin Brushing

Because our skin is the largest two-way eliminative organ in our bodies, flushing outwards by way of perspiration and absorbing nutrients and vitamins from natural sunshine, it is worth taking special care of it. The skin also breathes and absorbs oxygen while exhaling carbon dioxide formed in the body's tissues. The hundreds and thousands of sweat glands, which should operate to expel at least 1 lb (450 g) of waste products daily, regulate body temperature and act as miniature detoxifying organs working to cleanse the blood and free the system of suffocating poisons.

Help the skin to eliminate daily by dry skin brushing for 5 minutes followed by the seven times hot/cold shower routine (see below).

The benefits of skin brushing must be tried and tested to be believed. You will feel clean, refreshed and much more alert. Skin brushing stimulates the circulation, helping to pump the blood down through veins and up through the arteries, feeding those organs of the body which lie near the surface. It also stimulates the lymph and adrenal glands and, because of the hundreds of nerve endings in the skin, has a powerful rejuvenating effect on the nervous system.

By vigorously skin brushing over the major lymph glands, the dumping stations for waste fluids, you can stimulate the expulsion of mucoid lymphatic material or impacted lymph (more commonly known as cellulite). These lymph glands are situated behind the elbows and knees, under the arms, either side of the throat and, especially, in the groin. Skin brushing removes dead skin layers and other impurities, thereafter keeping the pores open and unclogged, and increases the elimination capacity of the skin. Used in conjunction with hot/cold showers it will help stop colds. It is important to remember that the skin brush is exclusively yours, not to be lent to or borrowed by others.

Five minutes of energetic skin brushing is equivalent to 30 minutes' jogging, as far as physical tone is concerned. It will build up healthy muscle tone and stimulate better distribution of fat deposits. All in all it can help you feel younger and gives a terrific sense of wellbeing.

You will need a natural bristle brush with a detachable long wooden handle. At my clinic I sell brushes made with Mexican tampico fibres which I import from Germany. The bristles are quite stiff to begin with and will soften with use, so start with a light pressure and increase it. Your skin should be nicely pink and glowing. Do not use it to brush the face — a softer and smaller brush is needed for that area. Nor should you use brushes made of nylon and synthetic fibres as they create static in the body, and you would need to scrub for 20–30 minutes with a loofah or hand mitt to achieve the same effect as just five minutes of brushing.

As your skin brushing is done dry brush on dry skin, it is important to maintain the brush properly. Wash it out once a week in warm soapy water, using natural soap. Rinse it well and dry in the airing cupboard thoroughly.

How to Skin Brush
Start with soles of your feet and a dry body. Brush upwards towards the heart from below and downwards from above.

Brush vigorously up the legs and over thighs, remembering to brush towards the groin where the lymph glands are. Use a circular clockwise movement over the abdomen, following the line of the colon and do this about ten times. Avoid the genital area and the nipples.

Brush palms and the backs of the hands, up the arms to the shoulders, then use downward strokes on neck, throat and over the chest. To stimulate the important lymph glands under the arms, you need to use your hands to create a pumping action. Lodge the thumb under the clavicle bone and with all the fingers grip the pectoral muscle, making sure the finger tips get right into the armpit. Squeeze and then release this area about fifteen times on each side.

Attach the handle on the brush so that you can brush across the top of the shoulders and upper back, then up over the buttocks and lower back.

This should take you about five minutes daily: first thing in the morning is the best time. Should you need to brush twice a day, do not brush too close to bedtime or you will not sleep. Brush every day for three months, then reduce it to 2–3 times weekly, changing the days each week. Never brush skin that is irritated, damaged or infected, or over bad varicose veins.

The scalp can be brushed to stimulate hair growth and to get rid of dandruff or impurities, or you may prefer to massage it with your fingertips to move the scalp skin.

Showering

After your 5 minutes' skin brushing, it is time to remove the dead skin cells by showering. Take a hot shower or bath for 2–3 minutes, followed by a cold shower for 20 seconds, and repeat seven times. Move the shower head from the feet upwards and then finish by holding it over the medulla oblongata at the back of the skull, letting cold water run down the spine. This method of hydrotherapy will alkalise the blood, clean the head and give a special boost to the glandular system and vital functions of the body.

A Summary of Ways to Look After the Skin

- Use only natural fabrics next to the skin, i.e. cotton, linen, silk, wool. That includes cotton or wool gloves and leather or canvas shoes.
- Use only natural organic soaps or olive-oil-based soaps, and natural oils which penetrate the skin rather than mineral or synthetic oils that lie on the surface only.
- Take regular exercise to promote breathing. Turkish baths and saunas also help.
- Encourage elimination by dry skin brushing daily. When fasting skin brush twice daily, morning and evening.

THE HEART

Post-menopausal women die from heart disease as rapidly as men do. Women beyond the menopause account for 51 per cent of all cardiovascular deaths, men 49 per cent. Remember too that HRT has been shown actually to increase the risk of stroke and heart attack (see

Chapter Two). Heart disease is the number one killer in the Western world, accounting for one in three deaths, but the reasons for its occurrence in women are not nearly as straightforward as generally postulated. Certainly oestrogen affects the cardiovascular system by increasing heart-protecting high-density lipoproteins that counteract low-density lipoproteins, but oestrogen also stimulates 400 types of cells that have oestrogen receptors, so administering it during the menopause has a ripple effect beyond the heart and blood. In addition, while high cholesterol is one of the top three risk factors for heart disease in men, this is not the case for women. The top three risk factors for women are untreated hypertension, smoking and too much fat carried over the belly.

It seems that 90 per cent of all heart disease can be prevented with lifestyle changes. A 'change of heart' is what is needed in all areas of one's life: a deliberate moving away from stressful work patterns and relationships, old eating patterns, old ways of celebrating (with lots of alcohol and rich food). Changes include eating a diet that is a low in fat, caffeine and salt, stopping smoking, keeping blood pressure under control, exercising regularly and gradually shedding any excess weight. Above all, one should practise compassion to oneself and others, a factor that is often neglected but incredibly important. Hard-heartedness can result literally in problems of the heart.

The following formula nourishes and protects the heart, safely relaxes blood vessels, and regulates tachycardia (erratic heart beat) while lessening the incidence of hot flushes.

HEART TONIC

Six parts of:
hawthorn berries.
One part of:
black cohosh, chaste tree
garlic, ginger, motherwort

Combine all these herbs as a tincture and take 20 drops three times a day with meals.

FOUR

THE POWER OF POSITIVE EATING

D ietary imbalances and unhealthy eating patterns can actually cause many of the supposed 'symptoms' of menopause. Body, mind, energy, emotions, spirit are all profoundly influenced by the food you eat. In short: garbage in, garbage out. How can you hope to build healthy living cells on dead, chemical-laden, processed foods?

Dr Max Bircher-Benner, Swiss nutritionist and visionary, understood this very well. 'Mangez vivant!' he would say to his patients, meaning 'Eat living food!'. He had no objections to eating meat as long as it was uncooked and in its entirety of blood, fat, bones, entrails, skin and flesh — in other words, the way a lion eats its prey in the wild. And how many of us would be willing to do that? He maintained that as soon as anything is processed in some way, it alters the state of the wholefood energy and produces ill-health. Later experiments with cats provided evidence for this view. Cats fed on a raw diet flourished over several generations, while those fed on cooked meat developed all sorts of malformations and health problems, including allergies and genetic defects. Dr Bircher-Benner maintained that while nutrition may not be 'the highest thing in life ... it is the soil on which the highest things can either perish or flourish'.[1]

The following nutritional steps are all invaluable to obtain optimum health during the menopause:

- Keep blood-sugar levels stable.
- Cut out dairy products, meat and salt.
- Avoid caffeine and alcohol.

- Ensure plenty of essential fatty acids in the diet.
- Eat organic food as far as possible.
- Keep nutritional supplements natural.

BLOOD-SUGAR LEVELS

Sugar is highly addictive. That is one of the reasons it appears in so many processed foods masquerading under all sorts of labels, including sucrose, glucose, dextrose, fructose, lactose, various syrups, honey, invert sugar (rather like synthetic honey), molasses, treacle, Sorbitol, Mannitol, Xylitol. Of the hundreds of pounds of sugar we eat on average each year, *seventy* are hidden in processed foods. Sugars are present in the form of preservatives, bulking agents, cheap sweeteners and give what food technologists call 'mouth-feel'.

You might expect to find sugar in soft drinks, but it is also present in some brands of frozen peas and the manufactured muesli which so many people eat, imagining it to be a healthfood. And have you ever thought how much sugar there is in an average-sized bottle of Coke? One tablespoon! This is more than enough to depress for several hours the ability your white blood cells have to engulf and destroy bacteria; and certainly enough to begin the long downhill slide to tooth decay.

In his eye-opening book *Sugar Blues*, William Duffey states that 'the difference between sugar addiction and narcotic addiction is largely one of degree'.[2] You may think this is extreme but have you ever noticed how hard it is to have just one bite of cake? Even a tiny amount creates a desire for more. And if you have ever tried to stop eating sweet things, you will experience strong cravings, along with lassitude, depression and possibly even fierce headaches.

Excessive sugar is one of the culprits in hypoglycaemia, diabetes, heart disease, dental caries, high cholesterol, indigestion, myopia, seborrhoeic dermatitis, gout, hyperactivity and an inability to concentrate, depression, anxiety, the crowding and malformation of teeth as well as the narrowing of bones in the jaw and pelvis, candidiasis and breast cancer.

The fact is we do not need sugar; it contains no additional nutrients. To make white sugar the juice is crushed out of sugar cane, leaving the fibrous bulk behind. It is then purified, filtered and boiled down into concentrated form till sugar crystals appear, and to facilitate these processes sulphur dioxide, milk of lime, carbon dioxide, calcium carbonate and charcoal (from burnt cows' bones) are used. While unrefined sugar does not have these additives, it is often contaminated with soil, mould and bacteria, while 'brown' sugars are merely refined white ones stained with additional molasses.

Artificial sugars are no better. Not only are they carcinogenic, but they actually encourage weight gain. Diet soft drinks are particularly high in them, contributing to the ubiquitous cocktail of excessive inorganic minerals and additives that overburden the liver and exacerbate the leaching of calcium from the bones, accelerating osteoporosis. In addition, the carbon dioxide present in fizzy drinks accelerates the speed by which these compounds are absorbed into the bloodstream.

If you need a sweetener, use date sugar (made from dried dates), organic maple syrup or honey, and use them very sparingly.

Hypoglycaemia

Otherwise known as low blood sugar, hypoglycaemia is extremely widespread in the West. I would estimate that some 60 per cent of my own patients suffer from it to some degree. Unhappily it often tends to go undiagnosed and its multitude of symptoms labelled merely emotional or psychological.

Blood-Glucose Levels

Usually blood-glucose levels are stabilised within a narrow band of variation by different hormones which react rapidly to the slightest changes. Insulin from the pancreas is released when glucose enters the blood from digested foods, so blood-glucose levels remain normal. The sugar is then stored in the liver and muscles as glycogen, or is converted to fat for later use. Cortisol and growth hormone counterbalance such insulin action. If any of these hormones are secreted too quickly or too slowly, the blood-glucose level becomes imbalanced. The most commonly involved glands and organs in this hypoglycaemic roller coaster are the adrenals, pancreas and liver. Hypoglycaemia is sometimes caused by a diet too rich in refined carbohydrates and adrenalin-producing caffeine and alcohol, as well as by stress. Caffeine stimulates the adrenal glands which try to mobilise the body's energy reserves in the liver and muscles, so removing its fail-safe mechanism for regulating blood-glucose levels.

Diagnosis

The symptoms of hypoglycaemia include irritability, fatigue, depression, an insatiable craving for sweets or carbohydrates, inability to concentrate, sweating, shaking, palpitations, tingling of the skin, lips or scalp, dizziness, trembling, fainting, blurred vision, nausea, rapid swoops and dips in energy particularly in the middle of the morning and mid-to-late afternoon, anxiety, indecisiveness and weeping. Symptoms are usually improved by eating. Hypoglycaemia can be accurately diagnosed using a five-hour blood-glucose test which can be conducted in hospital (although most hospitals do not even know of its existence) or in laboratories set up to deal with glucose-tolerance testing. A predisposition to hypoglycaemia can also be clearly determined by an iridology test.

Diet

The best diet to follow if you suffer from hypoglycaemia is one containing high-fibre, unrefined carbohydrates (hence slow to digest), along with adequate sources of non-animal protein. Meals should be small and spread out over the course of the day. It is important to avoid sugar in all its forms. Once the blood-sugar levels have been thoroughly stabilised, you can introduce a teaspoon or two of organic maple syrup daily. Anything refined should be avoided such as white rice, white flour and white bread, as should alcohol, coffee and cigarettes. Use whatever methods work for you for stress control and eat only when relaxed.

Many women whose energy levels are low during the menopause find following a hypoglycaemic diet extremely helpful.

Fruit

Fruit — dried or fresh — freshly pressed fruit juices and vegetable juices are all rapidly absorbed and therefore should be consumed moderately by sufferers from hypoglycaemia. It is advisable to dilute fruit and vegetable juices half and half with filtered water. When eating fruit it should be taken with a handful of nuts or soya yoghurt or a drink of soya milk. Fruit juice can be further fortified by superfoods that are high in plant protein, including spirulina, chlorella (see later in this chapter) and nutritional yeast.

Nutritional Yeast
Nutritional yeast (available from healthfood stores) is rich in elements such as chromium that help to stabilise glucose levels in the system and are essential for carbohydrate metabolism and proper insulin function. Take a dessert spoon of this three times a day. It is delicious stirred into soup, soya yoghurt or potassium broth (see 'Salt' below).

Fibre
Fibre will help the regular absorption of carbohydrate from the intestines. Foods which are particularly useful include whole grains, especially pre-soaked oats cooked at a low temperature, nuts, nut butters and nut milk (see 'Alternatives to Dairy Products' below), avocado, nutritional yeast and Jerusalem artichokes.

THE DANGERS OF A HIGH-FAT DIET

Our fat-laden, low-fibre diet is one of the contributing factors to the increase of breast cancer, endometriosis and uterine fibroids. Sixty per cent of all women's cancers, that is breast, ovary and uterus, are *directly* related to the level of fat in the diet.[3] Both benign and malignant tumours in the breast, ovary and uterus are closely associated with elevated oestrogen levels. Vegetables alter the metabolism of oestrogen in the bowel so that less is absorbed into the bloodstream through the colon wall and more is excreted. A vegetable-rich diet thus reduces oestrogen levels and, in turn, the risk of cancer.

High-fat diets stimulate sensitive breast tissue through excessive oestrogen production causing breast tenderness and the growth of cysts. The higher actual body fat and fat in the diet, the higher one's oestrogen levels and subsequently the greater risk of all gynaecological cancers. Body fat itself is capable of manufacturing oestrone, a kind of oestrogen, through the conversion of cholesterol to aldosterone. Decreasing the fat content of your diet to 20 g per day, which generally means cutting out dairy products altogether, will usually help alleviate menstrual cramping, the pain of endometriosis, allergies, sinusitis and even recurrent vaginitis.

DAIRY PRODUCTS
In the words of Dr Christiane Northrup:

> As a gynaecologist, I also see many problems associated with dairy food: benign breast conditions, chronic vaginal discharge, acne, menstrual cramps, fibroids, chronic intestinal upset and increased pain from endometriosis. I can't help but think there may be some correlation between the over-stimulation of the cow's mammary glands and subsequent over-stimulation of our own, resulting in benign breast conditions.[4]

I believe she is absolutely right. Imagine pushing a thick, dense substance like cheese or ice cream through a sieve. After only a short time the small openings would get gummed up, ruining the efficacy of the sieve. When we eat dairy produce precisely the same thing happens to our internal organs — the lungs, the intestines, the liver and particularly the kidneys. Burdened with an excessive amount of waste which the body is unable to handle, our organs literally clog up, unable to use the normal excreting channels and forced to use exterior ones — the skin and the linings to the mucous membranes. Any excessive matter that cannot be handled even in this way stays inside the body, turning into mucus and puss, the perfect breeding ground for bacteria. Dairy products are an ideal medium for infections and women suffer far more from the build-up and congestive effects of dairy products than men do, the subsequent problems taking longer to heal. This is not surprising when you think that milk is supposed to flow out of a woman's body, not into it. Reverse the flow and the energy system backs up so everything gets stuck.

The milk of any species was designed for one purpose only: to feed its young. Humans are the only creatures on earth who regularly drink as part of their normal diet the milk designed for another species.

The enzymes we need to break down and digest milk are rennin and lactose. By the age of four many of us lose the ability to digest lactose because we can no longer synthesise the digestive enzyme lactase necessary for its breakdown. This lactose intolerance results in diarrhoea, flatulence and stomach cramps. It has been suggested that some 90 per cent of adult Asian and black people and 20 per cent of Caucasian children are lactose intolerant.[5]

To the list of problems naturally inherent in the human consumption of milk designed for baby cows I can add a whole host of unnatural ones. Cow's milk contains the accumulated pesticides that have been sprayed on the grain fed to cattle, along with the female hormones given to cows to increase milk production and body fats. The relatively new use of the hormone bovine somatotropin (BST) in milk may change its chemical composition and present an uncertain and as yet uncharted danger to humans. Some milk has been shown to contain trace metals and radioactivity at higher levels than those permissible in drinking water. Around 20 per cent of milk-producing cows in the US are infected with leukaemia viruses which, because milk is pooled when collected, infects the whole milk supply. These cancer-inducing viruses are resistant to being killed by pasteurisation and have been recovered from supermarkets supplies. Surely it is no coincidence that the highest rates of leukaemia are found in children aged 3–13 who consume the most milk products, and in dairy farmers who, as a profession, have the highest rate of leukaemia of any occupational group?

Alternatives to Dairy Products

Despite all this gloomy news, there is some heartening information. There are many delicious and healthy alternatives to milk and dairy products. My favourite are soya products. Almost everything you can get as a dairy product is available in its soya form, including ice cream, cream, milk, yoghurt, cheese and butter. Some of these are even beginning to appear in supermarkets and all of them are available in healthfood shops. Certain soya yoghurts contain brown sugar but there are some which are sweetened with apple juice and taste very good. It is also possible to make your own soya yoghurt. Rice and oat milk can be found in some healthfood shops. Nut milks are a delicious alternative to dairy milk and are easily made at home, although one should proceed cautiously with children, who can be allergic to nuts of any kind.

ALMOND MILK

half a cup of almonds
4 cups (1 litre) of water
honey to taste.

Blend in a liquidiser and strain.
For a whiter, blander milk, skin the almonds first by soaking them in boiling water, draining them and pinching the fat end of each almond between the thumb and forefinger. The nut will simply slide out.

Other Sources of Calcium

Having been warned off dairy products, most menopausal women get understandably anxious about the link between calcium loss and osteoporosis and naturally ask about effective alternative sources of calcium. The logical reply is that women should obtain their calcium from precisely the same sources that cattle get it — dark-green leafy vegetables and whole grains. Other sources of calcium that are easily assimilable include sea vegetables — nori, wakame, dulse, kelp, hijiki — available from healthfood shops, seeds, soya products, nuts, nut milks and nut butters and carrot juice (which, pint for pint, contains eight times the calcium that milk does). The best herbal sources of calcium are nettles, parsley, sprouted alfalfa, comfrey, horsetail, sage, uva ursi, raspberry, cleavers, red clover, oat seed and oat straw, dandelion root and leaves, borage, plantain and yellow dock. To promote the production of hydrochloric acid (essential for the proper absorption of calcium), try taking these herbs as herbal vinegars. Select from the most flavourful of them and sprinkle on salads, add to soups and stews, or simply drink them in hot water sweetened with a little maple syrup or black strap molasses. Equally beneficial for good hydrochloric acid production is dandelion root tincture, 15 drops before each meal.

HERBAL VINEGAR

Pack a glass jar with the herb or a combination of herbs of your choice, bruising the leaves in a pestle and mortar. Cover to the brim with organic cider vinegar. Leave to brew for two weeks from the new to the full moon shaking several times daily. Strain, rebottle and remember to label.
One tablespoon (15 ml) of herbal vinegar provides 137 mg of calcium.

Points to Remember When Choosing Alternative Sources of Calcium

Organically grown vegetables have a higher nutritional content than those sprayed with pesticides or grown with artificial fertilisers.

The nutritional content of food depends on where the food was grown, when it was harvested and the quality of the soil. Healthy soil is one of the world's greatest natural resources and this rich, nutrient-packed layer of the earth's crust from which food crops draw their sustenance is currently being lost at the rate of 24 billion tonnes a year. One thousand million gallons of liquid pesticides are now being used yearly on Britain's farms. A report by the London Food Commission (*Food Adulteration and How to Beat It*) states that of the 426 main chemicals legally used in 3,009 brands of pesticides and fertilisers, 164 have been implicated in causing cancer, genetic mutations, irritant reactions and reproductive problems ranging from impotence to birth defects. Now you know why I am pressing you to eat organically.

When choosing fruit and vegetables for a calcium-rich diet, bear in mind that plants from the Solanaceae family — tomatoes, potatoes, aubergines, peppers and tobacco — affect calcium balance in the body. It has been observed that cattle feeding on a variety of plants from the Solanaceae family develop malformed skeletons and become so disabled that they are unable to walk and have to graze from a kneeling position.[6]

Other Foods to Avoid

There is a formidable list of foods that in one way or another affect our calcium balance. Some add calcium in an unbalanced context while others counterbalance these, and still more will drain calcium from the system. Others cause calcium to be pushed into inappropriate locations like the soft tissue of the body, so it is vital to understand that eating food high in calcium may not be enough in itself. *The body must be able to assimilate and utilise calcium appropriately.* For more on which foods to avoid, see Chapter Two.

FATS

Saturated Fats

In addition to the diseases outlined above, eating too much saturated fat leads to other health problems including plaquing of the arteries and raising of blood cholesterol, which can lead to heart disease, strokes and even cancer. It is present in all dairy products and animal flesh and in two vegetable sources — coconut and palm oils. A lot of saturated fat is hidden in sausages, baked goods and dairy products, which tend also to contain a great deal of salt and sugar.

It should be noted that some of the more persistent residues from pesticides latch on to animal fats. A government survey found pesticide residues in one-third of all the sausages and half of all the burgers and cheeses that were sampled. This is particularly worrying because, according to the London Food Commission, 40 per cent of pesticides currently in use are linked with at least one serious side-effect. Out of 426 chemicals tested, 68 were found to be carcinogenic, 61 capable of mutating genes, 35 to have various effects on reproduction ranging from impotence to birth defects, and 93 to cause skin irritations and similar complaints.

Unsaturated fats (mono- or polyunsaturated) are equally high in calories as saturated fats and should be consumed in moderation, but they do have a beneficial effect on the viscosity of blood fats. In addition, the more unsaturated fat in the bloodstream, the less room there is for saturated fats.

Butter Versus Margarine

Margarine is made by pushing hydrogen gas through the pure, liquid, unsaturated oil in order to harden it. This process, known as hydrogenation, converts the unsaturated oil to a totally saturated fat. It is one of the greatest unexposed and poorly misunderstood scandals in the history of the food-manufacturing industry. Besides this, margarine is very close to plastic in its molecular structure and is food entirely lacking in nutrients. It will not support any type of bacteria or fungus, nor will it melt naturally when you roll it between your fingers. Imagine, then, what it does inside your body. Not only will it will give you the same number of calories as butter, but it includes colouring (annatto), as well as mono- and diglycerides and maltodextrin, which encourage the development of arterial plaque. A study conducted by Harvard Medical School of 85,095 women over an eight-year period found that those eating margarine developed an increased risk of coronary heart disease.

The oils in margarine are so refined that their essential fatty acids (EFAs) are damaged, and solvents from petroleum are added to produce a lighter taste and colour. Often bleach is added to improve clarity, and this removes even more EFAs, trace minerals and vitamins. If you heat up this obnoxious synthetic substance, the remaining EFAs are almost annihilated and the resulting oxidation creates damaging free radicals in the body, dramatically increasing your need for vitamins and minerals.

During the process of hydrogenation transfatty acids (TSAs) are produced which have a different molecular structure from anything found in human tissues. Because of their plastic-like quality, the body has great difficulty in both eliminating and assimilating them. The danger of TSAs is a complex but important issue; mainly they seem to disrupt the body's use of cholesterol. Because our bodies cannot produce low-density compounds which carry cholesterol, the cells have to work harder to synthesise cholesterol, so raising levels of cholesterol in the blood.

It is best to avoid anything that has been hydrogenated and use with discrimination the few non-hydrogenated margarines now available. Never heat them up or cook with them. Watch out for hydrogenated fats hidden in baked goods, canned sauces, cheese snacks, potato and corn crisps and chocolate.

Essential Fatty Acids

These occur naturally in unprocessed sprouted seeds and grains, raw nuts and their oils, leafy green vegetables, spirulina (see below), breast milk, fresh sea vegetables, and fresh fish caught in deep, cold oceans. So called because our cells cannot function normally without them and our bodies cannot manufacture them, EFAs are the most important nutrient for building and maintaining strong, efficient cell membranes and for optimising the delicate balance between prostaglandins (hormone-like chemicals). Lack of EFAs have been implicated in breast pain, menstrual cramps, oedema, atherosclerosis (hardening and thickening of the arteries) and breast cancer.

Prostaglandin 1 (PG_1) and, to a lesser extent, prostaglandin 3 (PG_3) reduce inflammation and regulate the neurotransmitters in the brain, encourage a healthy immune system and increase the production of different hormones in the body, including sex hormones. All of this keeps the brain cells and hormonal glands ticking over nicely, so if you suffer from mental fatigue, emotional imbalances, chronic viral fatigue, or adrenal exhaustion, you should take omega 6 EFAs to boost PG_1 levels. These are richly present in breast milk, cold-pressed sesame, corn and sunflower oils, fresh corn on the cob, soya beans, raw nuts and pulses, leafy green vegetables, spirulina, lecithin (available from healthfood shops as granules or oil capsules), borage, evening primrose and blackcurrant seed oil.

As women reach the menopause their bodies become less efficient at manufacturing PG_1 and PG_3, which may result in aching joints. If the diet is also high in saturated fats, PG_2 production rockets and PG_2 is responsible for inflammation and pain. Many of my menopausal patients who are eating carelessly complain of headaches, rheumatism or arthritis and lumbago. If I find such aches and pains are the result of dietary indiscretion, I advise 4 pints (2.4 litres) of water and at least 1 pint (600 ml) of freshly pressed carrot and celery juice daily; plenty of nutritional yeast stirred into potassium broth; a daily liver flush (see Chapter Three) including omega 3 and 6 oils; and, of course, cutting out all saturated fats, including the coconut and palm oil often hidden in nut butters and baked goods. Omega 3 oils are found in fresh fish from deep, cold-water oceans, linseeds, pumpkin seeds and walnuts and their oils, leafy green vegetables, sprouted wheat, fresh sea vegetables and soya beans. I particularly like Udo's oil (available in some healthfood shops — see also Resources Directory), which not only is organic but has the perfect balance of omega 3 and omega 6 EFAs designed to create the optimal balance of prostaglandins.

Olive Oil

If you are wondering what fat to cook with, the answer is olive oil, which actually lowers your cholesterol levels by reducing the low-density lipoproteins (LDLs), which can contribute to arterial plaque and heart disease, and increasing high-density lipoproteins (HDLs), which clear the blood of excess cholesterol and fat, protecting us from heart disease. But remember olive oil is still high in calories, so use it sparingly and check it is cold-pressed (unprocessed). Refined oils are treated with chemicals (including caustic soda) to remove fatty acids, then bleached and deodorised by heating at high temperatures for up to twelve hours. Their chemical structure is so altered they have no health benefits. Heating any oil to a point when it is at smoking temperature distorts its chemical structure and encourages the proliferation of free radicals in the body, so deep frying is not a good idea. When heating olive oil it is best to put a little hot water in the bottom of the pan first and wait for it to steam before adding the oil. This will stop the oil from getting too hot.

Synthetic Fats

Food manufacturers are tumbling over themselves to develop 'non-fats' and so grab a slice of the extremely profitable slimming market. Avoid them. Fluffed up with cellulose, synthetic sweeteners and additives, they are entirely artificial and unhealthy.

If you want a trouble-free menopause, you would be best to cut from your diet all hydrogenated and processed fats and food containing them.

MEAT

The countries in which most red meat is consumed suffer proportionately the highest rate of deaths from heart attacks, strokes, cancer and diabetes. For the majority of the world's population meat is used as a condiment, not to provide the bulk of a main course. Most Britons and Americans eat much more protein than they need, and protein from animal sources is clearly linked to chronic disease. Studies conducted at Cornell University (the China Health Project) found that, in general, only 7–10 per cent of the protein in the Chinese diet comes from animals, compared to 70 per cent for Americans. As in the West, heart disease, cancer and diabetes, whose incidence is negligible in the poorer rural districts, flourish in the richer areas of China (particularly the large cities) where more animal protein is consumed as a result of people being able to afford to eat more meat.

MEAT AND DISEASE

The most widespread kind of cancer in men and women in the Western world is colon rectal cancer, which accounts for 60 per cent of all cancers. Red meat is heavily implicated in this type of cancer. The probable reason for this is that, when the cholesterol in meat is digested, by-products are created that are powerful carcinogens. For example, when beef is barbecued, the fat that spatters into the fire is changed by the heat into benzopyrene, a potent carcinogen. This chemical rises in the smoke and coats the surface of the steak; when the meat is chewed and swallowed, it is smeared against the bowel wall during the course of the digestive process.

A diet high in red meat increases the risk of breast cancer in women. This is because cows, lambs and pigs bread for slaughter are fed hormones and antibiotics, the residues of which remain in active form in the meat. Women who eat animal fat create high levels of the hormones oestrogen and prolactin, and these stimulate the growth of breast tissue, the lining of the uterus and many other tissues. As a result, women who eat red meat have higher rates of tumours and cancers both of the breast and the uterus.

All forms of concentrated protein (including chicken, fish and eggs as well as meat) injure the kidney filters, contributing to kidney failure, as well as leaching calcium from the bones, leading to osteoporosis. Some years ago, *The Lancet* reported that animal protein and animal fat actually aggravated arthritic symptoms, and every single one of a group in the reported study, when put on a pure vegan diet, noticed a significant improvement very quickly. Of asthmatics placed on a vegan diet, 80 per cent were able to reduce and some were able to discontinue their medication entirely.[7] It has been estimated that vegans account for only 40 per cent of the national cancer rate and have a lifespan six years longer than average.

In view of this overwhelming sea of evidence, Dr Campbell, who conducted the China Health Project at Cornell University, has advised a change in the Western diet 'so that 80–90 per cent of protein comes from plant products, only 10–20 per cent from animal products. We must come to realise that we are basically a vegetarian species. The study suggests that whether industrialised societies such as ours can cure themselves of their meat addiction, may ultimately be a greater factor in the world health than all the doctors, health insurance policies and drugs put together.'[8]

ALTERNATIVES TO MEAT

The alternatives to red meat are many and varied. Apart from preparing vegetables and pulses in interesting different ways, you can experiment with tofu, tempeh, texturised vegetable protein, quorn and quinoa. Dr William C. Roberts, professor of clinical medicine at Georgetown University and chief cardiology pathologist for the National Institute of Health, has remarked that 'although we think we are one and act as if we are one, human beings are not natural carnivores. When we kill animals to eat them, they wind up killing us because their flesh is never intended for human beings, who are natural herbivores.'[9]

FISH

I know I have already cited fish that swim in deep ocean waters as being high in omega 3 EFAs, but before you start including them in your diet consider this: rivers and oceans are often heavily contaminated with pesticides and toxic chemical residues, so much so that it is almost impossible nowadays to find fish from unpolluted waters. Bigger fish often eat little fish and, being at the top of an extremely long food chain, can have dangerously high concentrations of pesticides, insecticides and other toxic chemicals in their bodies. All fish are exposed to detergents, industrial effluence, oil spillage, harbour dredging, human and animal sewage, and ships' garbage. In view of all of this, unsurprisingly, fish have been found to contain toxins known to be carcinogenic, and to cause kidney failure, nerve damage and birth defects.

The fish themselves display high rates of cancer. Pollutants, such as polychlorinated biphenyls (PCBs), DDT and dioxin, concentrate in the muscle tissue of fish and it has been estimated that eating a 1 lb (450 g) fish from Lake Ontario is the same as drinking 1.5 million quarts of that polluted water. The problem is worldwide because carcinogenic hydrocarbons have been found in fish in rivers as far apart as Maryland in the US and the Nile in Egypt, and there are increasingly alarming reports of carcinogenic residues found in fish taken from the Mediterranean and Baltic seas. Mutagenic PCBs tend to gravitate to the flesh of trout, catfish, bass, carp, blue fish and mackerel, all of which are high in omega 3. In addition, mackerel are particularly fond of feeding off human sewage. Farmed fish like trout and salmon nowadays contain more saturated fat and less linoleic acid simply because of the food they are fed.

FISH OILS

Naturally high in omega 3 EFAs, fish oils have been praised over the last few years as being protective against clogged arteries and heart disease. But this needs careful thought. The liver of the fish, like the liver of any vertebrate, is the central organ for processing chemicals, so the chemicals which accumulate in the flesh of fish are particularly concentrated in its liver, and it is the liver of fish from which oil is extracted. Fish oils that are described as protecting the arteries actually decrease the blood's ability to coagulate to stop bleeding. While the rate of heart attacks among Inuits, who eat a great deal of fish, is very low, they suffer from the world's highest rate of cerebral haemorrhagic strokes, nosebleeds and epilepsy. Inuits also have the highest osteoporosis rate in the world. Besides all this, fish oil, like any other oil except olive oil, contributes to gall bladder disease and is high in cholesterol.

So by significantly reducing your consumption of fish, along with meat and dairy products, you will have an even lower risk of heart disease than the Inuits, and a much lower risk of osteoporosis.

EGGS

Eggs are fibreless and very high in fat and cholesterol. They contain eight times more cholesterol than the equivalent weight of beef and will increase blood cholesterol levels more effectively than pure cholesterol dissolved in oil. They are also regularly implicated in cases of salmonella food poisoning. As Annemarie Colbin observes: 'Because they are a product of the female hormone system (manufactured by the hen's ovaries), eggs may stress the human female reproductive system in some way. It is possible that they may overactivate it, and, on the reverse swing, weaken it. Women who have problems related to the ovaries may want to consider very carefully whether they need to eat eggs or not.'[10]

Between one and five colourants are fed to chickens to give a richer colouring to egg yolks; one of these, canthaxanthin, is actually banned by the British Ministry of Agriculture, Fisheries and Food for direct human consumption. Chickens are also fed arsenic (to kill parasites and stimulate growth) as well as antibiotics and hormones, so that their own hormone systems are overworked and they lay eggs at a much higher rate than is natural. All of these substances end up in the eggs that you eat. If you must eat eggs, ensure that they are entirely organic and free range. I have found soya cream is an excellent substitute for eggs in baking. (Use one level tablespoon in place of an egg.)

SALT

In its natural form salt keeps the bodily fluids in balance, and it is almost *never* nutritionally essential to add salt to food. The amount of salt needed daily by an adult in a temperate climate is 4 g and this can always be obtained from natural, unprocessed food. The majority of people add so much salt to their diet that their intake can be as much as 20 g a day. Ninety per cent of the salt you eat is actually hidden in food. Canned and processed foods invariably have added salt, and the additives in them — including monosodium glutamate, sodium bicarbonate, sodium nitrate, sodium benzoate, sodium propionate and sodium citrate — also contain salt. It may surprise you to know that other food like hard cheeses, dried, evaporated or condensed milk, baking powder and breakfast cereals also contain additional salt.

The problem with salt is the more you ingest, the more calcium you secrete, which exacerbates a predisposition to osteoporosis. In artificially fertilised crops the sodium content is higher and the potassium content lower than in organic foods, where the reverse is the case. Sodium and potassium are mutually antagonistic. The correct potassium/sodium balance should be 80:20, and when this is disturbed the body quickly fills up with toxins because the pressure between different body fluids is thrown out of balance. Symptoms of imbalance include general swelling as the result of water retention, chronic lassitude and poor immunity.

You should therefore aim to cut all forms of salt from your diet and try to avoid eating processed foods as these are too high in sodium and too low in potassium. There is, for example, a hundred times more sodium in a canned vegetable soup than in a fresh homemade one. A salt-free diet reduces high blood pressure and the possibility of strokes because high sodium intake has been found to interfere with the body's ability to clear fats from the bloodstream. Excessive salt is also implicated in kidney trouble, water retention, and even stomach cancer and migraine headaches. Using Japanese gomosio as a substitute is an excellent way of gradually weaning yourself off salt and is available from healthfood shops.

The potassium/sodium ratio in the body can be corrected not only by cutting out meat, fish, dairy products, alcohol, sugar and caffeine, but by taking a pint of potassium broth every day. This detoxifies the body and alkalises the system and is particularly helpful if taken during a fast (see Chapter Three). It makes a delicious addition to any cleansing programme and will flush your system of unwanted salts and acids while flooding the bloodstream with a concentrated amount of vitamins and minerals.

POTASSIUM BROTH

When making potassium broth it is important to use organic vegetables.

You do not want to consume any toxic insecticides or chemical fertilisers while you are on a cleansing and detoxification programme. Drink 1 pint (600 ml) or more daily, warmed. Add, if desired, extra nutritional yeast flakes. The strained excess may be stored in the fridge for up to two days in a glass container and reheated as needed.

Fill one-quarter of a large pot with thickly cut potato peelings, then add equal amounts of carrot peelings and whole chopped beetroot, chopped onions and garlic, and celery and greens.
Add hot chilli peppers to taste.
Add enough water to cover the vegetables and simmer on a very low heat for 1–2 hours, tightly covered.
Strain the liquid and drink only the broth. Put the vegetables on the compost.
Make enough for two days (refrigerate the leftover broth), then start a fresh broth.

WATER

'You are what you drink' would be an even more accurate dictum than 'You are what you eat'. Indeed we are pretty much a mobile water bag. In our bodies water composes

- 70 per cent of the weight of our brains
- 75 per cent of our muscles
- 83 per cent of our kidneys
- 22 per cent of our bones
- 72 per cent of our blood.

Water and Oedema

A well-kept secret is that water is an unbeatable natural diuretic. Far from bloating you, it does precisely the opposite and it is wonderful for ridding the body of cellulite — trapped toxic waste in the lymphatic system.

Few of us drink enough water and the quality of the inadequate amount we do drink leaves a lot to be desired.

WATER QUALITY

Millions of people in Britain are currently drinking water contaminated with levels of toxic chemicals that are frequently far in excess of international standards. So far, over 350 different manmade chemicals have been detected in British tap water. The drinking-water directive of the EC lays down standards for more than 60 features, including the quantity of disease-carrying micro-organisms, metals, natural chemicals, synthetic compounds, along with colour, taste, smell and electrical conductivity.

Britain committed itself to reaching EC standards by 1985. Yet government ministers and the independent water authorities both admit that some water supplies are still breaking legal safety levels.

Two million Britons are currently at risk from excessive concentrations of lead and/or aluminium in tap water. The British government was found guilty by the European Court of Justice of ignoring a directive to keep nitrate levels to 50 mg/l. At least 1.6 million people drink water that breaks EC limits for nitrates. Ten per cent of Britain's water plants contain concentrations of chlorinated solvents used in paper making, metal plating, electrical engineering and dry cleaning, above the level advised by the World Health Organisation. As yet we know far too little about the effects of such industrial chemicals on our drinking water except that they are acknowledged carcinogens.

In the alimentary tract ingested nitrate can break down to nitrite which is known to be toxic. In some cases when a person has diminished supplies of hydrochloric acid in the stomach (which happens naturally as part of the ageing process), nitrates can break down even further to nitrosamines, which have been shown to cause cancer in rats. Ingested nitrate destroys vitamins A and E and may give rise to mineral imbalances and hormonal disturbances.

The chlorine in water has been linked to high blood pressure, anaemia and diabetes and is a contributor to heart disease. Even in a minute quantity sufficient to kill germs, chlorine can undermine the body's defences against atherosclerosis.

Chlorine creates electrically charged molecules called free radicals, which can combine with natural vitamin E and eliminate it from our system, causing the body to lose too much vitamin E. In addition, free radicals directly damage the lining of blood vessels and so create a favourable environment for the formation of plaque. Chlorine also oxidises iron and so threatens haemoglobin levels in the blood, possibly leading to anaemia.

Lead and aluminium can be present in drinking water and both are neuro-toxins. Lead comes from antiquated lead piping and aluminium is added during treatment for the discoloration of peaty moorland water.

One astonishing statistic is that post-mortem examination of the bodies of people who lived in Weybridge has shown the thyroid gland in each case to contain twice the level of contamination as that of someone who lived near Sellafield, Britain's most polluted nuclear establishment. The Weybridge isotope, iodine-125, has been found in the local drinking water supplied from the Thames and in the thyroids of swans living on the river, and is assumed to come from hospitals flushing it into the sewers. An increasing amount of toxic discharge from radioactive sources — hospitals and research stations — appears to be being dumped into our water supplies, against the requirements of the Department of the Environment.

Our water contains other medical waste, including natural synthetic steroids, such as oral contraceptives, and certain anti-cancer drugs. Government bodies have concluded that the ingestion of hormones offers no risk, but they have recommended periodical analysis in case there is a build-up of synthetic hormones in re-used water sources. Yet there is already evidence that hormones present in water in large doses can have horrendous side-effects. In the Philippines, for instance, it was found that little girls drinking from a stream where hormone-injected chickens had been killed and washed were growing breasts and beginning periods at the age of five. Menopausal women should be concerned about the presence of hormones in drinking water as their own hormonal levels are particularly sensitive at this time.

FLUORIDE IN WATER
Contrary to popular belief, additional fluoride can be detrimental rather than beneficial to health and its presence should be of particular

concern to the menopausal woman. While fluoride increases the thickness of bones, it makes them break more easily, contributing to osteoporosis, and even very low levels of fluoride inhibit the ability of leukocytes (infection-fighting white blood cells) to migrate, causing depression of the immune system.

ENSURING DRINKING WATER IS CLEAN

Do not fill the kettle from the hot-water tap because this dissolves minerals, including lead, from the pipes much more easily than cold water does. Fill your kettle freshly each time you boil it. Repeated boiling merely increases the concentration of chemicals, particularly nitrates. Let the water run for some minutes first thing in the morning. Water that is hard due to increased levels of calcium and magnesium is actually healthier for you than soft water. Soft water is often higher in sodium than hard and can consequently interfere with the electrical impulses responsible for a regular heartbeat. Never drink water which has been processed by a water softener.

Water Filters

An under-sink filter that works by reverse osmosis contains a semipermeable membrane which will prevent the entrance into your water supply of most things: bacteria, viruses, hydrocarbons, pesticides and other complex chemicals including fluoride, chloride, detergents, hormones and tannin as well as poisonous heavy metals. It will not remove simple compounds like chloroform and phenols unless it has an additional carbon filter. (See Resources Directory.) However, reverse osmosis does leach out the organic minerals, so do ensure that you get a plentiful supply of these from other sources.

A *Which?* report (August 1990) rated Opella Castalla Filterclear as the only under-sink filter to remove 80 per cent or more of aluminium, lead and other heavy metals, organic chemicals and chlorine. Unfortunately, no filters are able to entirely remove every trace of added fluoride.

Distilled Water

You can opt for distilled water — not the sort sold in bottles at garages, but the type manufactured by a fractional distillation unit. It will not leach minerals out of the blood and bones as many of its adversaries suggest. The down side is that distilled water tastes poor — dead and flat.

Bottled Spring Water

Avoid Vichy St Yorre and Badois which contain higher concentrations of fluoride than recommended. Lowest levels of fluoride are to be found in Evian, Goccia, Highland Spring, Perrier and Prewett's. The *Which?* 1989 report found that several brands contain more bacteria than tap water does. Because bacteria is removed during processing, sparkling water is better on this count but it should be drunk in moderation because of the additional carbon dioxide — this being, after all, the major waste gas emitted by the body. France applies very stringent standards to its bottled spring water. Few other countries bother to regulate bottled water at all and what regulations there are tend to be even more sub-standard than those applied to tap water.

Drinking Enough Water

If you fail to drink enough water — that is, 6–8 big glasses daily, excluding any other liquids you may take in — saliva, which is vital for proper digestion, dries up. Water eliminates all sorts of waste from the body. The kidneys filter some 10 pints (6 litres) of urine daily, of which you should be getting rid of six or more glasses a day by urinating and a further two through the skin's pores (and this without any exercise), plus extra simply by breathing out moist air.

How thirsty you are is not a reliable indicator of how much your body needs. Athletes forced in a scientific experiment to drink more than they thought they needed while performing vigorous exercise showed no fatigue compared to those who drank only as much as they *felt* they needed, who collapsed from exhaustion.

CAFFEINE

Coffee contains caffeine, and filtered coffee contains even more caffeine than the instant variety. The methylxanthines in caffeine have been proved to exacerbate fibrocystic disease of the breast. Pre-menstrual breast discomfort after the age of forty can in some women become so severe that it turns into mastalgia. At this point the pain associated with it can become very intense and can appear at any time of the month.

Coffee stimulates the acid secretions of the stomach, encouraging ulcers and disturbing natural appetite-control mechanisms. Coffee also raises blood pressure and increases the risk of coronary thrombosis. Take five cups daily and the risk of a heart attack rockets by 60 per cent. Most importantly, as far as menopausal women are concerned, coffee acidifies the blood which then draws calcium from the bones to try and achieve a healthier acid/alkaline balance. In short, it would be best to cut out coffee altogether during the menopause, particularly as caffeine is also present in chocolate, cola, cocoa and tea.

Besides containing caffeine with all its attendant dangers, tea is full of tannin which prevents the absorption of minerals, particularly iron, in the digestive tract, resulting in indigestion and lack of energy.

As far as both tea and coffee are concerned, decaffeinated is not much better. Trichlorethylene was used to decaffeinate coffee until quite recently before it was discovered to be carcinogenic. Now petroleum-based solvents are often used, and my feeling is that these too will almost certainly be proved to be harmful. The only firm I know which does not use chemicals and which is prepared to divulge exactly how their decaffeinated coffee is produced is Nestlé. They tell me that their beans are flushed several times with pressurised hot water which dissolves the caffeine and drains it away. The green beans are then washed, ground and marketed as freeze-dried instant coffee called 'Descaf'. So if you must drink coffee, try this occasionally but remember that even decaffeinated coffee can upset the digestive process because it contains high levels of tannic acid.

ALTERNATIVES TO TEA AND COFFEE
There are some excellent alternatives on the market for both tea and coffee. These include grain coffees made from cereals and fruits, chicory and dandelion. Some dandelion coffee tastes sickly sweet because it is mixed with lactose (milk sugar) and I would not recommend this. It is possible to buy roasted ground dandelion root

from medical herbalists and other herbal suppliers. This needs to be boiled up for 20 minutes, using about half an ounce (15 g) of root to 1 pint (600 ml) of water and then thoroughly strained before drinking. The added bonus is that it is wonderfully cleansing and strengthening for the liver, as well as being a gentle diuretic and purifying the bloodstream. Do not mix it with soya or cow's milk as these make it taste decidedly odd. Drink it black and unsweetened because the bitterness is what stimulates the liver, or, if you are not concerned about this, you can add a touch of honey or maple syrup.

Alternatives to tea include Bancha, made from the twig of the tea bush, which contains no caffeine, and Rooibosch tea, made from the shrub *Aspalantus linearis* which grows readily in South Africa. This has a pleasant smoky flavour and is rich in vitamin C and trace minerals as well as being caffeine-free. Herbal tea to the uninitiated can take a bit of getting used to but there are some excellent ones on the market. My favourite brand is Celestial Seasonings — available from most healthfood shops. I also use a detox tea which actually not only tastes delicious but works on a medical level (see Chapter Three, 'The Liver'). Remember that most commercially available herbal teas have no medicinal affect on the body whatsoever because they are made so weak, but by drinking them you are at least avoiding the caffeine and the tannin contained in conventionally manufactured tea.

ALCOHOL

Apart from the bone mass of alcoholics being seriously reduced — which implies that alcohol is a contributing factor as far as osteoporosis is concerned — alcohol increases the risk of breast cancer, exacerbates low blood sugar, blocks the proper ingestion of minerals, especially zinc, and interferes with the metabolism of EFAs.

NUTRITIONAL SUPPLEMENTS

After many years in practice, I have observed that no one diet suits every single person. Our nutritional needs are as different and as individual as our fingerprints. One woman's peanut can literally be another's poison.

A woman's nutritional needs vary according to her lifestyle and stage of life and are certainly affected by such factors as stress, illness, puberty, pregnancy and lactation, the menopause and old age. What is less clearly understood is that structural and enzymatic differences, partially caused by genetics, determine how an individual will absorb a particular ingredient. You may be continually urinating a nutrient away simply because your renal threshold for it is very low, or you may have insufficient intestinal bacteria to ensure the absorption and manufacture of a certain nutrient. Or what a noted biochemist, Roger Williams, terms 'one of the fundamental wisdoms of the body ... the wisdom to eat' may be impaired by any one of a myriad of reasons so that you are unable to choose food wisely.

With the best will in the world, even given the finest organic diet you can muster, it is still best to supplement your diet with nature's 'superfoods' (see below). This is especially important during the menopause when, as the result of ageing, some women find that the levels of hydrochloric acid in their stomachs have depleted to such a degree that they cannot digest and assimilate foods properly. A natural digestive enzyme such as Biocare's Digest-aid (see Resources Directory), made from pineapple and papaya, can often be helpful in this instance, as can a teaspoon of cider vinegar taken in warm water before each meal.

THE VITAMIN AND MINERAL CONTROVERSY

Nearly all vitamin and mineral supplements are currently not made from food. If you were labouring under the illusion that manufacturers are grinding up fresh raw vegetables and organic fruits and grains, jettison that idea at once! In fact commercial vitamins and minerals are nearly always synthesised by the big pharmaceutical companies from exactly the same materials that drugs are made from — that is, coal tar derivatives, petrol products, animal by-products (which include parts of their bodies and their faecal matter), pulverised rocks, stones, shells and metal. The United States Pharmacopoeia simply states that if a product looks similar under a microscope, or any other form of laboratory analysis, it is the same product regardless of what it is made from. For example, salicylic acid is considered identical whether it comes from wintergreen leaves or from boiling coal in carbolic and sulphuric acid. It also contains glycerine, which may be obtained from fresh vegetable sources, or it could come from boiled-down animal carcasses, particularly the cartilage and hooves.

Most people are unaware that synthetic vitamin B_{12}, cyanocobalamin, is made from ground-up cows' livers or activated sewage sludge. These cows' livers are overloaded already with steroids and antibiotics and the pesticides the cows ingest while eating. Now I will readily admit that faecal matter is natural, but do you really want to eat it? Vitamin A is made from fish livers and the toxic overload from these I have clearly outlined earlier in this chapter. Vitamin D is made from radiated oil, vitamin C from acid blends which can irritate the lining of sensitive digestive tracts, and most minerals are simply made from pulverised and powdered shells and rocks. In today's environment where increasingly depressed immune systems are responsible for many serious illnesses, I can think of hundreds of reasons why all these materials pose a health risk rather than a benefit.

Synthesising Vitamins and Minerals

Vitamins and minerals naturally present in food are bound to food complexes along with carbohydrates, proteins and lipids, and the human body recognises only this entire food complex as a food. Nearly all synthetic supplements are combinations of isolated u.s.p. vitamins and minerals which are not bound to anything and may have an entirely different chemical structure than those found in food. Supplements are also formulated so that they can boast of containing 100 per cent of the daily recommended allowance of a particular vitamin or mineral. These synthetic formulae often ignore the antagonistic and synergistic effects of vitamins and minerals, both as far as absorption and metabolic reactions are concerned. The chelating agent in wholefoods that assists absorption may be missing, and synthetic calcium and iron are not well absorbed by women in any case.

Megadoses of vitamin and mineral supplements are largely excreted simply because the uptake mechanism in the intestines cannot cope with them. This is why B complex vitamins will turn urine yellow and make it smell strongly and iron will blacken the faeces. Megadosing is not simply a waste of money, it can also be dangerous. If the body relies on formulated supplements, it is possible that it may get lazy or forget how to extract the nutrients from food efficiently. In other words, megadoses may actually block the body's normal functioning. Bear in mind, too, that the clever technology which brought us chemical chelators, transporters and time-release agents in an attempt to get round this problem are, in themselves, synthetic. Such concentrates may affect sensitive people.

Clearly it is far better to get our nutrients from natural sources simply because our bodies are designed to absorb nutrients from food. It is not just how much you take of a nutritional supplement that matters, it is *how much you absorb*. Of all the vitamin and mineral supplements that I have tested on my vega machine I have yet to find any which are compatible with the human digestive tract.

NATURAL SOURCES OF VITAMINS OF HELP DURING THE MENOPAUSE

Vitamin E

Foods rich in vitamin E stimulate the production of oestrogen and help alleviate hot sweats. Vitamin E seems to exert a normalising effect on oestrogen levels and has the ability to increase the hormonal output in women who are deficient in it, while being able to lower it in those prone to an excess. Vitamin E is richly present in organic whole grains and oils extracted from them, as well as nuts and seeds.

Vitamin B

Foods rich in the B complex vitamins (such as nutritional yeast, wheatgerm, whole grains and seeds) enhance the effectiveness of oestogenic hormones and help prevent menopausal arthritis as well as oedema. B complex vitamins boost the thyroid gland, especially important during the menopause when the whole endocrine system is under pressure. A healthy thyroid gland is essential for normal sex-hormone production because the thyroid secretes thyroxin, which has a direct stimulating effect on the sex glands. An underactive thyroid gland will lead to depleted sex glands and insufficient output of sex hormones.

Zinc

This is necessary for reproductive hormone and enzyme production, for the formation of genetic building blocks RNA and DNA, and for the proper utilisation of vitamins and minerals, especially for the metabolism of vitamin A and for the synthesis of insulin and protein. Pumpkin and sunflower seeds are particularly high in zinc, while the vitamin and mineral content of any *sprouted* seeds is increased by up to 2,000 per cent.

THE SPECIAL PROTECTIVE SUPERFOODS

(See Resources Directory for suppliers.)

Spirulina

This is one of the most concentrated nutritious foods on earth. It is a blue/green alga, which was the original photosynthetic source of life on earth, 3 billion years ago; it nourished people in Central America and Africa for centuries. Because it has no hard cellulose in its cell walls, being composed of soft mucopolysaccharides, its protein is beautifully digested and assimilated in the human body. Spirulina has the highest level of protein of any natural food (65 per cent or more), far more than animal or fish flesh (15–25 per cent), soya beans (35 per cent), eggs (12 per cent), or whole milk (3 per cent). And 95 per cent of this protein is digestible. This is vital for those suffering from intestinal malabsorption (coeliacs, those affected by *Candida*, Crohn's disease, mucous colitis and many women over forty who have dwindling supplies of hydrochloric acid in their stomachs).

Life in the Fat Lane

Spirulina's fat content is a mere 5 per cent, far lower than almost any other protein source. One tablespoon has only 36 calories and almost no cholesterol. So spirulina is a low-fat, low-calorie, cholesterol-free source of protein. In sharp contrast a large egg yields 300 mg of cholesterol and 80 calories but only has as much protein as 1 tablespoon of spirulina.

Colon Cleansing

Engevita nutritional yeast, chlorella (see below) and spirulina are the only forms of protein that are not mucus-forming in the intestines. Spirulina acts as a metabolic activator directly on the body's tissues at a cellular level, promoting increased activity to burn up mucus-forming substances (such as the wastes from meat, eggs and dairy products). Spirulina acts as an aggressive cleansing herb that empties toxins out of the body's tissues into the lymph and is a superb addition in both fasting and colon-cleansing programmes.

Spirulina and Hypoglycaemia

The minimal amount of carbohydrate in spirulina, 15–25 per cent, consists of two polysaccharides which are easily absorbed by the body with minimum insulin intervention. Spirulina supplies rapid energy without taxing the pancreas so it will not precipitate hypoglycaemia. Indeed it is actively helpful for controlling the sweeping blood-sugar curves which so debilitate hypoglycaemics and this is one reason why it is so useful in a fast. It is also the richest source of B_{12} in food, higher than beef, liver, chlorella or sea vegetables, so it is highly recommended in a vegan diet. It actually reduces levels of cholesterol, triglycerides and LDLs (implicated in the build-up of arterial plaque). This may be partially due to its unusual and very high gammalinoleic acid (GLA) content. One tablespoon of spirulina provides 100 mg of GLA, and dietary GLA helps heart conditions, PMS, obesity and arthritis.

Spirulina and Immunity

The unique colour in spirulina, phycocyanin, has been proved to stimulate the immune system and accelerate normal cell control functions, to prevent the degeneration caused by malignancies such as cancer and to inhibit its growth or recurrence. In fact the National Cancer Institute in the US has found the glycolipids in spirulina to be remarkably active against the AIDS virus.

Spirulina actually encourages healthy lactobacilli by 327 per cent over a hundred-day period and increases the effective absorption of vitamin B_1 inside the caecum, the murkiest part of the colon most prone to encourage the breeding of parasites, by 43 per cent. Healthy lactobacilli mean better digestion and absorption, protect from infection and stimulate the immune system.

Spirulina and Anaemia

The iron in spirulina is twice as easily absorbed as the iron found in vegetables and meat and is therefore highly recommended for women prone to anaemia. Spirulina was used to treat the 160,000 children suffering from radiation poisoning at Chernobyl. Remember that in addition to the toxic waste produced by nuclear-power plants we are all constantly exposed to radiation from the atmosphere, leaking microwave ovens, electrical power lines, x-ray machines, illuminated neon clocks, clock faces, garage door openers and frequent flying. Spirulina also inhibits the growth of bacteria, yeast and fungus, which is why it is so important as part of any *Candida*-controlling programme and to heal internal bacterial infections. A diet of 30 per cent spirulina has been shown to decrease radically the toxicity of inorganic mercury and chemical anodynes, antibiotics and anti-cancer drugs which can cause acute nephrotoxicity (poisons in the kidneys).

One of the best ways of taking spirulina is in flake form because it is so easy to stir into drinks. The spirulina I import is some of the finest in the world, from Hawaii, and is totally organic. Some spirulina is harvested from dubious sites, such as near oil wells, so do be careful about your sources.

Chlorella

Another of the blue/green algae, this is second only to spirulina in its nutritional content. Its cell walls have to be artificially cracked to make the nutrients more available and increase its digestibility, so my first preference would always be for spirulina over chlorella simply because any substance which has had to be artificially messed about with takes it one step further from nature. Having said this, chlorella has some rather unique additions which spirulina lacks. Where spirulina is a multi-cell, spiral-shaped plant which grows on salty or brackish water, chlorella is a round, single-cell alga which grows on fresh water. It contains five times as much chlorophyll as spirulina and a substance known as chlorella growth factor (CGF). In a study conducted by Dr Yoshia Yamagishi and published in 1961, fifty ten-year-old students given 2 g of chlorella daily for 112 days outstripped their control group in height and weight over this period of time. Chlorella's capacity to stimulate growth in the young is probably due to its nucleic acid content of RNA and DNA, which are important building blocks for life. RNA and DNA both accelerate growth in the young and help repair damaged tissues in ageing adults.

It has been suggested that the loss of energy and physical deterioration associated with ageing is due to the increased breakdown of RNA and DNA which are needed to keep the cells healthy. As we age (from our twenties) our natural production of RNA and DNA become sluggish. A diet rich in RNA and DNA foods produces more energy and a more youthful appearance, and alleviates long-standing problems such as arthritis, memory loss and depression.

The Importance of Chlorophyll

All plant life depends upon the sun, and we depend upon those plants. Sunlight activates the green chlorophyll in plants to generate energy for them. Molecules of chlorophyll are constructed around magnesium and carry oxygen around the inside of plant cells which, in turn, create energy for the plant. It is this stored energy in plants which we eat and absorb to sustain us. Plant energy is the primal energy of life because even carnivores eat animals that eat plants.

Our vitality depends on a good supply of oxygen. Germs gravitate towards tissue which is oxygen deficient. Cancer tissues grow by a process which does not use oxygen. Whether taken internally by mouth, or rectally by enema, chlorophyll inhibits the activities of protein-destroying bacteria and of enzymes which make protein putrefy in the gut. It helps to make human saliva more alkaline, assisting in particular the digestion of carbohydrates. Chlorella can therefore be very beneficial in the treatment of allergies and for malabsorption problems.

The Advantages of Taking Chlorophyll

Over the years I have noticed that those of my patients prone to viruses such as colds and flu are generally either anaemic or smokers. Fewer haemoglobin molecules mean reduced oxygen-carrying capacity for red blood cells. Smoking makes the haemoglobin of red blood cells bind with carbon monoxide, found in cigarette smoke. Whenever oxygen is wanting in our cells, disease sets in. Both chlorophyll and haemoglobin molecules are capable of carrying oxygen to cells and in fact they are fairly similar in construction.

Many years of research have found that chlorophyll is not a chemical that fights specific disease but one that benefits the entire body, carrying oxygen to every cell. Consequently chlorophyll may help many different conditions including sinusitis, colds, rhinitis, respiratory infections, colon problems including ulcerative colitis, high blood pressure, skin infections, pancreatitis, peptic ulcers, gastritis, mouth sores and boils, fatigue, cancer, septic wounds, and it increases resistance to x-rays.

In addition, Japanese researchers have found that the juice of any green plant inhibits chromosome damage, which is one of the links in the chain of events leading to cancer.

All grasses contain fresh chlorophyll. As we saw in Chapter Three, the inhabitants of a village in Austria who were forced during the Second World War to live off grass not only thrived but many of their degenerative diseases began to heal completely. While you may blanch at the thought of eating grass, the good news is that other dark-green vegetables like spinach, cabbage and nettles all contain large amounts of chlorophyll as, of course does chlorella.

The CGF factor noted in chlorella is also present in wheat and barley grass. To obtain all its nutrients grass must be administered orally (in the form of a juice) or as a rectal implant (see below) and it must be made freshly. Synthetic chlorophyll will not do and is in fact poisonous.

Barley and Wheat Grasses

Naturally, the seeds of barley and wheat grasses can be sprouted, but when grown in soil they are more potent nutritionally than the grains themselves, richly abundant in vitamins, minerals and chlorophyll; barley is twice as rich in protein compared with wheat.

Growing your own grass in order to eat it may sound exceedingly eccentric but the dividends are well worth it. When using wheat or barley grass juice for the first time, it is a good idea to take it in very small quantities, perhaps only a tablespoon (15 ml) to begin with. Take enough to make you feel uncomfortable but not so much that you feel like vomiting it up again. Because both are such powerful cleansers, due to their high enzyme content, they will start immediate reactions with toxins and mucus in the stomach, often causing distress. This feeling of nausea merely proves that they are needed and should be taken regularly. Thirty minutes before taking any of the grass juice, drink the juice of a quarter of a lemon squeezed into a glass of water, or, if you have an acid stomach, mint tea. Both methods will clean out mucus from the stomach and minimise discomfort.

Grass juices in doses of 1–2 fl. oz (30–60 ml) can be taken immediately before sprouted seeds, which can then be eaten afterwards. Try and take any grass juice on an empty or nearly empty stomach. That way it is immediately absorbed. If you find in spite of all this that it is so potent you simply cannot swallow it, it may be taken by rectal implant, in which case use a minimum of 4 fl. oz (120 ml) working up to 8 fl. oz (240 ml) daily. Raw grass juices can be used as a mouthwash and are particularly helpful for periodontal disease. Remember chlorophyll will bring oxygen to the mouth and this is particularly helpful for anyone who has had thrush or *Candida* in their mouth or throat.

Sea Vegetables
The most popular sea vegetables available (which can usually be bought from healthfood shops or Oriental supermarkets) are combu or kelp, wakame, hiziki, nori and kanten, or agar, which acts like gelatine. Irish moss and purple dulse, commonly found in the British Isles, are also increasingly available, as are seaweeds like lava and kelp. Indeed things are improving even as I write this book: I was delighted to walk into Tesco's today and find both kelp and purple dulse fresh and packed in rock salt sitting on the shelves in the vegetable section.

Sea vegetables are an extremely concentrated source of nutrients. Purple dulse and nori contain up to 34 per cent protein and all sea vegetables are abundant in calcium, iron, phosphorus, potassium, sodium, zinc, manganese and, of course, iodine because they grow in sea water. They also contain good amounts of vitamins A, B, C and B complex, including the elusive B_{12}. Hiziki contains the highest amount of calcium and is therefore particularly useful for menopausal women. But all seaweeds aid the healthy growth of nails, hair, bones and teeth, ensure proper metabolism, reduce blood cholesterol, stimulate the reproductive glands, help digestion and act as antiseptics. They also neutralise strontium-90 by chelating and excreting it. My personal preference is for purple dulse because, unlike many of the other sea vegetables, it does not taste fishy.

Beetroot

Beets change inorganic raw elements into plant materials that are easily assimilated by us. Beetroot is particularly famous for its blood-building ability. It is used in the treatment of cancer and is a superb liver and blood cleanser. Raw grated beets and their juices were once used to treat tuberculosis, obesity and gonorrhoea. The plant pigments in beets are particularly helpful to both cure and prevent radiation-induced cancers.

Dark-Green Leafy Vegetables

All dark-green leafy vegetables, especially spinach, are high in calcium, iron and vitamin K as well as chlorophyll. When juicing any dark-green vegetables, use the juice in very small quantities as it is extremely potent. The organic oxalic acid found in beet greens, Swiss chard, kale, turnip greens, broad-leafed sorrel and spinach all in their raw state is excellent for constipation. Once cooked, the oxalic acid can settle in the joints, but serving these particular dark-green leafy vegetables with sunflower seeds counteracts this.

In the 1950s the British Ministry of Health and Public Service Laboratory admitted that spinach juice, cabbage juice, kale and parsley were far superior to milk for relieving excessive production of hydrochloric acid in the stomach.

Rosehips and Citrus Peels

These are some of the finest sources of vitamin C and contain the whole vitamin C complex, including the bioflavonoids rutin and hesperidin, calcium and all the trace elements that are now known to be vital in order to assimilate vitamin C. All citrus peels contain pectin which is known to remove heavy metals such as mercury and lead from the body, and even radioactive contamination like strontium-90. When you eat citrus fruit, always consume some of the white pith as it is particularly rich in bioflavonoids. Bear in mind, though, that the bioflavonoids in the pith of citrus fruit are highly active and unstable and easily destroyed by heat and exposure to the air. Be cautious about consuming too much orange and grapefruit *skin* (not *pith*) as it contains toxic substances.

In addition, all foods rich in vitamin C act as detoxifiers, rejuvenators and stimulants for the thyroid and sex glands. Such foods are an important addition to the diet during the menopause as vitamin C encourages the body to metabolise oestrogen while the bioflavonoids help, among other things (see below), to reduce hot flushes. A good way of ensuring that you get a daily dose of bioflavonoids is to put a thinly pared lemon into a morning liver flush (see Chapter Three).

Bioflavonoids

It has been known for some years that some of the bioflavonoids, particularly quercitin, are extremely active against viruses such as herpes. Two of the bioflavonoids, nobiletin and another closely related to it, appear to have even better anti-inflammatory properties than cortisone, while others, singularly or together, actively fight fungal viral and bacterial infection. Rutin, which can prevent bruising and is famous for elasticising arteries, also lifts depression by altering brain-wave patterns. It is richly present in buckwheat. Nobiletin, as well as being a powerful anti-inflammatory, helps the body to get rid of heavy metals and the poisonous substances from car exhaust fumes. Some of the bioflavonoids are believed to be anti-carcinogenic and methoxylated bioflavonoid stops red blood cells clumping together, decreasing blood viscosity by as much as 6 per cent. All bioflavonoids become far more active when the body is under stress, helping to combat fungi, viruses and bacteria. They are thus of particular benefit to women undergoing all the stresses and strains of the menopause.

As well as minimising hot flushes, regular ingestion of bioflavonoids improves vaginal lubrication and pelvic tone, strengthens the bladder, reduces oedema, eases sore joints, improves liver activity, reduces risk of stroke and heart attack as well as muscle cramping and improves resistance to bacterial and viral infections. Herbs rich in bioflavonoids include sprouted buckwheat, elderberries, rosehips, hawthorn, horsetail, shepherd's purse and nettles, although the inner skin of citrus fruits is undoubtedly the richest source of bioflavonoids.

Nutritional Yeast

There are literally hundreds of different types of yeast and they have various qualities. Many yeasts on the market today are the by-products of manufacturing processes in the brewing industry (hence the name brewer's yeast) or designed for the baking industry. In the past, some of these yeasts have been grown on rags and old newspapers; they are often used as food supplements. My feeling is that not only is their nutritional value suspect, but their quality is very poor and some are even toxic. Nature gives you a clue simply because they often taste bitter and unpleasant. More importantly, they are still active, meaning they are alive, and can be damaging to those people who have yeast infections and/or overgrowth problems with *Candida albicans*.

Saccharomyces cerevasiae nutritional yeast is grown solely for human consumption as a nutritional food supplement. It is cultivated on a base of pure beet and cane molasses and it absorbs the space in the same way as plants utilise minerals in the soil. Molasses is used because it provides the yeast with an abundant organic source of B vitamins and minerals. Once the yeast is harvested, it is thoroughly washed and dried, and during the drying process it is heated just enough to stabilise it, thereby rendering it completely non-fermentable. This process not only makes the yeast incapable of any further fermentation in the digestive tract, but helps it to be easily digestible and assimilable. It is therefore particularly recommended for women with internal bacterial fungal infections, including *Candida albicans*.

Soya Products

Japanese women who eat traditionally — tofu, kempeh, miso (see below) and natto — excrete oestrogen at a much higher rate than their Western counterparts and are well known for having a much lower rate of breast cancer. They also have very little trouble with menopausal symptoms, including hot flushes. All these products are made from soya beans and are rich in phyto-oestrogens (similar to the weak oestrogens found in plants). These appear to be protective against breast cancer partly because the weak oestrogen activity in them blocks oestrogen receptors on the cells of the body, preventing them from receiving too much oestrogen stimulation from other sources. Other foods which contain high levels of phyto-hormones include corn, wheat, apples, almonds, cashews, oats, peanuts, cucumbers, bananas, peas, yams, papaya and sprouted seeds, particularly those of lentils and red clover.

Miso

Miso is a fermented soy-bean paste which tastes deliciously savoury and is made simply by stirring a teaspoon of it into hot water. Available from some healthfood shops, it alkalinises the bloodstream, encourages the production of benign flora in the colon, reduces cholesterol and helps to negate many of the effects of environmental pollution on our bodies, including cigarette smoke and radiation, which is why 70 per cent of the Japanese include it in their breakfasts daily. Indeed, to achieve all these effects it must be taken regularly.

Flax

Flax, otherwise known as linseed, was revered by the Native American Indians because they felt it captured the sun's energy and that this was vital to the body's life processes. They were intuitively right. According to Dr Johanna Budwig, a meticulous researcher into the properties of fatty components in various materials, ingested flax seed oil partially migrates into the skin, acting as antennae for the photons in sunlight. Energy from the photons is then stored in chemical bonds for future use in vital biochemical reactions. Cancer patients often lack these oils in their skin and are allergic to the sun. Once put on a special oil-protein combination, they can be exposed to the sun, which actually helps to cure their cancer.[11]

Flax seed is an extraordinary food. The solid part of the seed is used in all digestive/eliminative toxic diseases of the stomach and intestines, including gastritis, ileitis and diverticulitis. It is one of the safest bulk laxatives and prevents cholesterol and bile acids from being reabsorbed into the body. It is packed with high-quality, easily digestible protein, contains almost every known mineral, all the fat-soluble vitamins, A, D, E and K, and some water-soluble ones, B_1, B_2 and C. It contains a perfect balance of omega 3 and omega 6 EFAs — 57 per cent of the former and 16 per cent of the latter. It is particularly rich in lignans which combine with beneficial intestinal bacteria to form compounds with antibacterial, antiviral, antifungal and anti-cancer effects. These compounds are especially helpful in combating cancer of the breast, colon, uterus and ovaries.

If you are buying the oil, it must be organic and freshly cold-pressed at temperatures of less than 33°C, and stored in a dark bottle to protect it from light. It should be kept in the fridge and used within three weeks. I find it delicious in a morning liver flush (see Chapter Three). If you cannot find a satisfactory quality of oil, use the seeds instead (golden or brown), pulverised in a grain mill or with a pestle and mortar, freshly as needed. Sprinkle a couple of tablespoons daily into soup, juice or cereal. Ensure the seeds are vacuum-packed and, once opened, store the packet, sealed, in the fridge. For the suppliers of the highest-quality seeds and oil, see the Resources Directory.

Garlic

Garlic is one of nature's miracle foods. The ancient Egyptians, Greeks and Romans all used garlic copiously to increase strength and fight disease and illness. Hippocrates employed garlic specifically to treat cancer. In the First World War the British government used garlic in the battlefield hospitals and it saved thousands of lives. It was used in numerous preparations to disinfect and heal battle wounds internally, and to treat typhoid fever and dysentery.

Today garlic is the leading over-the-counter drug in many European and Asian countries. It is an official drug in many countries and prescribed by medical doctors outside the US for a wide range of diseases, especially hypertension, high cholesterol and cancer, and as a broad-spectrum antibiotic, antiviral agent and fungicide. Indeed I prescribe it almost as a matter of course, trying to encourage my patients to eat between one and three cloves of raw garlic a day.

Garlic is famous for its healing power with heart disease. Countries where garlic consumption is high have a lower incidence of heart disease than average. Garlic lowers serum, cholesterol and triglyceride levels and, by increasing the blood levels of HDLs while lowering those of LDLs, reduces the build-up of atherosclerotic plaque in the arteries. Medical researchers have also found some substances in garlic that inhibit blood-platelet aggregation (the sticking together of blood cells). Because of its powerful effect on blood pressure, the Japanese Food and Drug Administration has approved garlic and it is now on the official drug list in the Japanese Pharmocopoeia.

Garlic is a highly effective cancer therapy. One-third of all the medical research into garlic is in fact cancer related. The National Cancer Institute has reported that cancer incidence worldwide is lowest in the countries where garlic consumption is highest. Garlic has been shown to help white blood cells combat cancer and increase the ability to destroy tumours. When the properties of garlic are present in the bloodstream, many aspects of the body's immunity are enhanced. Garlic has also been found to stimulate interferon production, enhance natural killer cells, stop tumour growth, and even reduce the associated pain of cancer. It has been found to reduce the incidence of colonic and rectal cancer and stomach cancer and has been shown to reduce stomach cancer ten times more effectively than in those who do not eat garlic. With over 80 different sulphur compounds, it is a free-radical scavenger. This is yet another way that garlic protects against cancer, even varieties that are chemically induced.

Garlic juice diluted one part in 125,000 has been found to inhibit the growth of harmful bacteria. The herb destroys both gram positive and gram negative bacteria, making it a broad-spectrum antibiotic. Garlic used as an antibacterial agent in Russia is so revered that it has been christened Russian penicillin. Unlike antibiotics, garlic is selective in its bacterial destruction, only killing bacteria that is harmful to the body. At the same time, it actually encourages the growth of friendly bacteria and improves the intestinal flora of the digestive tract.

Garlic destroys many types of disease-inducing bacteria including streptococcus, staphylococcus, typhoid, diphtheria, cholera, bacterial dysentery (commonly known as travellers' diarrhoea), tuberculosis, tetanus, rheumatic bacteria and many others. It is probably the most powerful cure for the common cold, effectively destroying different viruses that cause upper respiratory infections and influenza. It has been shown to destroy on contact the viral infections of measles, mumps, mononucleosis, chicken pox, herpes simplex 1 and 2, herpes zoster, viral hepatitis, scarlet fever and rabies.[12]

Garlic's antifungal ability is second to none. Laboratory tests have proved it to be more potent than any known antifungal agent, including Nystatin. Garlic will also regulate the overgrowth of *Candida albicans*.

SUGGESTIONS FOR A HEALTHY DAILY DIET

As we have seen, boosting your diet with nutritional supplements can be very beneficial during the menopause. Equally important is keeping to a basic healthy diet, adhering to the advice given throughout this chapter. Here are some suggestions for a daily regime.

On rising, drink a glass of pure filtered water, slightly warmed if desired, with freshly squeezed lime, lemon or grapefruit juice in it, or a large mug of herbal tea or a glass of freshly squeezed fruit juice from any whole fruits in season. The juice should be diluted half and half with pure water. (Do no use canned or frozen juices.) Squeeze it freshly in your juicer just before drinking. If you have catarrh, take one glass of hot water with 2 tablespoons of maple syrup, the juice of a freshly squeezed lemon and a quarter of a teaspoon of chilli powder. This will warm you up and shift the catarrh.

Take at least 40 minutes' brisk aerobic exercise combined with deep breathing and any stretching you can manage to fit in. If you live on a farm or own a garden, this is the ideal time to get in an hour's hard physical work to get your metabolism going. On your return from your exercise, skin brush vigorously (see Chapter Three) and follow this with the seven times hot/cold shower routine (see Chapter Six, 'Showers'). You are now ready for breakfast.

BREAKFAST
Eat fresh fruits of any sort organically grown in your own locality and

environment and in season. If you are very hungry try, after a 20-minute wait, sprouted seeds or a bowl of pre-soaked, low-heated (and therefore uncooked) rolled oats or pot millet with pre-soaked dried fruit and oat or rice milk added. Digest this for 2–3 hours before having as much freshly squeezed fruit juice and herbal tea to drink, until midday, as you desire. Alternatively, have a fruit smoothy (see Chapter Three) or banana milk.

BANANA MILK

3 sliced ripe bananas
2 cups (480 ml) of ice-cold water
1½ tablespoons of tahini
1 tablespoon maple syrup, barley malt or other sweetener (optional)
half a teaspoon of natural vanilla.

Liquidise until smooth and creamy.

LUNCH
Choose from the following:

- A large bowl of freshly prepared fruit salad (if not eaten for breakfast).
- Freshly prepared vegetable soup or any other cooked vegetable dish with one or two slices of wholegrain bread.
- Some rice cakes with vegetable pâté.
- A large salad with baked potatoes and an interesting vegetable filling.
- Pasta (try corn or rice pasta, not wheat pasta) with an interesting sauce and a large side salad.
- Vegan Middle Eastern or Italian mezzas and wholemeal pitta bread and salad.
- Stir-fried rice and vegetables, or stir-fried vegetables with seeds and nuts.
- Vegetable chilli or curry with rice, roti or nan bread and salad.

One of my favourite salad dressings, which is both tasty and nutritious, is two-thirds organic cold-pressed olive oil, one-third cider vinegar or freshly squeezed lemon juice, a generous teaspoon of grainy mustard, a teaspoon of maple syrup (preferably organic) or runny honey (preferably organic), two cloves of garlic and a heaped tablespoon of Engevita yeast liquidised together. Alternatively, omit the garlic and add freshly chopped herbs to your taste. This keeps very well in a screw-top jar in the fridge. (Please note, though, that in a diet low in dairy products vinaigrette dressing — as well as other naturally acidic products like wine and citrus juices — will decalcify the system so ensure that you consume nuts or nut butters at the same meal.)

MID-AFTERNOON
A glass of fresh fruit or vegetable juice or a cup of herbal tea or fresh fruit, or a tub of soya yoghurt with fresh fruit chopped into it.

DINNER
Try to keep this lighter than lunch and include, if you have not had it for lunch, a large bowl of salad with sprouted seeds. (Carrots, shredded beetroot and onions should be staples in every salad.) Or have a bowl of homemade soup with handfuls of sprouted seeds sprinkled into it and some oat or rice cakes to go with it. Try not to eat cooked food later than 7–8 p.m. and, if hungry beyond this time, take fruit or vegetable juice or fresh fruit.

BEDTIME
For a bedtime snack you can have a glass of freshly made nut milk or rice or oat milk with maple syrup and honey, if desired, or hot 'chocolate' made with organic soya milk and carob powder.

POINTS TO REMEMBER
- Whatever changes you make, bear in mind that the bulk of your diet should consist of seeds, nuts and grains and fresh vegetables and fruits, especially organically grown; up to 80 per cent of them, ideally, should be eaten raw. Eat the widest variety of available foods possible, but not in the same meal.

- Lunch and dinner menus are interchangeable, but keep dinner lighter.
- Remember to eat at least one large vegetable meal a day.
- Separate your protein and carbohydrate. The chemical processes involved in digesting these are incompatible. This leads to food being only partially digested which, in turn, can produce harmful toxins that place all sorts of strains on the body.
- Do not mix raw fruits and vegetables in the same meal because their enzyme combinations are incompatible for digestion. The exceptions are carrot and apple which combine well together.
- Do not mix fruit and starch. Fruit should be eaten in isolation and on an empty stomach because, being so high in water, it is incredibly cleansing, easily digested and leaves no toxic residue.
- Do not drink liquid with a meal as this dilutes the digestive juices. The exceptions are freshly squeezed vegetable juice or organic bottled vegetable juice or herbal teas (which count as medicinal).
- Drink between meals or 15 minutes before meals and try and ensure that you have at least six glasses of pure water a day. The brain is 70 per cent water so if you are starting to feel headachy or tired it is a very good idea to rehydrate yourself on pure, non-carbonated water. Carbonated water is more difficult to assimilate, as the gas pumped into it is precisely the same as the waste gas you are breathing out. Take carbonated water as fun liquidation; the serious option is plain filtered water.

Eliminate	Substitute
Salt	Flavourful kitchen herbs, spices, seaweeds, soya sauce, miso, sesame salt. (Sesame salt — eight parts sesame meal to one part salt — is very easy to make. Stir sesame meal constantly in a heavy-bottomed frying pan until thoroughly heated through and toasted. Decant. Heat up the salt and return the toasted sesame, stirring the mixture until well amalgamated. Decant again. Cool and store in a cupboard container.)

Eliminate	Substitute
Tea, coffee, alcohol	Herbal teas, dandelion coffee (avoid the ones with lactose added), grain coffees, potassium broth, warmed juices, miso, fresh juices. Both tea and coffee are high in tannin which neutralises iron, so both need to be eliminated when taking herbal supplements.
Sugar	Honey, maple syrup, dried fruits, date syrup, carob, fruit juices and sweet root vegetables.
Meat, fish, chicken, eggs	Tofu, nuts, seeds, spirulina, chlorella, Engevita yeast, high-protein substitutes made of soya.
Dairy products	Soya products, nut milks, rice and oat milks. Note that all dairy products can be substituted by soya, including ice cream, cheese, yoghurt, milk, custard and cream.
Flour, wheat pasta	Because wheat flour is mucus-forming, use chickpea, millet, spelt, quinoa, soya or rice flour. Try corn or rice pasta, not wheat pasta. If using wheat flour, opt for wholegrain fresh organic flour products without chemical additives and preservatives.
Carbonated fizzy drinks, fruit squashes, sugar-sweetened drinks, concentrated juices (which can contain sugar and the nutrients have been boiled away)	Filtered water with a dash of citrus to cheer up the flavour, if desired, herbal teas, fresh fruit and vegetable juices, potassium broth and miso.

CRAVINGS

It is very important that you continue to enjoy some of the foods you love or crave for, if you hold yourself under a very tight rein for too long, it is inevitable you will start to binge or reverse entirely into negative eating patterns. The superfoods, particularly spirulina and chlorella, will help to reduce craving. In addition, meditation, acupuncture, shiatsu and the practice of some of the Chinese martial arts may be helpful. Chewing (on highly nutritious sunflower seeds, for instance) will also help relax a jaw tightened with stress.

The best way is not to change your diet all at once. Alter one aspect of your diet at a time, such as giving up coffee. Once you have cut out the junk food from your diet and cleared the rubbish from your system, there will come a time when your body will be intelligent enough to tell you instinctively what it needs. At first you will find that instinct appears in fits and starts but, with persistence, you will eventually get the hang of it. When you have finally mastered the art of positive eating, it will transform your life.

FIVE

HEALTH PROBLEMS LINKED TO THE MENOPAUSE

THE IMPORTANCE OF A HEALTHY MINDSET

We create our own health, consciously or unconsciously, from the moment we are born to the moment we die. Bad health is not just something that happens to us, it happens *because* of us. The same applies to good health. This is an idea that many people find impossible to digest because it is so unpalatable to accept the part that each of us plays in creating our own illnesses.

Generally it happens at an unconscious level. The feelings embedded in our thoughts have such profound effects on us because they are literally wired into our bodies by way of our endocrine, immune and central nervous systems. Every feeling, whether vocalised or buried, has a physical effect in the body. The buried ones are tiny crucibles of illness waiting to surface, so I actively encourage the women I work with to observe the ways in which their own beliefs and behaviour perpetuate the system — medical, educational, communal, governmental — that hinders their health. As long as we women persist in believing that our diseases, symptoms and rites of passage are 'simply medical', we are participating in and perpetuating such systems, which rob us of our inner wisdom.

Our bodies have a blueprint for health and know exactly how to get well. Trusting that inner blueprint, that inner wisdom or knowing, is a way of joining the body with the soul and so achieving true health. All pain, all illness is the soul's way of waking us up and directing us, if we would but listen, towards better health.

As Dr Christiane Northrup has so wisely observed, 'For healing to occur we must come to see that we are not so much responsible *for* our illnesses as responsible *to* them [my italics].' She goes on to bid us 'be open to the messages and mysteries of our body and its symptoms. Be eager to listen and slow to judge. What you learn may have the capacity to save your life.'[1]

The self-healing capacity inside every one of us mirrors the energy it takes to get ill. By acknowledging that a large portion of any illness is self-caused, however unconsciously, you then reach the inescapable conclusion that you can actively choose to do something about it. This clear-sighted recognition lets you become responsible for yourself and puts you in control of your own healing.

But before you can take responsibility for the future you must take account of the past. Firstly, you need to accept that your actions were always your own. Once you accept responsibility for the old hurts, you can drop their burdensome weight and abandon the anger that still echoes around them. You must also come to accept that you must change the way you were in order to move on.

Above all, every one of us needs individually to change our belief systems and so demolish our cultural negativity about menopause and ageing. Instead we need to believe in our capacity to remain strong, vital, powerful and attractive throughout our lives. We must lose the fear we have of not living fully, of being hurt, of death, of loneliness, of losing the securities we have, of not being loved. Normally what we do with fear is invent belief systems to make it go away. But fear, properly handled, is a great psychological teacher. Experiencing our fear, living it so that the fear is us, empowers us, changes our awareness. And it is self-awareness we need in order to accept ourselves, whoever, wherever and however we are.

Not only self-responsibility but self-esteem are fundamental requirements for health and happiness, for all our problems stem from one basic problem, lack of self-love. In loving ourselves as profoundly, unconditionally and deeply as we would our truest lover we can find the power that will heal us. Self-love dissolves anger, fear and resentment. Through it the damaging thought patterns, resentment, self-criticism, guilt, fear and outmoded ideas that do not nourish and support us are transformed into positive attributes. Indeed there is no better way to become yourself, no better way to heal yourself, mind, body and soul, than through love.

SPECIFIC PROBLEMS AND HOW TO TREAT THEM

Before you scour through this section, I want to emphasise again that for the majority of women, perhaps as many as 80 per cent, the menopause is not a problem. As we have seen, post-menopausal health has as much to do with exercise, diet and lifestyle as it does with genetic make-up. There is absolutely no reason why a healthy, well-nourished woman should not have a satisfactory transition through menopause and, on the way, learn many joyful, empowering and liberating things about herself.

Bearing in mind the effect that negative thoughts and emotions can have on your body, you will appreciate that if you expect problems you may well create them. So please do be careful about your mindset. For an individualised list of herbs that will help during and after the menopause, see Chapter Seven.

The following sections are arranged alphabetically.

ACHING JOINTS

A lot of women suffer from aching knees, elbows and shoulders during the menopause. Aching in the hips, lower back and wrists may indicate osteoporosis or even dysfunction of the immune system, so have a check-up if you are concerned.

Treatment

- Moxibustion (a method of applying heat to treat aching joints) using burning sticks of dried wormwood (available from herbal suppliers of Chinese products) very close to but not on the skin of the affected joint is very helpful.
- A trauma oil made of equal parts of St John's wort, arnica and marigold is comforting and healing, as is tincture of cayenne massaged directly into the aching joint.

- Twenty-five drops three times a day of devil's claw tincture is helpful.
- Essential fatty acids are anti-inflammatory (see Chapter Four).
- Saunas, Turkish baths, mud baths, Epsom salt baths and mustard hand or foot baths all help.
- So does exercise, no matter how gentle or how little initially.
- Becoming a vegan and cutting out potatoes, tomatoes, aubergines, black pepper, bell peppers of all colours and chillies, as well as coffee and tobacco, reaps extraordinarily quick and long-lasting relief from pain.

The following anti-inflammatory formulation is extremely effective and works within a few minutes of ingestion.

Equal parts of the following tinctures:
black cohosh
meadowsweet
white willow
wild lettuce
wild yam
Quarter of a part of:
cayenne tincture.

Take 60 drops in some hot liquid every 15 minutes, if necessary, until the pain subsides. This is so effective that usually you will find 60 drops three times a day is perfectly adequate.

BLADDER PROBLEMS

Incontinence

Sixty-five per cent of women will experience one or more occurrences of stress incontinence after the menopause, but 5 per cent of young women have confessed to leaking regularly, so this is not just a menopausal problem.[2] Known causes of incontinence include weakening or damage to pelvic floor muscles as the result of pelvic surgery, precipitous birthing, many pregnancies, thinning bladder wall after the menopause, too much alcohol, urinary tract infections, constipation, fibroids and prolapse of the bladder. Surgical correction for the last problem can be very unpredictable. Properly performed pelvic-floor exercises are far more beneficial and should be the first resort.

Kegel Exercises

Dr Arnold Kegel was the first person to popularise the necessity of pelvic-floor exercises in preventing and treating incontinence. The pelvic-floor group of muscles supports the pelvic contents and when contracted restrains urine flow and prevents bowel movements. Women's anal sphincter muscles are generally very strong so they need to concentrate on the vaginal and urethral sphincters to help exercise the pelvic-floor muscles.

- Practise slowing urine flow and eventually stopping it to gain a sense of which muscles are involved. As you get better at this, practise stopping urine flow, holding it for 1–2 seconds, and repeat 6–8 times as your urinate but never do this with your first morning urination. Eventually you will find you should be able to stop urine flow quickly without any leakage and that you can slowly relax the pelvic-floor muscles in stages from full contraction to full relaxation.
- Using the same muscles, contract the pelvic floor throughout the day. Do this whenever and wherever possible but it should be repeated 6–8 times during each session, building up to 100 times a day. Hold the contraction 2–5 seconds and then relax.
- Contract the pelvic-floor muscles while making love. Ask your partner to tell you when he can feel the difference. Repeat many times whenever the opportunity arises.

Please note that while doing these exercises you should not hold your breath, bear down or contract the bottom, inner thighs or abdominal muscles. It is far better to learn to localise the contraction to the pelvic-floor muscles entirely and not to exhaust the pelvic-floor muscles in the early stages of your learning. Do as many contractions at a time as you can do at your maximum contraction and then add two more.

Other forms of exercise, especially yoga and swimming using breast stroke, will also strengthen and tone the muscles of the pelvic floor. Alternate hot and cold sitz-baths can help (see Chapter Six).

It is important to empty the bladder completely every time you urinate by pressing down behind your pubic bone with the flat of your hand or, if this will not fit, your fingertips.

I have known timed toileting to help some women. Go to the toilet once-hourly every day until you have achieved three consecutive 'dry' days (that is, with no leakage in between the hourly visits to the toilet). Then expand the interval by 30 minutes until you can handle three hours or more without leakage.

The following formulation is also helpful.

Equal parts of:
black cohosh
gravel root
juniper
lobelia
marshmallow
parsley.

Take 2 size 0 capsules three times a day with a cup of parsley tea.

Bladder Infections

It is tempting to douche if your vagina is dry, but please do not do this unless it is to relieve specific infection or inflammation, and even then only if it is deemed absolutely necessary. If bacteria is allowed to thrive in a dry or frequently douched vagina, it may cause infection of the bladder (termed cystitis) and of the kidneys (termed pyelitis and a much more serious complaint).

Cystitis

Cystitis simply means inflammation of the bladder and is not usually serious although it can be exceedingly uncomfortable. Common symptoms include pain and burning on urination, cloudy, sour-smelling or bloody urination, backache, chills and fever, none of which are to be taken lightly because of the pain, distress and complete disruption they can bring to a woman's daily life.

Cystitis is often the result of bruising or trauma of the urethra and bladder, generally as the result of vigorous sexual activity, including masturbation, which promotes the growth of any bacteria that may be present. Such bruising and trauma come about when a hand, penis or mouth produce enough pressure and friction on the urethra and bladder to cause reddening and inflammation of these sensitive organs. The penis can harbour and spread bacteria from an inflamed cervix, the anus or from vaginal infections and deposits from near a woman's urethral opening. In addition, pressure on the urinary tract from an over-full bladder or bowel, from a diaphragm or from a prolapsed uterus or vagina can increase the possibility of urinary tract infection.

Escherichia coli (*E. coli*) are the bacteria commonly responsible for cystitis. Women who are diabetic have glucose in their urine which enables *E. coli* bacteria to thrive. They grow well in blood and vaginal secretions containing yeast so it is particularly important to check if you are subject to repeated bouts of cystitis that you are not also infected with the fungus *Candida albicans* (see 'Candiasis'). Even if you are infected, it is very common to have negative bacteria counts on testing. Chlamydia can also cause cystitis.

Chemical foams, sprays and douches can irritate the urethral opening, and spermicidal jellies or creams as well as the latex in condoms can produce irritation affecting the urethral entrance. Obstructions in the urinary tract, like kidney stones, can cause irritation and provide a focus for the growth of bacteria. It is therefore absolutely essential that you do not leave behind any stagnant urine after urinating which can set off another attack of cystitis.

In many instances I have been aware of psychological factors in repeated attacks of cystitis and have never really understood why until I realised that stress and related moods of depression actually stimulate the production of hormones which cause body cells to retain water. Since fluid is retained by the body's cells, urine output is reduced and the bladder is flushed out less often, so creating a good environment for bacteria. If psychological factors appear relevant, I would recommend counselling.

Treating Cystitis

- Do not wear tights.
- Underwear should be made of natural fibres, i.e. cotton or silk, and always loose fitting.
- Avoid bleaches and detergents when washing clothes that are worn next to the skin. Avoid wearing fabrics covered by chemical dyes.
- Do not use soap to wash with; rinsing with cold running water, especially immediately after sexual intercourse or masturbation, is far preferable.
- Urinate frequently before and after sex. This helps to relieve pressure and reduces the likelihood of bacterial build-up.
- Do not use tampons or sanitary towels (see Resources Directory for alternatives).
- Constipation and liver congestion both cause toxins to be recirculated throughout the body, burdening the kidneys with excess work, so ensure that the bowel is working well. Do a liver flush once a month and as a preventative measure also do a kidney flush (see Chapter Three).
- After urinating or defecating, wipe from front to back using non-bleached, non-scented toilet paper, or use a bidet.
- In the event of an acute attack, take a hot sitz-bath every hour, if this is practical, with some tea tree oil in it, 10 drops to 4 pints (2.4 litres).
- Use a warm compress of fennel oil — 10 drops diluted in enough water to moisten the compress — over the bladder and wrap yourself up well, keeping the rest of the body warm.
- Fast on unsweetened cranberry juice, potassium broth (see Chapter Four) and parsley tea.
- Take 2 capsules of herbal antibiotics (see below) with half a cup of the kidney/bladder tea (see Chapter Three) every two hours.

HERBAL ANTIBIOTICS

Equal parts of:
chaparral
echinacea

> *goldenseal*
> *marshmallow.*
>
> *Fill size 0 vegetable gelatine capsules with the finely powdered herbs.*

Alternatively make the following tea up as a decoction and drink 1 cup (240 ml) every two waking hours until all feelings of discomfort have gone.

> *Four parts of:*
> *bearberry leaf*
> *echinacea root*
> *Two parts of:*
> *cramp bark*
> *lemon balm*
> *parsley root.*

For 7–10 days after the cystitis has subsided, stay on a vegan diet, taking in plenty of fluids, raw garlic and carrot juice. During this time continue with a kidney flush or take 20 drops four times a day of couch grass tincture in plenty of water.

In really difficult cases of cystitis I have found reflexology extremely helpful but if you get repeated or severe infections together with high fever or if the cystitis does not clear up in four days, please consult a qualified medical herbalist.

Burning Mouth

This is a symptom of an overworked liver, a common problem during the menopause. Take the herbs and liver flush recommended in Chapter Three.

Candidiasis

As hormones stop stimulating the reproductive organs, vaginal secretions become less acidic encouraging the growth of *Candida albicans* (commonly known as thrush) and *Monilia*. If menopause is induced by surgical interference or is particularly rapid, the upsurge in vaginal yeast can cause intense discomfort. HRT, antibiotics and diabetes can all exacerbate candidiasis.

Symptoms

- Vaginal infections characterised by itching, redness or a white discharge, like cottage cheese in consistency.
- Infections of the skin, showing redness, itching and swelling.
- Nails become hardened, thickened, grooved or often brownish coloured.
- Muscle weakness, painful or swollen joints and poor coordination.
- Mood swings, depression, lethargy, depersonalisation — that is, a sense of 'spaciness' — and, unsurprisingly, a loss of interest in sex as well as anxiety and irritability.
- Feeling tired or drowsy.
- A variety of food intolerances and uncomfortable reactions to things like perfumes or certain chemical smells.
- Bloating, heartburn, constipation, bad breath.
- Chest pains, shortness of breath, dizziness, easy bruising.
- Frequent headaches which manifest themselves as pressure above or behind the ears or eyes.
- Cystitis which in spite of testing shows up as negative.
- PMS or erratic periods.

When you look at this long list it reads like a hypochondriac's dream or an alternative therapist's nightmare. If you can say 'yes' to seven of these symptoms, please get yourself accurately diagnosed. Biolab have developed a gut fermentation test and refined it to a degree where they can distinguish yeast from bacterial growth (see Resources Directory). They can only accept references from doctors, however.

Treatment and Herbal Help

I treat candiasis with a good wholefood vegan diet, including at least 50 per cent raw foods and freshly pressed juices. Practitioners who preclude yeast, as so many do, puzzle me. The difference between food yeast and the *Candida* organism is rather like the difference between a bay tree and an oak. While I might advocate the exclusion of brewer's yeast and substitute an inactive nutritional yeast, I certainly do not exclude fresh whole fruits and vegetables from the diet. I do ask patients to take plenty of organic olive oil and eat lots of garlic. I have found a very good way of eating garlic in huge quantities is to slice up the raw cloves and eat them piece by piece with mouthfuls of ripe fresh pears. Another method is to liquidise the garlic with a cupful of organic apple juice, freshly pressed, and an inch of fresh peeled ginger. This actually makes a very pleasant drink.

Biocare's Candicidin attacks the fungus systemically. Their superb Probiotics are also extremely helpful. If the gut proves to be permeable, I have used their Butyric acid with great success. All are made from natural plant substances (see Resources Directory for Biocare's address). Sealing a permeable gut can be done successfully with Intestinal Corrective Formula No. 3 (see Chapter Three). Paracidin, again from Biocare, can be useful if the yeast spores have escaped into the respiratory tract or the sinuses. I do insist that patients avoid alcohol, tea, coffee and cocoa, all of which suppress the proper working of the immune system. I insist that all fruits be fresh and eaten whole as fruit juice is too concentrated in sugar unless it is being used as a vehicle to carry garlic (as above), and that any sweeteners — honey, maple syrup and molasses as well as sugar in all its forms — are entirely omitted from the diet.

Apart from garlic there is a wide range of herbs that are extremely effective in combating candiasis. These include black walnut, tea tree and horsetail. Herbal support of the immune system (like all infections, candiasis follows a prolonged siege of the immune system) includes echinacea, Pau d'arco and various medicinal mushrooms.

Being a trained colonic therapist as well as a medical herbalist, I have used colonic therapy with great success in treating candiasis, providing the gut has not proved leaky. Hydrotherapy, particularly pyrotechnic treatments, has proved invaluable for stimulating an exhausted immune system.

Sitz-Baths and Douches
Ten drops of tea tree oil or a cup of cider vinegar in a warm sitz-bath can ease the symptoms of thrush. If there is bacteria mixed in with the

yeast, the infection is much harder to clear it up because no matter how acidic you make your vagina with these methods, the presence of bacteria will undermine all your efforts. In this case insert a clove of peeled garlic, which should be bruised but not crushed, as high up into the vaginal canal as possible. If you are worried about not being able to retrieve it, wrap the clove in a piece of gauze 12 in. (30 cm) long and 1 in. (2.5 cm) wide. Fold this in half and twist it just below the clove to make a small tampon with a long tail and then dip the clove end in olive oil and insert in the vagina. Do this morning and evening, taking the first clove out before putting the second clove in, so the first clove is left in all day and the second clove left in all night.

CRAMPS

If you have suffered from cramps in the past, the nature of menopausal cramping may appear different, often more intense and accompanied by severe fatigue, nausea and faintness. Cramp bark tincture — 10 drops in hot water every few minutes if needed — helps. The best treatment is liferoot — 10 drops three times a day in the ten days leading up to your period, or as near as you can judge.

Post-menopausal women experiencing night cramps need to exercise their legs a bit more and should definitely not be smoking (see 'Smoking and its Ill-Effects on Health'), which impedes blood flow. If your legs twitch and feel restless, you may be anaemic, in which case drink a wine glass of beetroot juice daily or take 40 drops of yellow dock tincture morning and evening. While doing this, avoid all tea which, become of its high tannin content, blocks efficient assimilation. Ensure there is plenty of natural calcium in your diet and take 10 drops three times a day of *Ginkgo biloba* and 10 drops three times a day of Bioforce's Petesan (see Resources Directory), together with foods richly abundant in vitamin E (see Chapter Four).

DEPRESSION

Statistics show that women are far more prone than men to mental illness. The mentally ill occupy one-third of all our National Health hospital beds, the majority of these taken by women, and women are the largest user group of tranquillisers.

Depression comes as the result of oppression. Wellbeing comes as the result of being free from anxiety, feeling in control, able to accomplish anything and of being generally in good health, with lots of energy. Depression stems from not being in control of one's life. It affects women particularly badly because many women depend upon their husband for their income or rely on welfare or social security payments or low-paid jobs. A man's salaries is on average still two-thirds higher than a woman's in the equivalent job. There are still very few women who are completely financially independent in spite of the fact that now more than two-thirds of women work outside the home. In addition, as women grow older, they become increasingly dependent on their children, if not for money, for transportation, companionship or nursing when they are ill.

Pauline Bart, a feminist psychologist, defines depression as the response to powerlessness. She has compared women's feelings of passivity, fatigue and depression to the reaction of experimental animals who were subjected to electric shocks no matter what they did. I loathe this kind of experimentation and certainly do not condone it, but the dogs in the experiment behaved in ways similar to the ways people in depression behave. They did not learn but were passive, did not eat and did not even move much, and when they were able to move they did so with great difficulty. When Pauline Bart studied middle-aged women suffering from depression, she found that they were often over-involved with or over-protective of their children, not because they wanted it that way, but because society forced on them the restricting roles of wife and mother. When they lost either of these roles, they responded with a loss of identify, powerlessness and uselessness. It is Bart's feeling that society sets women up for depression by encouraging them, sometimes even forcing them, to put all their eggs in one or at the most two baskets — the mother role and the wife role.[3]

Certainly women are more likely to suffer from depression if they are isolated, have no close friends to confide in, do not work outside the home, live in poor housing, have financial difficulties, look after toddlers at home full time or lose their mother at an early age. Depression of course can apply equally to career women who may cripple themselves in the attempt to be superwomen, striving for perfection at work and in the home. Those who retire unwillingly are also notoriously prone to depression.

Depression is very common among women with induced menopause but menopause achieved naturally certainly does not contribute to poor psychological health (or poor physical health for that matter). In fact menopausal women aged 45–65 actually experience a lower incidence of depression than younger women.

A great number of middle-aged women are forced to confront and deal with the unfinished emotional business many of them have been avoiding for a large part of their lives. If a woman is brave enough to do this (and I have worked with many who have), no other treatment is usually called for. But occasionally depression can be the result of adrenal exhaustion (see Chapter Three), a thyroid imbalance, as a side-effect of HRT, poor diet over a prolonged period, food intolerances, heavy-metal toxicity, hypoglycaemia or candidiasis. All causes need to be appropriately checked and remedied. Certainly depression, whatever the cause, does not need to be treated with antidepressants (which, in any case, tend to have an adverse affect on women more so than on men). Acupuncture, bio-dynamics, cranial/sacral therapy and nursing in anthroposophical hospitals (run according to the principles of Rudolph Steiner — see Resources Directory, 'Residential Care') can be extremely effective forms of therapy, none of them involving chemical medicine.

Speaking up and standing up for yourself also helps. If your rights or dignity are being trampled on, summon the energy to stand up for yourself. Say what you mean, show your feelings. Purposeful activity helps too. Make sure it is something you enjoy and that will give you a sense of accomplishment. Do not hesitate to seek counselling if you feel it might be worth exploring (see Resources Directory). Valerianum Zincum (40 drops times three daily), available from Bioforce, can be helpful, as can the Bach Flower Remedies (see Resources Directory).

Physical exercise can be very beneficial, partly because it leads to chemical reactions which boost the nervous system. Two of the most common signs of depression are fatigue and inertia. Make your exercise programme regular and enjoyable and, given time, it will revolutionise your physical and mental wellbeing.

Digestive Problems

Some women get constipation or indigestion during the menopause or the menopause will exacerbate this tendency if they already have it because of the natural deceleration of the digestive tract. (Oestrogen in the pre-menopausal woman stimulates the gastrointestinal tract.) In addition, the liver has to work particularly hard during the menopause, which may exacerbate any constipation or indigestion. (For remedies for constipation, see Chapter Three.)

Indigestion

To my mind this is one of the easiest complaints to rectify, without even having to resort to herbal medicine, if eating habits are altered and the food-combining rules are followed (see Chapter Four, 'Suggestions for a Healthy Daily Diet'). Meals should always be eaten in a calm, quiet atmosphere and at a leisurely pace. Bear in mind the following:

- Chew food properly and thoroughly.
- Do not take liquid with meals unless it is a medicinal herbal tea or a potassium broth. If soup is being taken as part of the meal, leave a 15-minute gap before going on to the rest of the meal.
- Avoid salt and all spices, sugar, tea, coffee, alcohol, soda, refined carbohydrates, including fried foods, and anything else which you suspect acts as a gastric irritant.
- Do not eat excessively hot or ice-cold foods.
- Never eat if you are distressed. If you are really hungry, sip a glass of vegetable juice, which should be at room temperature, or a cup of potassium broth until you have completely calmed down.
- Do not eat if you are ill but drink plenty of fluids.
- Eat in unhurried, relaxed surroundings. No arguments at the table!
- Eat small meals and always leave the table feeling you have room for just a little more.
- If food is eaten too soon after a previous meal, the natural pace of the digestive process will be disrupted, so allow two hours respite after a fruit meal, three hours after a vegetable one and, if you have completely messed up your food combining, do not eat so much as a peanut for five hours. However, plenty of liquids may be taken.

- If none of this helps, investigate the possibility of an intolerance to dairy products or wheat, or check with a professional to see if you have candidiasis. Distortion of the thoracic vertebrae can affect the stomach and will need to be rectified by an osteopath.

As an iridologist I find it easy to determine if the stomach is too low or high in acidity. In my experience most people over forty become deficient in digestive enzymes and supplements of these will help in cases of low acidity (see herbal suppliers in Resources Directory). For high acidity try chewing 4 slippery elm tablets after meals, or 3 charcoal tablets, or drink an infusion of meadowsweet tea. If the indigestion is acute the obvious thing to do is not eat any more food and fast on something bland such as carrot juice with a touch of fresh ginger root in it if you are thirsty or hungry. A tea made of equal parts of fennel, peppermint and dill will facilitate digestion after a meal. This is much better for you than coffee which simply overloads and distresses the liver.

I absolutely abhor the use of commercial antacids. Those made of sodium bicarbonate are designed to relieve the excess acid which causes indigestion and heartburn by neutralising the gastric acid in the stomach. However, if used regularly they disrupt the natural acid–alkaline balance of the body, causing alkalosis which can, if exacerbated by a substantial intake of dairy products, result in irreversible kidney damage. Milk can actually increase hydrochloric acid secretion in some people which can make the symptoms far worse. Besides this, many antacids contain aluminium, an excessive intake of which is extremely poisonous. Aluminium accumulates in the liver and interferes with its function. It affects the kidneys, causing nephritis and degeneration, and may give rise to non-specific joint problems by affecting bone metabolism. This is because an aluminium overload also affects the central nervous system, particularly the parathyroid. So do please avoid antacids as far as possible.

ENDOMETRIOSIS
Endometriosis occurs when tissue like that in the lining of the womb is found in other parts of the body, most commonly the ovaries,

Fallopian tubes and peritoneum, but deposits have been found all over the body including the lungs and the eyes. Endometrial tissue has even been found in the pelvic cavities of infant girls. In adult women these deposits bleed during every menstrual period — that is, they behave just as they would in the womb lining. Bleeding causes inflammation and adhesions can form, which may make organs stick to one another.

Researchers are still investigating the causes of endometriosis. Interesting new research done by the United States Endometriosis Protection Agency suggests a close link between dioxin (toxic chemical) levels in the body and the severity and incidence of endometriosis. An experiment carried out on rhesus monkeys exposed to TCDD — the most toxic dioxin — found that the incidence of endometriosis was directly correlated with dioxin exposure. Further research showed the severity of the disease was dependent upon the dose administered.

If this is the case, it is doubly important that women do not use sanitary towels or tampons but find some other alternative (see below). Both forms of sanitary protection are made from synthetic fibres including rayon, manufactured from woodpulp-derived cellulose which can be subject to contamination with dioxins. In Sweden there is now concern that the dioxins used as part of the bleaching process of the cotton may contribute towards cancer of the uterus.

It is possible to buy unbleached sanitary towels (see Resources Directory) or to use natural sponges. If you do opt for a sponge, clean it by steaming it or letting it sit in very hot water with a generous dash of cider vinegar for disinfection. Boiling tends to destroy it.

Endometriosis is linked to an over-production of oestrogen, and as oestrogen is heavily present in dairy products as the result of added hormones used in the dairy industry, remarkable improvements can be observed when women cut out meat and dairy products altogether from their diet. Because of the oestrogen contained in HRT, it too can exacerbate endometriosis, as can being on the Pill. But the good news is that as oestrogen levels naturally decline during the menopause so does the discomfort of endometriosis.

There is some suggestion that endometriosis is also linked to an immune deficiency. Apart from implementing dietary changes, I have had considerable success in treating endometriosis by administering shitake mushroom tincture (25 drops three times daily) or by getting women to eat the mushrooms fresh each day because these inhibit the growth of abnormal tissue in the body. In addition, I use Pau d'arco tea, decocted, to boost the immune system and chaste tree tincture (dosage according to the condition) to support liver function. Hot and cold sitz-baths are often extremely effective, as the most common area for endometriosis to occur is behind the uterus in the area that lies between the uterus and the rectum — the pouch of Douglas. Add 10 drops of cypress oil to the hot water.

FIBROIDS

Fibroids may temporarily enlarge during the menopause, though many afterwards then shrink and disappear. They occur so frequently in women over forty — almost half — they might even be considered fairly normal. Fibroids are simply non-malignant growths of smooth muscle and fibrous connected tissue which can range from the size of a pea to the size of a grapefruit. Starting inside the uterus, many fibroids can often occur simultaneously on the uterine wall or on the outer surface of the uterus. Sometimes they can grow out from the uterus on a stalk and if the stalk twists, the blood supply can be cut off causing pain or vaginal discharge. They can cause very heavy uterine bleeding and discharge and heavy, painful periods. If very large, fibroids can press against the bladder causing frequent urination, against the colon, interfering with normal bowel movements, or against nerve endings, causing pain and an overall feeling of fullness in the abdomen. Fibroid growth is stimulated by hormones, particularly oestrogen, and with each menstruation fibroids can grow a little larger. The Pill can accelerate their growth, as can HRT.

I have been very successful in treating the problem herbally and with diet. The dietary change takes about six months to shine through as it is well known that fibroids (like endometriosis) are oestrogen sensitive. I advise a low-fat, vegan diet, high in complex carbohydrates and free of all refined sugar to decrease the amount of circulating oestrogens, together with plenty of the superfoods (see Chapter Four). Massage, t'ai chi, meditation, shiatsu, nightly castor oil packs (see

Chapter Six) and acupuncture are all useful to increase energy flow to the pelvis, as is aerobic exercise performed 3–4 times a week.

Caroline Myss believes that fibroids represent a woman's unexpressed creativity and may result from dead-end jobs or relationships which block her creativity.[4]

VAGINAL BOLUSES

A bolus is a way of administering herbs vaginally other than on a tampon or by douching. Boluses are made with healing herbs that draw out toxins and poisons so making the malfunctioning area healthy, their beneficial effects extending beyond the vagina or bowel to encompass the entire urinary and genital organs.

Equal parts of:
chickweed
comfrey
goldenseal
mullein
slippery elm
squawvine
yellow dock.

Combine these together in finely powdered form and then melt down enough coconut butter to mix in well so that the whole mass has the texture of pastry. Now roll it between the hands until you have a pencil-like bolus as thick as your thumb and about an inch (2.5 cm) long. Round off the ends gently with your fingers and put all the boluses you have made on a greased baking sheet in the fridge where they will harden (and where they can be stored for up to six months). Insert one of these boluses before bed, protecting your knickers with a sanitary towel, for six nights a week and fast on the seventh day. Overnight the coconut butter will melt, leaving only the herbs, which are easy to douche out. The following morning lie on your slant board (see Resources Directory) and inject with your douche applicator half a cup of the following mixture:

Six parts of:
comfrey
oak bark
Four parts of:
yellow dock
Three parts of:
marshmallow
mullein
walnut
One part of:
lobelia.

Make as a decoction and strain well before use. Hold this mixture in the vagina as long as possible before voiding and while doing so knead and massage the abdominal area, as well as doing your slant board exercises (see below), so that the herbal tea can be assimilated by the body.

Using this treatment six days on and one day off, I have helped women to remove their fibroids altogether. Certainly, upon repeated physical examination, they become smaller and smaller and eventually disappear altogether. Please note that the treatment may need to be continued for up to six months, so you need to be patient.

Slant Board Exercises
To perform these exercises, one end of the slant board should be elevated to a height of about 12 in. (30 cm) while the other should remain firmly on the ground. You should lie on the slant board so that your feet are at the elevated end.

1. Lie on your back on the board with your arms by your sides for at least 10 minutes. This will allow gravity to help your abdominal organs to get into their correct positions.
2. Raise your arms directly above your head, making your body into a straight line. Repeat this exercise 10–15 times; this will stretch the abdominal muscles and pull the abdomen towards the shoulders.

3. While holding your breath, move your abdominal organs towards your shoulders, by contracting the abdominal muscles, then allowing them to relax. Repeat this exercise 10–15 times.

4. Pat your abdomen vigorously with both hands, then lean first to the left side and then to the right, each time patting the stretched side 10–15 times. Using your abdominal muscles, bring your body to the sitting position, then return to the lying position. If possible, do this three times. Then lie down flat and roll a ball around the abdomen, pressing deeply and following the shape of the colon from left to right.

5. Bend your knees and raise your legs at the hips, drawing them towards your chest. While in this position, turn your head from side to side 5–6 times, then lift your head slightly and rotate 3–4 times.

6. Lift your legs so they are almost at right angles to your body. Make outward circular movements 8–10 times. Increase to 25 movements after a week or two of exercising.

7. Bend your knees. Straighten one leg and raise it slowly about 10 in. (25 cm) from the slant board, keeping your back firmly on the board. Repeat ten times, then change legs.

8. Raise your legs in the air and make circular movements as if you were riding a bicycle. Do this 14–25 times.

When you have finished your slant board exercises, relax and rest, letting the blood circulate in your head for 10 minutes.

HEADACHES AND MIGRAINES

If you have always suffered from migraines, the menopause may actually bring relief from them. Other women can begin to get headaches, often quite severe ones, for the first time during the menopause as the result of fatigue, stress and rapidly changing hormone levels as well as surges of *kundalini* moving into the crown of the head (see 'Hot Flushes'). Headaches and migraines can also arise as a side-effect of HRT. Chronic headaches can sometimes be triggered by reaction to certain foods, the most suspect being citrus and dairy foods, red wine, all additives, artificial sweeteners, sugars and all members of the Solonaceae family (see Chapter Four).

If the headache has arisen simply as the result of tension, try a few big, slow, half-head rolls from side to side, while sitting upright with the shoulders relaxed. Alternatively place a steaming hot wet towel around the back of the neck and simultaneously put your feet in a basin full of hot water. Or try a brisk walk, making sure your hands, feet, head and neck are well covered and breathe deeply while doing so. On your return take 10 drops of black cohosh tincture or vervain tincture as often as needed and if necessary every 15 minutes. Putting the tinctures in hot liquid accelerates their passage into the bloodstream.

Migraine

This is a particularly severe form of headache that recurs and is usually accompanied by visual and/or gastrointestinal disturbances such as nausea, vomiting and an inability to look at light. Attacks can be preceded by flashes of light, the result of intercerebral vasoconstriction, followed by severe head pain confined to one side of the head or eye due to dilation of the extracerebral cranial arteries. It is important to get a correct diagnosis before proceeding with treatment since a migraine is much more deep-seated than other forms of headache and will take longer to heal. I have found an iridology test particularly useful for ascertaining whether there is any liver congestion, intestinal toxaemia or hypoglycaemia, all of which can be the underlying cause of migraine. If I can catch a migraine early enough, I can use lobelia in emetic doses because the induction of vomiting will often help to forestall a severe migraine. Please note, though, that this herb is only available on prescription from medical herbalists.

Cranial/sacral therapy may be indicated if muscular spasm and arthritis is present. If liver congestion is indicated, as it very often is, a three-day fast coupled with liver detoxification, castor oil packs and liver-cleansing herbs is recommended. Intestinal toxaemia calls for fasting and the use of enemas, chicory root enemas being particularly helpful. They can also be used in the early stages of a migraine and sometimes may stop it dead in its tracks. Other herbs which help include violet, peppermint, lavender, feverfew, rosemary, valerian root, vervain, dandelion, motherwort, centaury, ginger root and skullcap.

Ginger root is effective as an antiplatelet aggregatory as it seems that the blood platelets of migraine sufferers spontaneously come together more than normal between attacks. So ginger tea taken on a regular basis may prove very helpful in these instances. If you have the kind of migraine which is relieved by a hot-water bottle placed on the face or the neck, use herbs which will assist to expand the blood vessels in the head — such as peppermint, lavender, rosemary or feverfew. However, if you have the kind of migraine that is relieved by ice packs, use instead valerian, skullcap or motherwort. Infuse or decoct as appropriate any of these as teas and drink 3 cups (720 ml) per day. In addition, Bioforce's Migrane Echtroplex is extremely helpful (see Resources Directory). The usual dose is 30 drops three times daily.

HEART DISEASE
(See Chapter Three, 'The Heart'.)

HOT FLUSHES
These are the only 'true' menopausal symptoms. Most women will have had at least one by the time they reach sixty. A single hot flush which sweeps through the upper body to the face, reddening the skin, or making it blotchy, and causing sweating may pass in a few seconds or last up to fifteen minutes. Rarely will it last more than an hour. Eighty per cent of those women who do experience hot flushes have had them for between two months to two years and a small percentage persist with them right into their eighties.

The Mechanics of Flushing
A hot flush begins in the hypothalamus which, among its other tasks, controls body temperature and regulates oestrogen levels. As the output of oestrogen begins to stutter during the menopause, the hypothalamus sends gonadotropin-releasing hormone to the pituitary gland, instructing it to send follicle-stimulating hormone (FSH) to the ovaries. FSH in turn tells the ovaries to produce oestrogen but during the menopause the ovaries may not be able to do so through lack of viable eggs. However, if an egg follicle does develop, the resulting higher levels of oestrogen instruct the brain to stop sending FSH. If

ovulation does not take place, no oestrogen is produced and there is no consequent feedback to the brain to tell it to stop sending FSH. The pituitary, unused to this new situation, causes FSH to soar trying to meet its normal goal of stimulating more oestrogen. At this point the body responds to the low levels of oestrogen by whipping the hypothalamus with adrenalin which in turn resets the body's thermostatic control to high so that a hot flush floods the body. As blood vessels dilate, the body is cooled by sweating and a new lower temperature is set.

Hot flushes are exacerbated by stress, by any form of heat — whether weather, water or body generated — and by coffee, chillies or any other hot spices, alcohol and nicotine.

Think of a hot flush as a release of what Hindu philosophy terms *kundalini* — cosmic electricity — which sweeps up from the earth and evaporates to the cosmos. *Kundalini* naturally begins to rise in women by the age of forty, activating the *chakras* through which it passes. (There are seven *chakras* representing different areas of energy flowing through the body.) Caroline Myss believes that hot flushes are related to blocked *kundalini* and are a classic symptom in menopausal, non-orgasmic women whose sexual pleasure has inevitably been limited.[5]

Herbal Help

Herbs that assist adrenalin function — Siberian ginseng, nettles, borage, liquorice — stimulate the production of a little more oestrogen, helping to decrease the incidence of hot flushes. Nervines such as vervain, valerian and lemon balm calm the body. Liver herbs such as dandelion and Oregon grape root help to support the liver's natural work of metabolising the hormones still circulating in the body. The following formulation is Dr Christopher's (see Chapter Three for his intestinal formulae) and is excellent for combating hot flushes.

CHANGEASE

Equal parts of:
black cohosh

> *false unicorn*
> *holy thistle*
> *liquorice*
> *sarsaparilla*
> *Siberian ginseng*
> *squawvine.*
>
> *Take 2–3 size 0 capsules of the finely powdered herbs morning and evening.*

Many of my patients find drinking 3 cups (720 ml) of sage tea daily, infused, is also very effective.

HYPERTENSION (HIGH BLOOD PRESSURE)

Let me start by saying that high blood pressure is not a disease. It is simply a defensive and corrective measure deployed by the body; a means of dealing with pathological conditions like toxaemia (overall poisoning of the body as the result of the failure to remove toxic waste through the eliminative channels), glandular disturbances, defective calcium metabolism, malfunctioning kidneys, degenerative changes in the arteries, obesity and emotionally caused physical dysfunction. Often high blood pressure has no obvious medical cause at all and yet there are hundreds of thousands of people who take drugs for high blood pressure every day, assuming they will need them for the rest of their lives. To my mind it is a complete waste of time lowering the blood pressure unless the cause of the condition can be removed. An iridology test will often get to the root of the problem. Once the cause has been identified, the vast majority of hypertensive people can be helped by a simple naturopathic approach, although this does require dedication and persistence on the part of the patient.

I have found a supervised juice fast for 3–4 weeks is an excellent way of bringing blood pressure back to normal and it certainly produces a very rapid reduction in the systolic pressure (the rate at which blood bounds outwards from the heart through the arteries). The juices I use are citrus, blackcurrant, grape, carrot or spinach. Spinach juice, being very powerful, must always be mixed in a carrier base of carrot juice.

Vegetable juices can be spiced with a dash of onion or garlic. A brown-rice fast works equally well (where boiled brown rice is eaten in small bowlfuls whenever required, supplemented with drinks of mineral water or homemade potassium broth) but most people, in my experience, prefer a juice fast. I must emphasise that if you are going to go on such a prolonged juice fast, you must do this under professional supervision with somebody experienced in the field.

A simple way to regulate either high or low blood pressure is to take a teaspoonful of cayenne pepper in a glass of warm water three times a day. You will need to build up to this dosage gently because initially it can taste fiery. Include lots of garlic, buckwheat (for its rutin content), sprouted alfalfa and raw foods in the diet and entirely cut out salt, tea, coffee, chocolate, cocoa, alcohol and all strong spices and flavourings except cayenne and garlic. Meals should be small and taken often, and weight needs to be controlled. A diet high in potassium and low in sodium is essential in any case for the maintenance of healthy blood pressure, so ensure you drink a pint (600 ml) of potassium broth daily. Taking vitamin E during and after the menopause reduces the risk of a heart attack by 36 per cent. (For vitamin E rich foods see Chapter Four; see this chapter also for the section on fats and oils.) It should be noted that vegans rarely have high blood pressure.

Exercise is of paramount importance in lowering blood pressure, although this should be done under supervision if obesity is a problem. Aim for a minimum of 40 minutes 3–4 times a week. In addition, avoid hot showers and baths and use instead warm showers alternated with cold showers of 2 minutes each, repeating several times and finishing with a cold shower.

Lecithin will help emulsify fat in the bloodstream and is available in the form of granules from healthfood shops. Garlic has the same effect, and is an excellent supplement for combating high blood pressure and heart disease generally (see Chapter Four, 'The Special Protective Superfoods').

Always remember that high blood pressure can be triggered by strong emotional responses, fear, stress and prolonged nervous tension. These need to be taken into consideration and reduced wherever possible. Deep relaxation and alternate nostril or pranayama breathing, as taught in hatha yoga, calm the sympathetic nervous system, relaxing the capillaries and permanently lowering blood pressure. I am a manual lymphatic drainage (MLD) therapist and have found a course of MLD, with regular top-ups, achieves similar results.

TONIC FOR HIGH BLOOD PRESSURE

This formulation regulates high blood pressure gradually, while strengthening the heart, protecting the arteries and improving the circulation.

Six parts of:
hawthorn berries
Three parts of:
motherwort
One part of:
dandelion
hyssop
nettles
rosemary.

I make this up as a tincture and generally prescribe 60 drops three times a day. If further help for the kidneys is needed, I also prescribe the kidney detox routine (see Chapter Three).

INSOMNIA

This is not uncommon if you are waking at night soaked in sweat and having to change the bedclothes and your nightwear. Remember always the internal processes occurring during the menopause demand a tremendous amount of energy which can leave you feeling very drained unless you nourish yourself particularly well, rest often and use your energy discriminately.

A warm bath (94–97°F/34–36°C) before bed with 10 drops of lavender or chamomile oil added helps to relieve congestion of the brain and spinal cord. Once in bed, take twenty deep slow breaths of fresh air, which means leaving your window slightly ajar. If safety precautions preclude this, have an ioniser plugged in beside your bed at night.

Cut out caffeine, salt and nicotine, because all of these can affect your sleeping pattern. Overeating before bed can make getting to sleep difficult, as can a nightcap of alcohol. Nutritional deficiencies, particularly those of the B complex and calcium, are a common factor in insomnia. Allergic reactions to food additives, colourings, preservatives and pesticides may cause tachycardia (abnormally rapid heart action). One of the simplest and main causes I have found in cases of insomnia is people going to bed at erratic times. I particularly noticed this as far as the many air crew I have treated. Their odd working hours leave very many of them stressed, fatigued and sleepless. The important thing here is to follow your own body rhythms and sleep regularly at a time that is comfortable for you. Do not worry if that is well after midnight. Six hours of refreshing sleep as part of a regular sleep schedule is much better than lying awake tossing and turning. Exercise is also terribly important. Remember too that sleep problems can often be connected to the side-effects of various drugs. Relaxation exercises, autogenics or some other form of meditation (see Resources Directory), and bio-feedback all help.

Take a cup of lemon balm or lime flower tea before bed. Lemon balm tea is delicious but needs to be made from fresh leaves as dried leaves are a dusty, flavourless disappointment. If using lime flowers, ensure that your sources are fresh as ageing flowers can be poisonous. Olive is a wonderful Bach Flower Remedy for exhaustion (see Resources Directory). A decoction of skullcap tea placed in a flask besides the bed is particularly helpful for those who wake up suddenly in the night full of unnamed fears and premonitions of calamity; it can be especially helpful if you add the Bach Flower Remedies aspen and walnut.

MEMORY LOSS

There is absolutely no evidence to support our cultural belief that senility comes with age. Women do complain to me about fuzzy thinking and memory loss during the menopause, but when I question them closely, it seems their long-term memories become sharper by the year and that, while their brains *feel* fuzzy, it is only because they are leaving behind a life-long attachment to left-brain thinking — the logical, masculine way of solving problems — and evolving a more feminine right-brain pattern of thought, involving a greater reliance on feelings and intuition. I encourage such women to take advantage of this and get involved in creative pastimes which thrive on right-brain activity rather than reaching for the *Ginkgo biloba.* Slant board exercises (see 'Fibroids') will also help to increase the flow of blood into the brain.

MENSTRUAL IRREGULARITIES

Rarely does a woman's period stop dead in its tracks. Generally the menstrual cycle becomes erratic. Missing periods is normal as are floods and trickles, and spotting during ovulation. All is well if it feels well to you, so tune into your body and listen to it. Draw more love to yourself in your spiritual, social and personal relationships and rest, rest, rest! I observe too many women ploughing on relentlessly through the menopause instead of honouring the changes they are feeling. It takes a lot of energy to journey through the menopause. Feeling tired is not unreasonable so when your body bleeds, take time to rest. Use sister moon to help you regulate your cycles by sleeping where a full moon can shine on your face and stimulate your pineal glands.

TREATMENT FOR IRREGULAR CYCLES

This formulation will also help with spotting and heavy bleeding. Mix together the following tinctures:

Four parts of:
tormentil
Two parts of:
blue cohosh
chaste tree
lady's mantle
One part of:
sage.

Take 40 drops three times a day and, if you are flooding, 40 drops every half an hour in hot water.

Please note that it is not normal to flood hugely with every period, so do get this checked by a doctor. Heavy bleeding can be a symptom of fibroids, endometriosis, ovarian cysts, polyps, pelvic infection or occasionally, but rarely, even cancer. There may also be emotional causes behind heavy bleeding, notably depression, and sterilisation sometimes causes heavy bleeding.

Reflexology
Reflexology can often be very successful in treating heavy periods. You can have a go at this yourself.

- Sit comfortably on a couch and put your foot in your lap so that you can easily reach the sides. The reflexology pressure points for the genitals and female organs are situated around the ankle.
- With the flat of your thumb press on a spot on the inside of your foot about half way between your ankle bone and the bottom of your heel. This is the uterine pressure point.
- Press on the corresponding spot on the outside of your foot — the pressure point for the ovaries.
- Squeeze and pinch either side of your Achilles tendon about 3 in. (7.5 cm) up from your heel. This will also affect the uterus. If it feels tender or hurts, go gently but do not stop.
- Work on these points throughout the month but not during the actual flow as this will make it even heavier.

OEDEMA (WATER RETENTION)
Fluid retention may indicate a weakness in the kidneys and adrenal glands, and even the heart. Nettle tea nourishes the kidneys and adrenals, so drink 3 cups (720 ml) a day, infused. Dandelion tincture is particularly effective — take 20 drops three times a day — as well as the kidney cleanse (see Chapter Three). Manual lymphatic drainage is very beneficial, and any form of exercise will stimulate fluid movement.

PALPITATIONS

Palpitations are not indications of heart disease and tend to accompany hot flushes. Occasionally a woman may have had a minor heart prolapse (this affects 10 per cent of the population in general as they grow older) and it may manifest during the menopause in the form of pain or palpitations. Fluid loss from heavy sweating can cause palpitations so drink lots of water, nettle tea, which is particularly helpful, or diluted organic grape juice. Valerian, liquorice, hawthorn and especially motherwort all help to ease palpitations. Take them in tincture form 25–50 drops times three daily and more often if needed. Avoid taking liquorice if you have high blood pressure or suffer from fluid retention.

PRE-MENSTRUAL SYNDROME (PMS)

If nothing is done to heal PMS, it often gets worse over time and so rages particularly hard during the menopause if you are prone to it.

Physical and Emotional Symptoms

Many of the physical changes manifested during PMS are the results of a shift in fluid balance in response to progesterone which is produced in large quantities after ovulation. Physical changes may include swelling of the breasts, feet and hands, haemorrhoids, abdominal bloating, weight gain, migraines, backache, cramping, painful joints, marred skin and lank hair, asthma, hay fever, hoarseness, nausea and red eyes. Emotional problems may include food or alcohol cravings, depression, loss of concentration, fatigue and irritability.

Diet

A hypoglycaemic diet is ideal for PMS sufferers. The craving for refined carbohydrates, including sugar, rockets by two and a half times during a bout of PMS. It seems it is not the hypoglycaemic state itself that causes PMS because its symptoms disappear soon after food is eaten and in any case never lasts for days on end. What hypoglycaemia does is to overburden the adrenal glands as they struggle to stabilise drastically fluctuating blood-sugar levels. Distressed adrenal glands need an abundance of B complex vitamins and vitamin C.

These vitamins are essential for carbohydrate metabolism and are often missing in a typical Western, highly refined diet, which produces hypoglycaemia in the first place. So women with cravings for refined carbohydrates get stuck in a vicious cycle generating hypoglycaemia and adrenal exhaustion. This is why vitamin supplements of B complex and B_6 have been so successful in treating certain cases of PMS.

Many PMS sufferers eat four and a half times more dairy products than women not affected by this syndrome. Saturated animal fat inhibits the formation of PGE_1, which is an anti-inflammatory prostaglandin deficient in PMS sufferers. Oil of evening primrose, blackcurrant or borage all enhance the production of PGE_1. Vitamin E is also useful as an inhibitor against the formation of a PGE antagonist derived from meat.

Other Forms of Treatment for PMS
Osteopathic adjustment may be necessary to relieve bloating, and exercise certainly helps.

Different Types of PMS
There is not one, but four different types of PMS. Women with PMS-A have abnormal hormone levels that are high in oestrogen and low in progesterone, and suffer from anxiety, irritability and nervous tension as a result. PMS-H sufferers have problems of water retention with subsequent bloating and breast pain. Those with PMS-C crave refined carbohydrates and feel weak and prone to headaches. Those with PMS-D can get profoundly depressed, forgetful and confused because progesterone levels are too high and oestrogen too low. Women with PMS-A tend to eat large amounts of dairy produce, while those with PMS-H eat too much refined carbohydrate and those with PMS-C too much animal fat. Sufferers of PMS-D are especially vulnerable to the effects of environmental lead. All PMS sufferers are deficient in B complex vitamins and magnesium, both of which are closely involved with the mood-altering chemicals in the brain. A magnesium deficiency is exacerbated by a diet high in dairy products, which also allows more lead to get into the body.

I have found that severe candidiasis can exacerbate PMS, so it is worth having this checked.

Apart from following all the advice on a hypoglycaemic diet in Chapter Four, take the following pre-crash tonic in the ten days leading up to your period.

PRE-CRASH TONIC

Equal parts of:
blessed thistle
blue cohosh
chaste tree
cornsilk
cramp bark
dandelion
false unicorn
ginger
sage
sarsaparilla
squawvine
uva ursi
valerian
wild yam.

Make as a tincture and take 15 drops three times a day in a little water.

Once the period starts, switch to the changease formulation (see 'Hot Flushes') or use Higher Nature's Pre-mens Prevention (see Resources Directory). I have found a combination of changease and pre-crash tonic an extremely successful formulation if followed faithfully over a period of some months together with the advice given in the above section.

SEX DURING THE MENOPAUSE
Women vary as much during this time of their lives as they do at any other. Some have such diminished *chi* — internal vitality — as the

result of years of self-sacrificial care-taking of partners, families and communities that they have nothing left over for sex. But others tell me that because they are finally free of the fear of unwanted pregnancies, they feel liberated enough to express their true, uninhibited sexuality at last. Sex drive is certainly not related to waning oestrogen levels.

For a woman, organism, emotion and mood come in an indissoluble package, and this is part of the reason why women have more difficulty than men climaxing in each and every sexual encounter. Of course most of you already know this, intuitively understanding that conditions have to be right and your lover has to give you half a chance if you are to have an orgasm. Most women are content to finish sex at the plateau arousal phase from time to time, but if this happens too often or all the time, naturally it causes both physical and emotional problems.

The single most common cause for a woman failing to achieve orgasm is inadequate stimulation. Often the man gets blamed, verbally or silently, for coming too soon. But just as often it is not really his fault and a woman must share some of the responsibility of bringing herself to orgasm. She has to, in her own way, give directions if she wants to get to her destination, so to speak, and to do this she has to feel free to speak up, say what feels good, change positions, move a man's hand (or her own) down to her vulva and teach him how to stimulate her entire genital area in the way she is used to having it stimulated through her own masturbatory experience.

If a woman's sex life was happy and fulfilled before menopause, it will almost certainly go on being so after menopause. And the converse is also true of course. If a woman's sex life has been uninteresting, unsatisfying, done as a duty for a rather insensitive partner, she may welcome menopause as an excuse not to bother with sex any more. A woman who does not have a sensitive partner or any partner at all may decide that sex just is not that important.

Unsurprisingly, the things that determine whether a woman will enjoy sex as she grows older are the very same things that determine whether she enjoyed it when she was young. It all depends on her attitude (seeing intercourse and masturbation as natural and fine —

the less guilt she has, the more responsive she is), overall health (a woman is unlikely to feel sexy if she is not feeling good in other ways too) and whether she has a sensitive, caring partner (making love with a man who is attentive and appreciative of her will naturally enhance her self-esteem).

Remember, too, that a heterosexual woman's partner, if he is her own age, may be having difficulty maintaining an erection for various reasons including the side-effects of certain chemical medicines, a poor diet and lack of fitness. All can be remedied sensibly.

Smoking and its Ill-Effects on Health
Consider some facts about smoking.

- Cigarettes reduce blood flow, particularly to the hands and feet. It takes six whole hours after the last cigarette to get the blood flow back on an even keel. So if lighting up is the first thing you do when you get out of bed and the last thing you do before sleeping, your circulation is probably normal for about only two hours a day.
- Smoking depresses the immune system and this process takes three months to reverse once you have given it up.
- Osteoporosis has been proven to be aggravated by smoking.
- Menopausal problems are made worse by smoking.
- Smoking inhibits the pancreas and may lead to hypoglycaemia.
- Smoking forces the heart to accelerate to after only one cigarette, so more oxygen is needed, yet the bloodstream is depleted of oxygen by the carbon monoxide in the cigarette smoke. As the result of a reduced supply of oxygen in the bloodstream, function of all the organs is impaired, causing extensive damage in the long term.
- Statistics show that death from lung cancer in women will overtake death from breast cancer by the year 2000.

I am well aware that the majority of smokers are desperate to break their addictive habit and also that smoking has been shown to be more addictive than heroin and cocaine, but consider the following.

Life Expectancy
If you need an incentive to spur you on, sit down and work out when

you expect to die. Alter the years into months and by doing so your remaining lifespan will appear much shorter. If each cigarette smoked is estimated to take away eight minutes of life, this means that someone who smokes twenty a day will lose a month of life for every year they smoke. If you smoke forty a day, this adds up to sixteen years deducted from your life. If you do not give up, the quality of life left to you will be severely diminished in any case. Cigarettes contain over 4,000 known toxic poisons, any one of which can kill if taken in sufficient quantity.

Giving up Smoking

Only 3 per cent of smokers are able to stop smoking on their own. So you might as well relax and recognise the fact that you will almost certainly need professional help and guidance as well as high motivation which only you can supply. Sign up with any programme that has been recommended to you as effective for giving up smoking. Check that it uses the combination of aversion therapy and behaviour modification.

In the initial stages of giving up smoking a prolonged fast, professionally supervised, of between seven to twenty-one days certainly helps to overcome nicotine craving and detoxifies the body rapidly. This is probably best done in a residential naturopathic clinic or a health farm. Any form of hydrotherapy which makes you sweat will help you get rid of nicotine through the skin. Colonic irrigation is also helpful and should be conducted twice a week for several weeks. Lobelia, which contains lobeline and can be prescribed by a medical herbalist, has a very similar action to nicotine but is non-addictive. The general dosage prescribed is 15 drops six times a day, but you may take more every time you feel a craving for a cigarette. Taken in excess lobelia will cause nausea and may act as an emetic and induce vomiting. This is no bad thing because not only will it clear the stomach of poisons but it will act as an aversion therapy associated with cigarettes.

Passive Smoking

Passive smoking greatly increases the risk of lung cancer as well as heart disease, nasal-sinus cancer and brain tumour. If you are unfortunate enough to work in the same room as someone who smokes thirty cigarettes a day, you will have passively inhaled a total of five of those cigarettes.

At the end of the first month of kicking the nicotine habit, I encourage any women courageous enough to give up to go out and buy something extravagant with the money she has saved on cigarettes, or to invest it in a yoga or a martial arts class. Both disciplines are not only invigorating but also empowering.

Sore Breasts

Menopause usually brings welcome relief from chronically tender breasts and nipples but for those still battling with this problem ensure that you take very high doses of natural calcium, and foods rich in vitamin E and B complex, in addition to oils rich in gammalinoleic acid. Avoid all caffeine including that in colas. Take 40 drops of chaste tree tincture twice a day or, if you are predisposed to flooding, 20 drops of Dong Quai morning and evening.

Sweats

A sweat is the equivalent of a hot flush but it happens at night and by no means do all women have them. Use sheets made of cotton or silk and try a natural-fibre mattress, like a futon. Go to bed in silk nightwear as sweat evaporates through silk much more easily than through cotton. Keep a pile of fresh linen by the bed so you can change quickly and easily. Having a tincture of motherwort or sage on standby at night can be very effective in reducing nightly sweats, as can additional vitamin E. Rest during the day and drink oatstraw tea, decocted, to calm and strengthen the nervous system.

Vaginal Changes

The vagina continually sheds its epithelial cells. Harmless bacteria in the vagina help to decompose cell detritus, producing lactic acid which protects against harmful bacteria. But as oestrogen levels fall in the menopausal woman, the climate in the vagina changes dramatically. The cells of the lining thin and dry out and are unable to fend off invading bacteria. As a result offensive vaginal discharges are much more common during the menopause and afterwards. This in turn can cause pain during love making and, unsurprisingly, can put a woman off sex altogether. Synthetic hormonal creams are not the answer. Hormone replacement therapy is dangerous when administered in this way or by transdermal patch (plasters containing HRT chemicals which are applied to the skin), because it goes straight into the bloodstream in an uncontrolled fashion. In any case it is not lack of oestrogen which makes vaginas dry: dryness is simply caused by under-use.

Regular sex, or masturbation if you do not have a partner or do not feel like sexual intercourse, keeps the vagina in good working order. Lubrication has much less to do with the intensity of stimulation than with its duration, so if you find yourself getting into difficulties, please share this information with your partner. However, experimenting must be done gently. In the post-menopausal woman the clitoris is more exposed because of labial atrophy, so this sensitive area will become more vulnerable to direct stimulation through intercourse. Indeed any very intense stimulation, far from being exciting, can be distressing and painful.

Treatment
- Saliva or KY Kelly helps with vaginal lubrication.
- Take 600 iu's of vitamin E daily (but avoid it if you have high blood pressure, diabetes or rheumatic heart disease).
- Drink at lease 10 pints (6 litres) of water daily.
- Slippery elm mixed into a thick paste with aloe vera juice is both cooling and soothing. Apply this inside the vulva and as high into the vagina as possible. This is particularly helpful for vaginal or vulvar itching and burning.
- Biocare make an excellent cream, Cervagyn, which comes with an internal applicator and helps maintain the proper balance of lactic acid in the vagina.
- Exercise pelvic-floor muscles daily (see 'Bladder Problems — Incontinence').

The following formulation improves circulation, general nutrition and hormonal balance and so minimises the thinning of the vaginal lining.

> *Four parts of:*
> *wild yam*
> *Two parts of:*
> *lady's mantle*
> *nettles*
> *sarsaparilla*
> *all in tincture form.*
>
> *Take 40 drops in water four times a day.*

Post-Menopausal Vaginal Bleeding

Benign causes include a sudden boost in the diet of superfoods (see Chapter Four) or a switch to a particularly healthy detoxifying diet including herbs, raw, fresh and added to foods or taken as medicine. This may just stimulate one or two recalcitrant eggs to develop, causing a normal menstrual cycle. I have seen periods begin again in post-menopausal women who fall in love and resume a passionate sex life. Note that blood spots during or after sexual intercourse will very often come from tiny tears in delicate, friable, older vaginal tissue or as the result of cervical polyps. If you are in any doubt about the cause, please seek immediate medical help.

WEIGHT GAIN

If you are overweight, do not try to lose weight suddenly. You can afford to gain half a pound a year without increasing the risk of an heart attack. Alternate bingeing and purging unbalance the body's electrolyte levels, causing weakening of the heart muscle and damage to a healthy heart.

Most obese women show abnormal glucose tolerance and have raised blood levels of cholesterol, triglycerides and free fatty acids. The fact that many obese people say that they do not eat any more than other people is very often true. A thin person may simply have a different, rather than a better biochemistry. So no real progress will ever be made unless the actual biochemistry of an obese person is changed. For this reason I suggest that anyone trying to lose weight should initially eat only whole grains that are very lightly cooked and still chewy but not soft. There should be no unrefined grains, such as wholewheat bread, in the diet at all at first. Then all sugars and saturated fats should be cut out of the diet, including natural sugar from juices. Only whole fruit should be eaten.

This regime should be coupled with sufficiently prolonged aerobic exercise to alter the biochemistry of the body. Begin with 12 minutes, building up to 20–40 minutes at least five times a week. The type of exercises considered aerobic are fast walking, jogging, running, skipping, cycling, rowing, cross-country skiing, roller skating or aerobic exercise classes. While swimming is an aerobic exercise, it is not recommended for weight loss since the water temperature is usually colder than that of the body and will then signal the body to store fat for insulation — clearly not what is desired. However, as a cardiovascular exercise for the entire body, it is excellent.

True aerobic exercise changes the body on a biochemical level, altering the deeply entrenched way anyone who is overweight metabolises carbohydrates and fats, as well as stimulating the endocrine system.

A basic diet should include plenty of raw fruit but no fruit juices and only one banana a day. There should be plenty of raw vegetables, which are particularly beneficial if eaten at the beginning of a meal, as well as a smaller proportion of lightly cooked vegetables. All potatoes should be eaten with the skins on, baked or steamed, but should be limited to three servings a week. Beans, sprouted seeds and sprouted beans may be taken in quantity as desired but nuts must be kept low in the diet. You would be better off coming off animal proteins altogether while dieting. All refined carbohydrates should be avoided completely. Among cereal-based foods, eat only *whole* grains that are lightly cooked — unrefined brown rice, barley, millet, rye, buckwheat, wheat, bulgur and corn. Let your teeth do the grinding and take bread and breakfast cereals made from *whole* grains only. Use cold-pressed unsaturated oils for salad dressing, particularly walnut, olive and flax seed oil, in moderate amounts mixed with lemon juice or cider vinegar and use for cooking in very conservative amounts.

It is also far better to eat 4–5 smaller meals a day than 2–3 large ones, the main meal being taken at midday. Eat in situations where there are no mental distractions such as television, radio or books. You should aim to drink at least eight large glasses of water a day which will help to dilute the many toxins produced by the breakdown of proteins and fats for energy and the toxins stored within the fat cells themselves which are liberated as the fat stores melt away.

Alternate hot and cold showers (see 'Hypertension') will stimulate the circulation in the endocrine system. Saunas or Turkish baths are beneficial, too, and ideally should be taken several times a week. Spinal manipulation and massage may be indicated once or twice a week. The superfoods (see Chapter Four) are extremely helpful for weight loss, particularly purple dulse, spirulina and chlorella. I know of one woman who lost over 200 lb (90 kg) by taking fruit smoothies with two heaped tablespoons of the superfood stirred into it twice a day, eating salads and whole grains for her third meal.

SIX

HERBAL PHARMACY

PREPARING HERBS FOR EXTERNAL USE

WATER-BASED PREPARATIONS

Fresh herbs should be crushed to break down the cellulose of the plant which releases the active principles. Use a stainless-steel knife, your fingers or a pestle and mortar to do this. Dried herbs should be chopped or pounded in a pestle and mortar. Alternatively, put the herbs in a sealed plastic bag and pound with a rolling pin. Remember that water-based herbal preparations decompose rapidly so they need to be made fresh each day. The exception to this is a decoction of the herbs boiled for 10–20 minutes before being strained out of the liquid. Such prolonged boiling is usually only used for roots, barks and berries and helps to preserve the herbal mixture for 3–4 days. However, delicate parts of the herb, like the flowers, leaves and stamens, need to be steeped in water for 20 minutes. Use 1 oz (30 g) of the herb (remember fresh herbs will take up 3–4 times the room that dried ones do) and pour over them 1 pint (600 ml) freshly boiled filtered water which has first been allowed to stand for 30 seconds. If you use water that is actually boiling, it will be too harsh and destroy the potency of the herbs. Then stir the preparation thoroughly with anything that is not aluminium. Cover the container closely and leave to steep for 15 minutes, then strain through muslin, nylon, a stainless-steel or silver tea-strainer or, for a large quantity of herbs, a fine sieve.

Seeds, roots, bark or very tough leaves like bay leaves need very vigorous processing to make them surrender their medicinal properties. Their cell walls are so strong that more heat is needed here than would be for flowers, leaves and stamens to ensure that the active constituents are transferred into the water.

Put 1 oz (30 g) of the herbs in the bottom of a glass, enamel or stainless-steel saucepan, add 1 pint (600 ml) filtered water and cover with a tight-fitting lid. Bring to the boil and simmer very gently until the water is reduced by half. Generally this takes about 15 minutes. Strain and use as required.

Should you need to use both the tough parts of the herb and the flowers in one mixture, it is better to make an infusion and decoction separately and then combine them. An *infusion* is the term used for preparing easily damaged herbs and a *decoction* used for the more rigorous process of boiling up tough herbs. Remember all seeds, roots and bark need to be well crushed using a pestle and mortar or coffee grinder; burdock root and cinnamon only need steeping in freshly boiled, not boiling, water; valerian root should be steeped in cold water for twenty-four hours to ensure that the valerian acid and essential oils are not lost. Decoctions will stay fresh for 3–4 days while infusions tend to only last for a day and a half at most.

Store what you do not need immediately in the refrigerator in a glass jar covered with muslin or linen to allow the water-based preparation to breathe. Try not to use plastic. Fine bubbles popping up to the surface are a sign that the preparation has begun to ferment, so throw it away — your garden will be grateful for it! However, if you make only 1 pint (600 ml) at a time, you will generally find you will finish the mixture within a day or so, so this should not be a problem.

ALCOHOL-BASED PREPARATIONS

The advantage of these are, first, that alcohol is a better solvent than water on certain types of plant constituents and, second, that they can be kept indefinitely if properly stored. An alcohol-based preparation is known as a *tincture*.

Use good-quality brandy, gin or vodka. Never use alcohol in the form of surgical spirit or methanol as these are poisonous when drunk. All alcohol needs to be at least 30 per cent proof. In general you will find that the final amount of alcohol is only one-third of the original amount by volume as any herbs used, once strained out, absorb much of it. (My teacher Richard Schulze, in the United States, has started to make what he calls 'industrial strength' tinctures and does so by filling the entire jar with herbs and then covering it with alcohol. He uses only organically grown or wild-crafted herbs for all of his tinctures, and, made in this way, their efficacy is extraordinary.) The conventional way to make a tincture is to use one-third of powdered or very finely chopped herbs to two-thirds alcohol by volume. Some herbalists use one-third alcohol and two-thirds water but I find this less effective. Combine 5 oz (150 g) powdered or very finely chopped herbs with 1 pint (600 ml) alcohol. Keep the container somewhere warm — an airing cupboard is ideal. Shake vigorously at least once daily (twice daily if you have the time) and strain through muslin after fourteen days.

Tinctures should be started with a new moon and strained with a full moon fourteen days later. The power of the waxing moon helps extract the medicinal properties. There is much published evidence to support this theory. In her book *Moon and Plant*, Agnes Fyfe discusses the moon's nodal cycle in relation to both the earth and the plants on it. Over her lifetime she conducted 70,000 consecutive single tests on plant sap which proved irrefutably that the moon has a chartable influence on the way the sap rises and falls in plants. She was aware that medicinal plants were gathered in the past at particular times according to some faculty and knowledge now lost. Her experiments prove that such practices were not simply arcane but vital if herbs were to be used at their most effective.[1] You can buy diaries which chart the course of the moon in your local stationery shop.

If there are still bits floating around in the tincture once you have strained it through muslin, strain it a second time through coffee filter paper (preferably unbleached) and cap the resulting mixture tightly. For external use tinctures can be rubbed on to the skin directly or applied on poultices previously dampened with water. Applying tincture of plantain to insect stings or bites or rubbing myrrh tincture into a gum boil is extremely effective.

Now that you have learned three ways of preparing herbs for external use, let me explain their application.

APPLYING HERBS FOR EXTERNAL USE

Poultices

These may seem rather old-fashioned but they are, in fact, a very useful form of treatment for external wounds or grazes, for ulcers and for drawing out boils. Additionally, they supply nutrients to the skin by way of the lymphatic and blood circulatory systems to the tissues and organs beneath. Poultices are also a good way of softening and dispersing material that has become hardened, such as breast lumps. In addition, they are often very effective on limbs being treated for varicosity, thread veins, eczema, psoriasis and ulcerous conditions. You need the following:

- Herbs: fresh herbs need to be liquidised in a little water at high speed, while dried ones should be macerated (soaked) in a little hot water. Powdered ones can stay as they are.
- Slippery elm powder, cornflower or arrowroot as a carrier base.
- Cider vinegar, preferably organic.
- A fine white cloth. A large handkerchief is often ideal, depending on the size of the area to be treated, but for a large area gauze is also suitable and is available from chemists everywhere.
- Two large plates and a large saucepan of boiling water.
- Plastic sheeting such as a piece of bin bag or any large clean piece of plastic or clingfilm. You will also need to have on standby a supply of stretchy cotton bandages (the amount will vary depending on the area to be treated: applying a poultice to the whole of the abdomen, for instance, it is going to take a lot more bandage than a poultice applied to your wrist) and safety pins.

Estimate how much of the herb will be needed to treat to a depth of a quarter of an inch (6 mm). Mix the herb with an equal quantity of your chosen carrier base and add just enough cider vinegar, a little at a time, to form a thick paste. Mix in a china or glass basin with a stainless-steel or wooden spoon. Spread out the piece of cotton on a plate over a saucepan of boiling water. Scrape the mixture on to one half of the cotton only, keeping it from the edge so that it does not squelch out when you use it. Fold the other half of the cotton over the top and press the edges together. Cover the whole poultice with the other plate and allow it to become really hot. Remove it and apply as hot as is bearable to the affected area (do not burn yourself). Cover the poultice with plastic and secure it with bandages and then safety pins, or, if the area is very large, a thin towel. Leave it on all night. If the poultice is to be applied somewhere on the trunk, wear a tight-fitting cotton tee-shirt to hold it firmly in place.

Next morning peel your poultice off and wrap it up again using the plate method. While waiting for it to warm, cleanse the area by bathing it with half and half diluted cider vinegar and hot water. Re-apply the poultice but this time use the other side against the skin. Repeat again in the evening using a completely fresh poultice and reusing the other side again in the morning until the area is healed. In other words the poultice will need to be refreshed and the contents inside the old poultice thrown away every twenty-four hours. The cloth used for the poultice can simply be scraped free of its contents, rinsed, boiled and dried out for repeat use.

Castor Oil Poultices

Castor oil may be bought from most chemists, but the best cold-pressed variety is available from the representatives of the original inventor of the castor oil pack, Edgar Cayce (see Resources Directory). Cold-pressed castor oil has been processed in a way in which has not been heated up and so contains significantly more of its original healing properties. The absorption of the oil via the skin into the lymphatic system softens, relaxes, nourishes and balances the sympathetic and parasympathetic nervous systems. It also disperses congestion and tension, and slowly helps to release the blockages in bowel pockets and to get rid of hardened mucus in the body, which may appear as cysts, tumours, or polyps. However, using castor oil can be pretty messy, so do not wear clothing that you want to keep in good condition, and protect your furniture and bedclothes from it with biodegradable plastic sheets (bin bags do beautifully).

Directions
- Gently heat up the castor oil in a saucepan containing no aluminium or copper, soak a pure cotton flannel in it and place this

over the entire abdomen. (The Edgar Cayce representatives sell unbleached woollen flannel for precisely this purpose which is even better than cotton flannel — see Resources Directory.)

- Cover with a second moist flannel to provide wet heat, topped with two layers of plastic.
- Place a heating pad or a hot-water bottle on top.
- Cover it all with a thick towel, wrapping it around to hold everything in place.
- Enjoy this soothing and relaxing pack for one and a half hours, three days in a row. For an even better effect, leave the pack on all night, taking it off the next morning.
- For the next three days, massage the entire area with olive oil.
- Rest on the seventh day, then repeat.
- Remember to use towels, bed sheets and flannels that you do not mind getting messy. Continue applying the oil every night for at least a month for chronic degenerative illnesses. Acute illnesses such as swollen glands, chest infections and digestive upsets can be treated for three days, during which time the castor oil will have generally cleared them up. There is no need to wash the flannel — simply put it back into the castor oil-filled saucepan the next day, covering with fresh castor oil if desired and reheating. Once the pack has been used for an entire month, by all means wash the flannel in natural soap by hand, rinsing it out well by hand, or simply buy a new piece of flannel.

COMPRESSES

These are like dilute poultices designed to be used over very large areas. They assist the circulation of the lymph or blood to a specific area, so relieving swellings like varicose veins, goitres and muscular aches. Cold compresses ease head congestion, insomnia, fever, indigestion, sprains, bruises and sore throats. Many of my patients grumble about going to bed accompanied by the unromantic rustle of plastic bin bags (the plastic is necessary to hold in moisture from the compress) but having applied them faithfully, they finish up agreeing that they are extremely effective. Compresses have the added advantage of often giving almost instant pain relief. As well as being made from fresh, dried or powdered herbs, they can be made from warmed oils, plant juices or tinctures diluted in water. Plant juices can be extracted from mucilaginous plants such as comfrey or aloe vera, by putting them through a juicer.

Hot Compresses

Make a double-strength herbal decoction by using 2 oz (60 g) herbs to 1 pint (600 ml) water and strain, mashing the herbs well down in the sieve to extract all the goodness from them. (Powdered herbs are particularly effective for this.) Reheat the liquid and dip into it white, pure cotton cloths (bits of old sheet will do nicely), wringing them out lightly but firmly. Wrap around the parts to be treated and secure with bandages and clingfilm or a piece of some other plastic. This will keep the moist heat of the compress intact and protect the bed sheets from seeping dampness. You may also need to protect the bed with a towel to prevent it from staining, especially if you are leaving the compress on all night.

If the compress needs to be reused, the simplest is to turn a slow cooker or saucepan on high and drop in the damp compress, leaving the lid off. The compress will heat up very quickly and if you need to alternate compresses one can be kept hot and within reach in this way while the other is being used. If applying a compress for more than an hour, it may be necessary to refresh it with enough herbal decoction or infusion to re-dampen it.

If you are treating a whole arm or a leg with the compress, soak either cotton tights or a long cotton glove in the herbal mixture. This cuts down on bandages which, if they have to be wrapped all the way up the arm, puttee style, are often awkward to remove. Silk stockings, although difficult to find, are a good alternative to cotton tights, although any natural fibre will do. If you need to apply a poultice to your trunk, it is better to use a close-fitting white cotton tee-shirt. You will need to sustain the heat over the area concerned for as long as you can with hot-water bottles. Do not use an electrical heating pad.

Cold Compresses

These are made in exactly the same way as hot ones but allowing the liquid to go cold before dipping the cloths in. The cold compress is generally applied for between 5 and 15 minutes and encourages the blood to move quickly to the surface in cases of high temperature, sprains and bruises. For fever it is necessary to change the compress every 5–10 minutes as it heats up. A cold compress left on for 20–30 minutes will relieve indigestion and insomnia and may be repeated if necessary once every two hours. A cold compress left on all night will relieve a sore throat and bring down the swelling, and is also particularly effective for swollen joints. Cold compresses can be used in conjunction with applications of hot water. For example, a cold compress applied to the back of the neck at the same time as a hot foot bath relieves headaches and congestion, particularly sinus congestion, very quickly. Hot and cold compresses, 3 minutes of the hot and 2 minutes of the cold, are often used alternatively for the first forty-eight hours of an injury until healing is complete and are especially effective for sprained ankles.

BATHS

Therapeutic baths should last for only 2–10 minutes. They are not at all like the long luxurious baths you treat yourself to at home. Very hot immersion baths, if taken daily, encourage debility, mental lethargy, physical weakness, poor circulation and even depression.

The best way to take a hot bath is to enjoy a deep, hot one, interspersing it with showers of ice-cold water. If you do not have a shower as part of your bath, use one of those rubber ones you can purchase from a chemist and attach it directly to the tap. If you have a mixer tap and such an apparatus will not fit, keep a couple of large plastic buckets of cold water on standby.

The only instance in which prolonged hot baths may be beneficial in medical terms is if they are taken when menstruation is late, for dysmenorrhoea (painful menstruation) as an antispasmodic, or as a pyretic for the treatment of fevers.

Herbal Baths

Add 1 gallon (4.8 litres) of strained herbal decoction or infusion to a half-filled bath. Immerse as much as possible of the body under the water for 15–20 minutes, protecting the head on a folded towel or bath pillow to make a comfortable resting place.

Remember to clean the skin *before* you take the bath by vigorously skin brushing (see Chapter Three) and washing any really dirty bits with a natural soap or flannel. Never use soap *after* any sweating therapy as it prevents the cholesterol coming out through the pores. Depending on the herbs used, herbal baths are extremely effective for insomnia, for quickly reducing acute pain such as that induced by strained or pulled muscles or cramping and for the unbearable itch of eczema, poison oak or nettle rash.

Epsom Salt Baths

This treatment is not to be used for people suffering from high blood pressure or heart conditions but it is an excellent way of dispersing acidity from the system, soaking up aches and pains, getting the skin to work properly, inducing a short sweat for therapeutic purposes and cleansing the system of fungus. It is also a wonderfully effective bath to be taken at the onset of a cold and is particularly beneficial for any kind of deep purification and healing. I have used it often over the years in my own practice for people who are particularly toxic, especially those suffering from heavy metal poisoning such as the result of dental amalgams. Epsom baths need to be taken on alternate days for six days, resting on the seventh day and on this day detoxifying the body with a fast on fruit or fruit juices.

Buy 1 lb (450 g) of Epsom salts and mix them with enough almond oil to give them the texture of wet sea sand. Carry this mixture into the bathroom in a large basin and rest it on the side of the bath. Now plug the bath while it is empty and stand in it massaging yourself all over with the mixture, using small circular movements working upwards towards the heart. This exfoliates dead skin. Let the salts and oil fall into the empty bath and step out, then fill it as deeply as possible with hot water, adding an additional generously heaped cup of Epsom salts and one of cider vinegar (do not worry about the dead skin cells; they are invisible to the naked eye and will, in any case, disappear down the plug hole when you drain the bath away). Stir with the hands to dissolve the salts thoroughly and soak yourself in the bath for 30 minutes adding hot water as it cools. While you do so, sip as many cups of any diuretic herbal tea (ginger mixed with a little maple syrup and lemon is my favourite, but peppermint and elderflower are also particularly pleasant-tasting). Elimination through the skin is vital. Normally the skin does only one-twentieth of the work of kidneys but by speeding it up with herbs and hydrotherapy it can take on one-tenth of their work, so relieving the kidneys of any added burden.

Have some ice cubes on standby in a bowl and a couple of flannels to apply to the face, neck and forehead if you feel dizzy, faint or sick. While the water is draining out of the bath, run a cold shower over your face and body to encourage it to cool down thoroughly. Alternatively, fill up plastic buckets with cold water and pour it over your body. Go to bed warmly dressed in natural fabric and pack yourself round with hot-water bottles to encourage free perspiration. Some of my patients sweat so prolifically that they need to get up in the middle of the night to change into fresh nightwear, which is all to the good. Do not wear any kind of body lotion or oil after this treatment. It will stop the skin breathing freely. If you are using a deodorant, make sure that it is a natural one. Having sweated profusely during the night, take a hot shower followed by a cold one the next morning or (preferably) seven hot/cold showers, finishing up with a cold one.

TURKISH BATHS AND SAUNAS

In the 1950s and 60s many local councils built excellent public baths equipped with steam rooms (often known as Turkish baths) saunas, icy-cold plunge pools and showers. Entrance is often very reasonably priced and I generally try and get down to my local one once a week. Turkish baths and saunas increase circulation, skin function, respiration and general vitality, as well as stimulating the nervous and hormonal systems and encouraging mental relaxation and sleep. While in a Turkish bath, throw basins of cold water over yourself and, in a sauna, you will need to come out and take cold showers or plunges into ice-cold water every 2–3 minutes after perspiration becomes noticeable. Skin brushing either before or after such baths is particularly helpful for stimulating the nervous and hormonal systems and increasing the circulation.

For those with bronchial congestion or sinus problems, a few drops of eucalyptus, peppermint or wintergreen oil mixed with water, which can be dashed over the coals in a sauna, is helpful, but some people find that as it evaporates it makes their eyes sting, so take care. In a Turkish bath, use a small cotton cloth soaked in a few drops of one of these oils and hold it to your face. In either instance breathe in deeply through the nose and out through the mouth.

SITZ-BATHS

These can be awkward, but they are often the most rewarding hydrotherapy of all. A sitz-bath increases the circulation of blood and lymph to the pelvic region, removing internal congestion and improving tissue vitality and nutrition.

In health institutions that use hydrotherapy there are often specifically designed sitz-baths which tend to look like two water-filled armchairs facing one another. One is filled with very hot water, the other with icy cold. You can sit with your bottom in the hot and feet in the cold for 3 minutes and then do the reverse, leaving your feet in the hot for only 1–2 minutes. Alternate back and forth from hot to cold for three immersions in each temperature, finishing with your bottom in the hot bath. After drying vigorously with a rough towel, you then exercise until sweating is produced. A simple way to do this is to jog up and down on a trampoline. Alternate hot and cold sitz-baths are useful for any disorders of the uterus, ovaries or Fallopian tubes, for prostatitis, constipation and digestive disorders.

It is possible to imitate these baths at home. Use two large plastic tubs or galvanised wash basins (baby baths do very nicely). They need to be big enough to accommodate the bottom easily and hold enough water to cover you from navel to mid-thigh. The hot-water temperature should be as warm as the body can comfortably bear and the cold should be very cold (if necessary, melt ice cubes in the water). For maximum benefit, carry out these baths at least once and sometimes three or four times daily as instructed.

Cold Sitz-Baths

A simple way to make a cold sitz-bath is to fill your bath tub with 6 in.

(15 cm) of cold water so that when you sit in it the water comes up to your navel. Now climb in, sit down and raise your feet to above the level of the water, resting them on the edge of the bath. If this is tiring you can put an up-ended plastic bucket as a foot rest. Let your knees fall apart and sweep up handfuls of water, vigorously splashing it over the abdomen while you count slowly to 60. A cold sitz-bath is especially useful for bed wetting, impotence, difficulty in conception and any difficulty with the position of the womb. When you get out, wrap yourself in a towel without drying yourself and lie down for at least 10 minutes. If you feel a nice warm glow after this, gradually increase to a slow count of 180 over twelve sessions or more, so that eventually you are sitting in a bath for up to 3 minutes at any one time.

Hot Sitz-Baths

These are conducted in exactly the same way as cold sitz-baths but the duration can be longer, anything from 3 to 10 minutes. It is important to take the bath as hot as you can manage it without burning yourself. It is useful to treat colic and any kind of muscle spasm in the abdomen, lower back pain, haemorrhoids and intestinal disturbances.

Anyone with rectal pain which is so bad that sitting in a hot bath is unbearable should fold two towels into quarters and place them one under each buttock. This will help to turn a hot sitz-bath into a more enjoyable experience and is a particularly useful way of treating haemorrhoids externally.

SHOWERS

Hot/Cold Shower Routine

This is an easy and very beneficial routine that I put nearly all of my clients through. The hot/cold shower routine stimulates and rejuvenates all the body functions but particularly the adrenal and other endocrine glands. It is also an unbeatable way of revitalising skin activity and improving the circulation.

Having thoroughly done a dry brush massage first (see Chapter Three), take a warm shower for 3 minutes, if necessary using a natural soap to clean any parts of you feel are really dirty. Rinse the soap off well and then switch to the coldest water you can for up to a minute.

Switch back to hot water for a minute and repeat this seven times so that in all the shower lasts for slightly less than 20 minutes. If there is a particular area in your body which is affected with illness, pay special attention to it, massaging it vigorously while under both hot and cold. After the hot/cold shower routine warm yourself up by rubbing down with a coarse bath towel.

Cold-Shower Treatment
Dr Lindlahr, a famous nature-cure pioneer, believed that there was no such thing as a cure-all but if there were it would have to be cold water properly applied. You too will find this routine extremely effective once you have tried it.

A cold-shower treatment is like a tonic, exerting both rejuvenative and healing effects on the entire system by stimulating the circulation and increasing muscle tone and nerve force. It stimulates the entire glandular system, improving digestion, and speeds up general metabolism. It also increases resistance to infections and colds if used regularly. It has a powerful influence on the central nervous system, on the brain and on every organ in the body. It actually increases the blood count and has an electromagnetic affect on the entire body, stimulating the flow of life energies and increasing the intake of oxygen to a remarkable degree.

Set your cold shower to the most forceful flow possible because the harder the stream the greater the therapeutic value of the shower. Stand under it and let the stream pound over your entire body for as long as you can manage but no less than 10 minutes. If it is too tiring to stand up for this length of time, place a plastic stool or chair in the shower. Benedict Lust, another famous nature-cure pioneer, used to administer this to his patients for up to 10 or 12 hours at a time while they were lying in a plastic cot, turning them over in the cot and exposing every part of their body to the forceful stream.

Salt Glow
This is an effective way of dislodging superficial catarrh in the tissues and I strongly recommend patients of mine who suffer from chronic catarrh which nothing seems to move to carry it out 3–4 times a week.

I have found it extremely successful.

Stand naked in an empty shower tray (or bath) and shower the skin all over with warm water. Mix 1 lb (450 g) of fine salt with enough water to turn it into a soft slurry and pick up palmfuls of this at a time massaging vigorously into the skin with brisk circular movements. Start with the soles of the feet, moving upwards towards the heart. Areas above the heart should be massaged downwards towards the heart. Do not massage the salt into the scalp or the face and avoid the genital area and nipples. Rinse off the salt with a forceful warm shower followed by a brisk icy-cold one. Stand under the cold shower for as long as you can manage until you are breathing very deeply. Get out of or shower (or bath) and dry vigorously.

VAGINAL DOUCHES

Douches reduce the instance of non-specific vaginitis, relieve painful periods and are essential after the use of vaginal boluses (see 'Pessaries and Boluses' below). They are a very active form of treatment so only use mild herbs, well strained, at body temperature unless otherwise directed and never take more than two douches daily. Even this is only permissible when trying to contain infections. Stop douching as soon as the infection clears, otherwise the delicate balance of natural bacteria in the vagina will be altered. The addition of a tablespoon (15 ml) of cider vinegar or a teaspoon (5 ml) of fresh strained lemon juice to every 2 pints (1.2 litres) of herbal infusion or decoction will help to maintain the correct pH balance.

Your douche kit needs to be kept scrupulously clean. Do not share it with anyone else. Make an infusion or decoction (depending on the herb chosen) and strain through coffee filter paper. Allow it to cool to body temperature. Hang the douche bag (the ones I sell in my own clinic have a strong hook attachment) on the wall over the bath, about 2 ft (60 cm) above the hips. Climb into the bath and lie down. (It helps to warm the bath up first by running hot water around it and then letting it drain out.) Insert the nozzle gently into the vagina so that it actually touches the cervix (which will feel a little like touching your nose with a piece of plastic) and lie back. Now release the closed tap slowly allowing the herb tea to flow into the vagina. Then using both hands feel the vaginal opening around the nozzle so that the vagina literally becomes flooded. If you do this correctly you will feel a slight sensation of pressure as the vagina expands to accommodate the fluid. When not sexually aroused the vagina is a bit like a squashed corrugated toilet roll, hence the feeling of expansion once filled with fluid. When it feels full shut the tap with one hand, releasing your hold with the other, and allow your vagina to drain. If you do it correctly the liquid will be rapidly expelled with a big swoosh. Now repeat the whole procedure until all the tea is used up.

Douching while sitting upright on a toilet or bidet is useless because so little actually gets to bathe the vaginal walls before seeping out. Always douche lying down.

Note: pregnant women should *never* douche and should avoid douching for at least four weeks following delivery. The only exception is if they are haemorrhaging, in which case a douche using cayenne pepper in warm water can be very effective.

ENEMAS

These are used to treat nervous complaints, pains and fevers; to cleanse the bowel and stimulate detoxification by the liver, spleen, kidneys and lymph; and to carry nourishment into the body. Most women who have experienced an enema at all have usually done so just before childbirth, in an atmosphere of fear and discomfort. Often soapy water is used which induces violent and painful peristalsis as well as wiping out all the benign bacteria from the colon. I am not, therefore, at all surprised when I mention enemas, particularly to women, that most of my patients get very apprehensive. Happily enemas are no longer routine before childbirth.

Please let me reassure you: an enema is really easy and comfortable to administer if done correctly. Give yourself plenty of time and privacy and lay everything out in advance because the more relaxed you are the easier the whole process is.

Contrary to popular fantasy, enemas do not make a mess. Your anal sphincter will hold the liquid in the colon until you decide to release it. Initially the stimulus the enema fluid gives the bowel may make you want to rush straight away to the toilet and release it, but you will acquire more self-control with practice and persistence.

Taking an enema is perfectly logical. No sensible person would attempt to unblock a drain from the top end of the waste pipe. Using the same analogy a blocked colon needs to be relieved from the bottom end. In the event of a fever an enema is the quickest way to relieve the bowel of toxic waste. If you are so weak that you cannot eat, then an enema of spirulina or slippery elm will supply some nourishment.

How to take an Enema

You will need the following:

- Three and a half pints (2 litres) of a herbal decoction or infusion made with filtered water. (Cool enemas are used for cleansing and warm ones for treating nervousness and spasms.)
- An enema kit (see Resources Directory).
- Olive oil, Vaseline or KY jelly.
- A large bath towel or a piece of plastic sheeting.

1. Fill up the enema bag with your chosen infusion or decoction at the right temperature and hang it from a hook in the bathroom at shoulder height.
2. Lubricate the tip well with Vaseline, olive oil or KY jelly.
3. Lie down on your right side with your knees tucked up to your chest and gently push the lubricated tip of the enema tube into the rectum. (Do not worry — it will not slip in too far because it is joined to the kit with a tap which acts as a barrier.)
4. Release the tap and allow the liquid to flow slowly into the rectum. If the liquid encounters a block of impacted faeces, you will feel marked internal pressure so turn off the tap and massage the area in an anti-clockwise direction.
5. When you are half way through the mixture (you will know this by keeping your eye on your bag suspended from your hook), carefully roll over on to your back with your knees bent and place the soles of your feet flat on the towel or plastic sheet beneath you. When the enema pack is emptied of its contents, turn off the tap and remove the nozzle tip.

6. Carefully stand up and wrap yourself in a bath towel, then go and lie down on your bed with your bottom raised on some pillows. If you are nervous about spilling any of the enema mixture on to your bed, cover the bed first with a plastic sheet.

7. Retain the enema for 20 minutes if you can. Get up and release while sitting on the toilet.

Note: enemas should *never* be relied upon in place of a proper bowel movement, nor should they be abused by over-use.

Herbal Oils

These are easily obtainable from healthfood shops and your local medical herbalist. Garlic oil can be bought in capsules, as can borage and evening primrose oils, though garlic oil is extremely easy to make at home. Cover 4 oz (120 g) of fresh garlic with 1 pint (600 ml) of virgin or almond oil and liquidise it at high speed. Add 1 tablespoon (15 ml) of cider vinegar to assist the breaking up of the cellulose in the garlic. Pour this mixture into a glass jar, leaving a gap at the top so that the contents can be shaken vigorously. Ideally the jar should be placed outside in strong sunlight while embedded in fine sand which attracts and holds the heat for hours after the sun has disappeared. Bring the jar in at night. Shake again and store it in the airing cupboard until the morning. Keep this routine up for two weeks from the new moon to the full moon, then strain the oil through muslin initially, then coffee filter paper. (Given the British climate, you will probably have to resort to keeping it in an airing cupboard as you would a tincture.) Bottle the resulting strained oil in dark glass and label.

This process can be speeded up by using artificial heat but I have never found the results as good. Place the jar in a pan of boiling water and keep the water just below boiling point for two hours. Top up the water as needed. This will need more or less constant attention. Strain and bottle when cool. Garlic oil is wonderful for any kind of internal infection as well as for earache and any sort of external sepsis.

Using the yellow flowers of the herb, I have made St John's wort oil, which is very effective for burns. It comes out a glorious rich ruby red and is also part of the formulation for my deep-heat treatment oil for pulled muscles.

When buying an essential oil, always dilute it before applying it to the skin. Essential oils should not be taken internally except under the supervision of a medical herbalist. Do not get undiluted essential oils anywhere near mucous membranes as they will sting.

OINTMENTS

These are easy to obtain from your local healthfood shop and local medical herbalist. They are particularly useful for their protective and emollient effects and are usually made with herbal oil and beeswax or cocoa butter. Ointments are good for dry cracked skin. They need to be applied generously, rubbing in thoroughly. If you want to have a go at making your own ointments, it is not too difficult. Use 1 pint (600 ml) of herbal oil to 2 oz (60 g) melted beeswax or cocoa butter, beating vigorously while the mixture cools and thickens. Add essential oils when the mixture has cooled considerably, but before it begins to set. Beeswax gives a stiff pastry consistency while cocoa butter gives a rich oily one.

CREAMS

Creams are better for treating sore, chapped skin and protecting and moisturising healthy skin because they are lighter and more easily absorbed. Their moisturising affect is enhanced if you spray the skin first with flower water or diluted cider vinegar.

It is possible to make your own creams in the same way as you would an ointment but while emulsifying you also add water, flower water or cider vinegar. These are very tricky to make at home to the right consistency and there are so many excellent ones on the market it is probably better that you buy them, providing you are sure that the ingredients in them are all natural.

PESSARIES AND BOLUSES

These are simply internal poultices and can be used locally to relieve irritation, itching and soreness. Vaginally they will help to relieve chronic reproductive conditions and discharges. The bolus also influences conditions held deep in the tissues such as tumours, cysts, inflammation, sores and cervical dysplasia (growth abnormality), sending the nutrients to heal the specific area affected. This is possible because the herbs are absorbed into the mucous membranes and spread through the capillary blood circulation and lymph into the pelvis. When the bolus is supported with herbal nutrients taken internally, total healing should be possible.

Pessaries are made by adding to gently warmed cocoa butter enough finely powdered herbs to form a doughy paste. A vaginal ovule or bolus should be shaped into a sausage the size of a regular tampon with the ends slightly softened and rounded. A pessary should resemble your little finger in size and if it is being used to treat the colon, not only the rectum, it should be at least 2 in. (5 cm) long and two should be inserted one behind the other. The best way to roll out the paste is on an oiled marble slab or inside a plastic bag. The pessaries or boluses can then be left overnight on a flat surface in the refrigerator to harden and then stored in sealed plastic bags, each pessary or bolus wrapped in greaseproof paper.

Once unwrapped, the pessary or bolus should be inserted as deeply as possible into the rectum or as high into the vagina as possible, just before bed. The body's own heat will then gently melt the cocoa butter and release the herb. Bedlinen should be protected with an old towel and you should wear cotton knickers with a press-on sanitary towel. Alternatively, you can insert half a tampon or natural sponge vaginally to hold the bolus in place. Rinse the anus or the vagina well the next morning, preferably in a warm followed by a cold sitz-bath. A new pessary should be inserted after every bowel movement, a new bolus on the evening of every second day. To prevent it coming out while having a bowel movement, insert your finger into the vagina to make sure it stays in place. You should douche on alternate evenings (not the evenings on which you insert a bolus), resting from both douching and the boluses or pessaries on the seventh day.

Often patients will say to me that the bolus has disappeared and wonder how that is possible. It is simply because the body in its own wisdom will absorb as much of the herb as necessary and may reject the rest. But if it is very much in need of the entire contents of the bolus, all of it will disappear. Sometimes the bolus comes out looking more or less unused and this may be a sign that the treatment is coming to an end and the bolus is no longer needed by the body.

HERBAL TREATMENTS FOR INTERNAL USE

There are almost as many ways to administer herbs internally as there are externally and these include those based on water, alcohol, sugar, honey and glycerine, all preparations where the herb is being used fresh or in its dried finely powdered form.

HERBAL TEAS

To prepare a herbal tea follow the instructions above for water-based preparations but avoid powdered herbs which quickly turn into a muddy and unappetising soup. Keep a teapot especially for your medicinal tea. Your ordinary teapot will tend to get stained with tannin and if you brew an iron-rich tea like yellow dock in such a pot, the iron from the herb and the tannic acid from the staining will bond to form tannate of iron, a very strong styptic (an agent that is extremely stringent and contracts tissues, specifically a haemostatic agent which stops bleeding by contracting the blood); this can induce acute constipation and digestive problems. Always used boiled, filtered water (see Chapter Four).

The quantities of a medicinal tea are always the same unless otherwise specified. These are 1 oz (30 g) to 1 pint (600 ml) of water. The usual dosage is 1 cup (240 ml) of the strained herbal tea with every meal. Many medicinal herbal teas drunk at this strength taste very strong and somewhat unpalatable so can be sweetened with honey, maple syrup, date sugar, liquorice or a dash of apple or grape juice or even grape sugar, but there are certain instances when a tea should not be sweetened, such as in the case of hypoglycaemia. Decoctions are particularly strong-tasting and so may need this additional help. If a tea is specifically designed to act on the digestive system, particularly the stomach, liver or pancreas, it may be necessary to drink it without any masking with sweet additions. Teas can be drunk hot as well as cold. Some people find cold decoctions more palatable than hot ones; however, hot teas are more stimulating and will act more quickly on the body.

ALCOHOL-BASED PREPARATIONS

These are made in exactly the same way as tinctures are for external use (see above). If you are teetotal and cannot face the thought of alcohol even for medicinal purposes, simply add the tincture to a little freshly boiled water which will evaporate most of the alcohol out of it. In many instances the use of alcohol to extract a specific property from a herb is essential. (For example, the diosgenin in wild yam is only soluble in alcohol, not in water.) But the actual amount of alcohol per dosage is so small that there is more in some commercial mouthwashes than in a herbal tincture. Herbal tinctures are perfectly safe for anyone who is healing themselves of alcoholism. The dosage for tinctures is generally 1 teaspoon (5 ml) or 15 drops in a cup (240 ml) of water three times a day with meals, but in chronic conditions (such as a diseased heart) I will administer 500 drops of hawthorn tincture daily to a patient and in some acute conditions such as infection I will use 360 drops of echinacea per day to clear it up.

GLYCERINE-BASED PREPARATIONS

It is possible to base a tincture on glycerine which treats the digestive tract more gently than its alcoholic counterpart, but such tinctures have the disadvantage of not dissolving oily or resinous materials as effectively.

To make a glycerine tincture, mix one part of glycerine with four parts of filtered water so that you make up 1 pint (600 ml) of the mixture in all. Add 4 oz (120 g) of the dried, ground herb and leave it in a well-stoppered container for two weeks, shaking it vigorously at least daily (twice if you have the time). After two weeks, strain and press or wring the mixture out in the cloth, catching it in a large basin. Coffee filter paper in this instance is not helpful as the glycerine will not pass through it. Please ensure that your glycerine is entirely vegetable based in order to avoid any worries about possible BSE infection.

SYRUPS

These can be a good way of preparing medication for children as the syrup masks the strong taste of the herb. To a strained decoction trickle in a quarter of its weight in liquid honey slowly over heat. Stir with a wooden spoon until the mixture turns syrupy. You will need to skim off the rising scum from time to time. Alternatively, mix one part of the tincture with the equivalent weight of honey, stirred over a low heat if necessary to amalgamate the two. Decant into a labelled glass bottle. Take 1 tablespoon (15 ml) as needed.

Syrups are an excellent basis for cough mixture. They are also very pleasant to gargle if diluted in their equivalent volume of hot water.

DRIED PREPARATIONS

My favourite way of administering herbs is in their dried, powdered form. This is probably the most potent and effective form of herbal medicine because the whole herb, rather than an extract, is used. In my own clinic, herbs are generally encapsulated in gelatine capsules but I wish I could get more patients to take them simply in their powdered form mixed with a little water because this is the only way that some of the bitter-tasting herbs can be effectively utilised: their effectiveness depends on the neurological sensation of bitterness in order to stimulate the digestive tract.

Dried herbs swallowed in this way take longer to be absorbed by the system because they are unprocessed by water or alcohol, but this may be just as well because the action is ultimately far more powerful. If you find you cannot take powders in liquid or in capsules because you have difficulty swallowing, or because you have a particularly sensitive digestive system, you can swallow them with a slippery elm drink. Mix the dried herbs with honey or maple syrup or take the tinctures or extracts made from the powders in juice. If you can swallow herbs in their naked, powdered form, you can buy them direct from the suppliers listed in the Resources Directory. Alternatively, you can powder your own by putting them through a coffee grinder with a very powerful motor. Even this, however, will not touch some of the very hard roots and barks, which have to be purchased in their powdered form. Do check that they are as fresh as possible.

GELATINE CAPSULES

These are small cylindrical capsules made up of animal or vegetable gelatine in which the herbs are compressed. There has, understandably, been a big swing towards vegetable gelatine capsules since the scare about BSE. All capsules are available in sizes ranging from 00 to 4. The stock size is 0, the correct size for an adult. It is easy to fill capsules. Simply separate them and press both halves firmly into the powdered herbs until each is as full as possible, then close the capsules carefully together so that one side slots into the other.

The normal dosage for size 0 gelatine capsules is 2–3 to be swallowed at the beginning of each meal with liquid, preferably herbal tea, fruit or vegetable juice. The food that then follows will ensure their complete assimilation and easy digestion.

Should you have difficulty in swallowing capsules but can manage tablets or visa versa, it may be because you are using the same swallowing technique for both. For a tablet or pill, place it in the mouth with a small amount of water and tilt the head backwards. You will find that this way you can swallow more readily. Follow with more liquid. This method does not work for a capsule which, because it is lighter than water, will float forwards and so be difficult to swallow. Instead tilt the head or upper part of the body forwards, then the capsules will float backwards and be swallowed easily.

PILLS

These are helpful when herbs cannot be finely powdered but can be roughly chopped and for those who do not have the dexterity or patience to fill capsules. Mix 1 oz (30 g) of the herbs with enough firm set honey or slippery elm powder to make a malleable paste. Divide the paste into 100 equal-sized portions by rolling it into thin sausages, then cut it into pellets and shape it into balls. Roll each ball so that it is smooth and easy to swallow. Store the capsules that you are going to be taking over the next two days in the fridge and deep freeze the rest in a plastic bag until needed. Because there are no preservatives in either the slippery elm and water mixture or the honey mixture, they will spoil even if kept chilled in the fridge after two days.

Note: hypoglycaemics, diabetics and anyone with pancreatic malfunction should not use honey or maple syrup, nor should people who are trying to lose weight.

DOSAGE

As a general rule, the dose of any herbs should follow the body weight. Doses in this book are for adults weighing 150 lb (75 kg). Bear this in mind and adjust the dose accordingly. I have found in my own clinic that for people who are underweight or highly strung or possibly both, the best way to take herbs is to spread the dose of the herb out on a more continual basis throughout the day. This way one capsule, for example, can be taken six times a day with juice or food, rather than three times a day.

HERBAL TEAS
One cup (240 ml) with meals three times a day.

POWDERED HERBS
Two or three size 0 capsules before meals three times a day. This is the equivalent of about 1 oz (30 g) a week. This amount can be increased for a nutritional or rejuvenative formulation such as adrenal or nervine (using calming herbs such as vervain, valerian and lemon balm) formulations. In this instance, you can take anything from 4 to 8 oz (120–240 g) a month. I also increase the dose if my client is large or very active or actively wants to pursue a dedicated programme of purification and regeneration. In this instance I start off with average amounts and then escalate the dose upwards depending upon results.

MONTHLY DOSE FOR CHRONIC CONDITIONS
If my patient has a chronic condition such as arthritis, rheumatism, colitis or nervous exhaustion, I may go as high as 3 oz (90 g) of herbs per week or as much as they can take individually. Much depends on digestive capability, food habits, symptoms, age, levels of pain and discomfort. At this dosage my patient would be taking 6–9 capsules with each meal. The bowel formulations in this book are to be taken according to individual need (see Chapter Three for dosages).

SYRUPS
One tablespoon (15 ml) between meals three times a day.

TINCTURES
One teaspoon (5 ml) or 15 drops in a little cold or freshly boiled water, allowed to cool, three times a day.

STORING FORMULATIONS

Always sterilise containers before use by boiling thoroughly, and screw on sterilised lids or plug uncapped bottles with generous swabs of cottonwool. Corks will need to be boiled first and then sterilised in diluted cider vinegar. Anything made with vinegar will keep for well over a year if stored in firmly stoppered opaque glass bottles and a tincture made with alcohol will keep for up to five years in these conditions. Dried herbs should be thrown away once they have passed their first birthday. Syrups will keep up to five years but should be stored in a refrigerator, tightly covered, preferably with a vacuum seal. Essential oils will keep indefinitely in small sterilised opaque glass bottles but air gaps should be eliminated by transferring them into smaller and smaller bottles until they get used up. Poultices and compresses should always be freshly made and cotton or gauze bandages should be well boiled after use, dried and stored in sealed plastic. If they become sticky with ointment and almost unwashable, throw them out. Castor oil will often need to be washed off with soap, and then boiled to remove it from poultices.

Any herbal preparation which has gone rotten will smell odd, fizz or turn ominous colours; throw it on your compost heap.

WHEN NOT TO ADMINISTER HERBS

The strict rule when using herbs at home is that no herb should ever be taken even in small quantities unless you are personally totally familiar with its properties and any contraindications. For those who have experience in using harmless herbs for bodily correction, there is no need to justify their use. If in doubt, *ask for professional help.*

One of the enormous advantages of herbal medicine as a therapy is that it is completely safe — when correctly administered. In general, herbs are safer than orthodox medicines and many still provide the raw materials for today's allopathic remedies. But I have known amateur herbalists to run away with the erroneous belief that all herbs are benign and beneficial and consequently to administer them in a spirit of cavalier abandon. This is irresponsible and dangerous. It should be remembered that herbs are very potent healing tools and there are many which are poisonous and should not be used at all.

Occasionally, amateur herbalists poison themselves or, worse still, someone else, by ingesting poisonous plants. (When I was at university many years ago there was an epidemic of hemlock poisoning, the result of enthusiastic students on a 'Food for Free' kick eating what they thought was wild carrot.) You must remember that many plants have not yet had their biochemical qualities, both toxic and therapeutic, fully documented. There are, for example, 200 species of lupin, two species of laburnum and many others which are intensely poisonous even when taken in minute quantities. What constitutes a toxic dose of a normally therapeutic herb depends largely upon the herb. Often the toxic dose may be 300 times the medicinal dose and herbs in this quantity would be extremely difficult to ingest. There are other herbs that have a toxic dose so close to the therapeutic one that any attempt by the amateur at self-medication may end in disaster. These are listed below. I have also included warnings specifically about treating pregnant women and other medical conditions like diabetes. In general it is best to treat an acute condition without any herbs at all. Instead fast on fruit or vegetable juices. Fasting is the best medicine of all. However, if you are confident about managing fever there are herbs which are useful for accelerating the patient through this stage.

Qualified herbalists know that when two or more herbs are married in one prescription their individual properties react together in such a way that other effects are produced that are not normally found when either of the herbs is prescribed separately. This marvellous internal cooperation between herbs results in the extraordinary situation of two plus two equalling five. So if a formulation is given in this book which includes more than one herb, please do not change it unless I give you an alternative. Never alter the dose of any herb.

CONTRAINDICATIONS OF HERBS

This is a check list of herbs that are contraindicated. Read through this section carefully before embarking on taking any of the herbal medicines in this book.

The following herbs have contraindications but are covered fully in Chapter Seven (Helpful Herbs): aloe vera, cascara sagrada, chamomile, cayenne, false unicorn, garlic, ginseng, guelder rose (cramp bark), goldenseal, liquorice, nettles, raspberry, sage, sassafras, shepherd's purse, valerian, yarrow.

ACONITE
There are some 100 species all containing the deadly poisonous alkaloids aconitine and pseudoaconitine. If these are ingested in anything but the most minute quantities, the results are fatal. *Please do not use this herb at all.*

ASTRINGENT HERBS
Very prolonged use of any astringent herb that contains tannin has been associated with throat and stomach cells becoming cancerous so herbs rich in tannin are all best used only for the short term. These include bayberry bark, blackberry, sarsaparilla and yellow dock as well as peppermint, cleavers and uva ursi.

BELLADONNA
This should be used *only by a qualified medical herbalist* as it is part of the Solanaceae family and one of the better-known plant poisons.

BROOM
This should not be used if there is high blood pressure. Nor should it be used during pregnancy.

BUTTERCUP
The sap is *extremely dangerous* taken orally.

CELERY
The problem here is the seeds are often dressed with a poisonous fungicide so buy organic celery if you possibly can. It is a uterine stimulant and so should be avoided during pregnancy.

CLOVER

Some varieties of white or Dutch clover contain hydrocyanic acid which can break down into prussic acid in the digestive system and become *extremely poisonous*. Ensure that you use red clover only. If using clover externally on the skin, it is advisable to mix it into a carrier base such as slippery elm or marshmallow as prolonged contact externally can cause burning and soreness.

COLTSFOOT

Both *Patasites* spp. and *Tussilaga* spp. contain pyrrolizidine alkaloids and should be *strictly avoided* during pregnancy. Other plants in the species are not contraindicated.

COOKED SPICES

Most spices if cooked, as in a curry, aggravate. They are much more therapeutic if taken raw.

FOXGLOVE

If taken in excess it is *deadly*, so it should not be used by amateurs.

GREATER CELANDINE

This has been called both the best and most wicked of herbs and in large doses it is *extremely poisonous*. Its sale is restricted to medical herbalists only.

GROUNDSEL

Excessive doses over short periods of time may cause cirrhosis of the liver.

HAWTHORN BERRIES

These are not to be used if you have low blood pressure.

HEARTSEASE

Excessive doses can cause a cardiac reaction. Take this *under the supervision of a medical herbalist*.

HEMLOCK
Most people are familiar with the fact that this is *poisonous*. Also avoid water hemlock, which is equally deadly.

HOLLY
The leaves are sometimes used to treat rheumatism but the berries are *poisonous*. Make sure no one nibbles them over Christmas.

HORSETAIL
This should always be used with a demulcent herb to soften its effect. (Slippery elm and marshmallow are excellent demulcents.) Horsetail contains silicic acid, saponins, alkaloids and a poisonous substance called thiaminase which causes symptoms of toxicity in both humans and animals. Thiaminase poisoning causes a deficiency in vitamin B and can lead to permanent liver damage.

JUNIPER BERRIES
Juniper berries are wonderful for clearing up a brief attack of cystitis but should be used only for this kind of emergency, *never* for prolonged treatment.

LIME TREE FLOWERS
Always ensure your supplies of these are fresh. Old fermenting leaves and flowers can cause hallucinations.

LOBELIA
This is *only available to qualified medical herbalists.*

MISTLETOE
Government authorities in the West are sensitive about this herb, mainly, I suspect, because of its anti-carcinogenic reputation. The berries also contain large amounts of viscotoxins and so are restricted to use *by medical herbalists only.*

NUTMEG
It is perfectly acceptable to use nutmeg in small quantities in cooking

but in large quantities the poisonous alkaloid, strychnine, can result in fatalities. It should not be used during pregnancy because it can cause abortion.

Pennyroyal
The essential oil is an abortifacient and should be avoided by pregnant women. The powdered herbs or leaves made into a tea are much milder and can be used in the last six weeks of pregnancy.

Pilewort
This should never be ingested fresh or rubbed on to the skin fresh because it causes irritation. Once dried the toxins in the plant break down, making it safe to use.

Poke Root
The leaves are *extremely poisonous*. They contain mitogenic substances (that is, substances that distort cell structure). This should be taken *under the guidance of a medical herbalist*. Properly administered it is an unbeatable cleanser for the lymph and the blood, and is excellent for chronic catarrh and benign cysts.

Rue
If inhaled in large amounts, it is hallucinogenic.

St John's Wort
In tea or tincture form taken internally this can cause skin reddening and soreness in some susceptible individuals. The oil used externally on the skin can cause puffiness and swelling. Avoid sunbathing while using this herb in any of its forms.

Senna Pods
Used over a prolonged period (upwards of a year), these will actually discourage peristalsis.

Squill
This can cause drastic diarrhoea and retching, and must be given *only by a qualified medical herbalist*.

TANSY
This should not be used during pregnancy as it stimulates the uterus.

TOBACCO
Chewed raw or taken as a tea, this can cause vomiting, convulsions, respiratory failure *even in minute doses.*

VIOLETS
Always use the fresh and not the dried flowers.

WHITE BRYONY
In large doses it is *toxic.*

WARNING ABOUT ESSENTIAL OILS

It takes 7,000 or more flowers to make a single drop of undiluted essential oil, so you should treat all essential oils with a great deal of respect and caution. This applies to both their internal and external use. If in any doubt at all, *please consult a qualified medical herbalist or aromatherapist.*

POISONING BY PLANTS

Induce vomiting as quickly as possible by the age-old method of sticking fingers down the back of the throat (unless the herb was taken several hours beforehand in which case vomiting is a waste of time). In either case, *you will need to telephone the doctor as quickly as possible.*

Keep the patient calm. Panic only increases the speed by which any poison will invade the system. Do not clear up any vomit until the doctor has inspected it. Undigested plant material in the vomit can give important clues about the nature of the toxic material swallowed. Do not try to induce the vomiting more than once.

QUALIFIED MEDICAL HERBALISTS

Choosing a competent medical herbalist is tantamount to walking through a therapeutic minefield. There are still some excellent herbalists in practice who have no formal qualification whatsoever, just many years of experience, but these are dwindling in numbers. There is a distressing number who have little or no experience and hide behind a list of weekend certificates that mean absolutely nothing. (For a list of qualifications to look for, including medical herbalists that I have personally trained myself over the years, send me an SAE — see the Resources Directory for my address.) As in every profession, the skill of a medical herbalist will vary. Choose someone who will fit into your lifestyle but, whoever you choose, look for, and expect, absolute professionalism. I always think the best way to make a choice is to talk to other patients working with a practitioner you have in mind. If a patient has been going to see a practitioner for the last two years and is not improving, there is something wrong. It obviously means that the disease is not being helped. Even those with entrenched illnesses like multiple sclerosis who may need to see a medical herbalist for a long period of time should be experiencing some relief.

Many medical herbalists like to see patients for a yearly check-up on a purely preventative basis. I much prefer to work with people who are basically healthy and want to stay that way rather than those who are on their last legs and have tried every other form of medical help before coming to see me. Choose someone who specialises in one field only. A jack of all trades and master of none will be no good to you. Be prepared to work with someone who will open-mindedly refer you on to another branch of natural healing if necessary. Herbalism is not the panacea of all ills. Neither is acupuncture, homeopathy or osteopathy, though, judging by the jealous way they cling to their patients, some practitioners evidently believe so.

SEVEN

HELPFUL HERBS

ALFALFA

Alfalfa, a member of the pea family, is one of the oldest cultivated plants on earth. Its tap root can extend deep down into the earth to a level of 40 ft (12 metres) to extract nutrients. The Arabs refer to it as the 'father of all foods'. The sprouted seeds of alfalfa are bursting with essential nutrients, including protein, zinc, calcium, iron, potassium, silica, beta-carotene, vitamins C, D, E and B, which make them a very good multi-vitamin and mineral supplement. The plant tops contain phytosterols (plant steroids) which have hormonal balancing properties, as well as optimising oestrogen levels. Alfalfa is also an important source of dietary fibre, ensuring proper bowel function as it can get right into the small diverticular pockets that may be present in the bowel and clean them out thoroughly.

DOSAGE
Tea: 2 oz (60 g) of the herb, infused. Drink 3 cups (720 ml) a day.
Tincture: 1–2 teaspoons (5–10 ml) diluted in water, three times a day.

ALOE VERA

Like comfrey, aloe vera is a plant very rich in allantoin, a cell proliferant. Unlike comfrey, it does not grow naturally in Britain, preferring hotter climates. The fresh juice or gel from this cactus plant is the part that stimulates cell proliferation. Aloe vera, taken as a juice, is also very nutritious, increases digestive function, boosts the immune system and has an anti-inflammatory action, healing internal ulceration. (The juice is obtainable from healthfood shops, but see Resources Directory for suppliers of the best-quality juices.) Like the juice, the quality of aloe gels varies enormously, so it is often an advantage to buy your own plant to have a convenient fresh supply of leaves (see Resources Directory). A cut leaf from the living plant can be rubbed on the skin to treat burns, rashes, psoriasis, insect bites and itching. Aloe gel is very effective in treating an itchy, sore or dry vagina, or thinning vaginal tissues, and is extremely soothing the moment it is applied.

DOSAGE

When taking aloe vera as a juice, follow instructions on the side of the bottle for dosage.

CONTRAINDICATIONS

Aloe juice should not be confused with the whole herb or with aloe gel, both of which are potent in their action and should *never* be used internally. If you ingest the whole plant, it will cause internal ulceration and piles. Normally it is the dried sap of either Curaçao, Barbados or Cape aloes that is used internally, but this needs to be mixed with other herbs to counteract the griping effect it has on the bowel and, in any case, should never be used by pregnant women.

BETH ROOT

Beth root is a traditional Native American remedy for all manner of menstrual complaints, especially conditions involving pain, heavy bleeding, PMS, amenorrhoea and haemorrhoids. It is usually found in a damp woodland habitat and is a member of the lily family. The root and rhizome are full of steroidal saponins which contain diosgenin. These act as precursors for sex hormones (that is, they create the right conditions in the body for hormones to be built from them), helping with menopausal symptoms, especially excessive menstrual bleeding. Externally beth root applied as a poultice will have antiseptic properties and help with vaginal discharge including thrush as well as trichomonas, ulcers, varicose veins and insect stings.

DOSAGE

Tea: boil the root as a standard decoction (see Chapter Six for standard

measures) and take half a cup (120 ml) morning and evening.
Tincture: 15 drops twice a day.

CONTRAINDICATIONS
Not to be used during pregnancy.

BLACK COHOSH

Also known as black snake root, this herb is a firm favourite in the Native American herbal tradition. A study carried out in Germany in 1988 proved that black cohosh tincture was as effective as HRT in alleviating common menopausal symptoms such as hot flushes, joint pain, water retention, fatigue and headaches.[1] Using 10–15 drops of the tincture twice a day for several months significantly reduces LH but not FSH (see Chapter One), thereby reducing the intensity and frequency of hot flushes. Black cohosh helps to counteract menopausal prolapses because it strengthens the pelvic muscles. It relieves menstrual pain and irregularity, along with headaches, arthritis and rheumatism because the aspirin-like salicylates present in the herb dilate the blood vessels while other substances soothe the central nervous system. Black cohosh has a cardiotonic effect on the body, lowering blood pressure and improving circulation while thinning the blood and dilating the blood vessels. It also alleviates water retention and breast tenderness and is useful in the treatment of incontinence because it nourishes both the kidneys and adrenal glands while discouraging oedema.

DOSAGE
Tea: up to 1 oz (30 g) per day of the root and rhizome (the underground stem), decocted. Drink 1 cup (240 ml) three times a day.
Tincture: half to 1 teaspoon (2.5–5 ml) three times a day.

CONTRAINDICATIONS
In large doses of over 2 teaspoons at a time it may cause headaches and it is contraindicated in pregnancy unless under the supervision of a professional medical herbalist.

BLESSED THISTLE

Also known as holy thistle or Our Lady's thistle, the entire plant is used medicinally. Due to its astringent action, it helps alleviate menopausal and other hormonal changes by reducing heavy and painful periods. It assists liver function, clearing any sluggishness in the system, and acts to reduce water retention through its diuretic effect. It has also been proved to expel abnormal cells from the body and is antibacterial.

If you are thinking of growing it, it is best not to plant it in your herb garden but put it in a distant patch, well walled around with deeply embedded roof tiles to make sure it does not spread all over the garden.

DOSAGE

Tea: make a standard infusion and drink 1 cup (240 ml) morning and evening.

Tincture: make a tincture from the whole plant, preferably fresh, but the dried herb works well too. Take 20 drops in a little water before each meal three times a day. As it has a distinctive bitter taste, it makes a useful digestive aid before meals.

BORAGE

Borage is an excellent restorative herb for the adrenal glands, helping the body after steroid use and countering stress. Borage leaves, flowers and seeds stimulate the adrenal cortex and this is especially useful during the menopause when the adrenal glands take over oestrogen production. Borage acts as a mild antidepressant for which the juice of the whole flowering herb is used. It is always best to use the fresh herb, and as the flowers contain more active ingredients than the leaf, a mixture of two-thirds flowers and one-third leaf and cut stem is optimal.

The seeds are a very rich source of gammalinoleic acid, which is a natural plant oil also found in flax seed, blackcurrant seed, evening primrose oil and spirulina. Gammalinoleic acid helps to regulate prostaglandin production in the body. Excessive prostaglandins in the bloodstream are often the culprits for flooding periods, mood swings and menstrual cramps.

DOSAGE

Tea: 1–2 oz (30–60 g) of the dried flowering herb, infused, per pint (600 ml) of water. Drink 1 cup (240 ml) three times a day.

Tincture: 1 teaspoon to 1 tablespoon (5–15 ml) diluted in water three times a day.

CALENDULA

Calendula, also known as pot marigold or simply marigold, is an effective wound and trauma healer when applied externally as a cream or as an oil. It is extremely effective when applied to burns, damaged tissue, ulcers and badly healing wounds. To make the oil, pack the freshly picked flowers in olive oil and place the mixture in an airing cupboard or on a sunny windowsill (out of direct sunlight), from the new moon to the full, until it turns a deep golden orange in colour and very fragrant, then strain. The oil can be applied directly to a sore, itching rectum or to thin vaginal tissue, or it can be rubbed into bruises and quicken their healing.

Taken internally calendula is a powerful lymphatic decongestant, helping to ease fluid retention and breast soreness as well as enhancing immune function. The herb stimulates the liver and has an affinity for the female reproductive system, regulating menstruation and cramping. Its astringent properties stem excessive menstrual bleeding and tone the uterine muscles. In addition, calendula contains phytosterols — plant steroids which can help to reduce menopausal difficulties.

DOSAGE

Tea: infuse the dried petals in a standard measure (see Chapter Six) and drink 1 cup (240 ml) three times a day.

Tincture: 5–20 drops in water, taken three times a day.

Fresh: sprinkle discriminately on to salads (too much will make the salad unpalatably bitter).

CASCARA SAGRADA

Cascara sagrada is the 'aged' bark — bark that is dried and stored for at least a year — which is used in herbal medicine as a corrective treatment for the colon. In addition, it enhances liver and pancreatic function; clears gall bladder congestion; supports the nervous system; helps with insomnia and to control hormonal imbalance as a result of underfunctioning of the pituitary gland. Cascara is abundant in nutrients such as beta-carotene, B complex vitamins, calcium, potassium, magnesium, iron, selenium, sodium, silica and vitamin C.

DOSAGE
Cascara is most effective when used in its dried, finely powdered form. Take a quarter of a level teaspoon three times a day. Remember that it will cleanse the colon so if as a result of this dosage you get diarrhoea, reduce the dose accordingly.

CONTRAINDICATIONS
If this herb is used over a prolonged period (upwards of a year), it will discourage peristalsis. It should not be used during pregnancy.

CAYENNE
Cayenne is similar to garlic in its wide range of beneficial effects on the body. It will rapidly improve problems of the circulation (blood and lymph), heart and lungs, heal infection and ulcers, stop both internal and external bleeding, as well as preventing blood clotting, aid digestion, enhance immune and liver function, relieve cramping and pain, and help with the elimination of toxins through the skin by encouraging sweating. It can even be used as an effective eye wash. Cayenne is rich in vitamins C and E, as well as calcium, beta-carotene and many other essential nutrients.

DOSAGE
Begin with a quarter of a teaspoon of the powder in tomato juice three times a day and gradually work up to 1 full rounded teaspoon three times a day.
Tincture: 10 drops, diluted in water, three times a day. For treating shock, it can be used neat on the tongue.

CONTRAINDICATIONS
Always take cayenne pepper uncooked. It can cause burning on

defecation and this will be helped by mixing it half and half with slippery elm.

Menopausal women should bear in mind that cayenne can occasionally cause bladder irritation if taken neat and activate hot flushes, as can other spices such as ginger and black pepper.

CHAMOMILE

The flowers of chamomile are revered for their calming effects on the nervous, digestive and genito-urinary systems, as well as for soothing muscles. Chamomile is therefore particularly useful for easing pain, for dysmenorrhoea, menstrual cramping and PMS, as well as for treating insomnia, depression, irritability, anorexia and vertigo. It can even calm the irritation caused by intestinal parasites. Use externally in compresses, chamomile can be used to treat conjunctivitis and for itchy skin, particularly pruritis vulvus (itchiness of the vagina that can occur with or without infection). A few drops (up to 10) of the essential oil in a hot bath can ease stress and pain.

Chamomile can be used to treat many of the symptoms of the menopause and menstrual difficulties in general. It also possesses diuretic properties which may help with menopausal hot flushes and night sweats. Making up an infusion of the herb releases the anti-inflammatory constituent azulene, which is not active when the herb is used fresh.

DOSAGE
Tea: make a standard infusion and drink 1 cup (240 ml) three times a day. Please note that chamomile does not extract fully in glycerine.
Tincture: take 5, working up to 20, drops three times a day. When making or buying a tincture, make sure the water in the extraction process is hot and let the mixture cool down completely before adding alcohol or glycerine to preserve it.

CONTRAINDICATIONS
Over-strong infusions can cause nausea, so proceed cautiously at first to see what strength suits you.

Anyone who is sensitive to ragweed and chrysanthemums (part of the same plant family) may be allergic to chamomile, although the azulene present in the herb has been shown to have an anti-allergic effect. If a skin rash or other allergic symptoms appear when you use the herb, discontinue use.

CHASTE TREE

Vitex (from the botanical name *Vitex agnus castus*), or chaste tree, is native to the Mediterranean region. The berries are the medicinally active part of the plant. The herb acquired its name because it was fed to temple priestesses to subdue libido and used by monks and priests to lessen sexual desire. The Arabs used it to cure insanity and on a recent trip to Egypt I found it available in bazaars sold as a calming agent for hysteria. It has been used since the time of Hippocrates for exactly the same conditions it is used for today and is completely non-toxic.

Numerous clinical studies have proved chaste tree's stimulating effect on the pituitary gland, working to regulate and normalise hormonal function. Chaste tree can increase the production by the anterior pituitary gland of luteinising hormone, enhancing the progesterone cycle, and at the same time it inhibits the release of FSH, thereby regulating the oestrogen cycle. As it increases progesterone levels slowly and naturally, it keeps bones and vaginal tissues strong and healthy.

Chaste tree can also help to support ovarian function, normalising hormone production in the second stage of the menstrual cycle. Because of its pronounced anti-inflammatory effect on the endometrium, it relieves chronic menstrual cramping. It also helps to relieve the symptoms of PMS (for which it needs to be used for at least six months after the relief of all symptoms, to prevent relapse) and to regulate such problems as amenorrhoea (lack of periods) or heavy blood loss. It is useful in treating endometriosis and reducing the size of uterine fibroids, often eliminating them. In addition, chaste tree can re-establish hormonal balance in women who have stopped taking the Pill and it will help to stimulate the flow of breast milk for nursing mothers because it encourages the production of prolactin.

In women without ovaries the herb appears to dampen the extremes of hormonal imbalance, probably through its indirect effect on the liver, circulation and endocrine system. Chaste tree stimulates the liver because of the bitter element in the plant. Because of its calming effect, it is very useful for treating menopausal depression and mood swings. It helps with other menopausal symptoms, too, such as hot flushes, hormonally related constipation and water retention.

Overall, chaste tree is rightfully known and highly regarded as a special remedy for female ailments because it can rectify imbalance in the hormonal patterns of a woman's body. It is a slow-acting tonic, however, with results only becoming evident after three months of daily use. It is most effective when used for at least a year.

DOSAGE
Tea: 1–2 teaspoons of crushed berries boiled in half a pint (300 ml) of water for 10 minutes in a tightly covered saucepan. Take 1 cup (240 ml) three times a day, served hot.
Tincture: 30–60 drops diluted in water three times daily.

COMFREY
Comfrey is a plant rich in a substance called allantoin which encourages cell proliferation. It helps to repair and accelerate regrowth of damaged body tissues and bones as in the case of broken bones, inflammation, bruises, torn cartilage and general connective-tissue weakness. Some of comfrey's old country names — knitbone and boneset — suggest these healing properties, which are particularly useful if there is danger of osteoporosis. The root and the leaves of the plant also contain steroidal saponins, which assist in correcting hormonal imbalance. The plant is high in mucilage which helps to heal damaged or inflamed mucous membranes. In addition to comfrey's many healing properties, it is a very nutrient-rich vegetable packed full of protein, zinc, calcium, beta-carotene, iron and B vitamins, all essential during the menopause.

Comfrey has gained a reputation as a dangerous plant despite centuries of safe use throughout the world, thanks to erroneous animal tests and an isolated constituent of the plant, pyrrolizidine alkaloids. In 1968 an independent Japanese scientist first reported finding these alkaloids and regarded them as potentially hepatoxic and carcinogenic.

Austrian studies confirmed the Japanese reports but since then the company that conducted these tests in Austria has verified that such tests were inconclusive and in Japan doctors still continue to recommend comfrey for cirrhosis of the liver.[2]

The truth of the matter is that most plants contain chemicals that are potentially harmful but if the herb is used in its whole form the synergistic relationship between various chemicals in the plant often nullifies or strengthens certain aspects of one another. It is the total of these hundreds of chemicals within a plant that determines the complete 'personality' of the plant, and judging a plant's actions simply on the basis of a single chemical component is rather like judging a person's character on the basis of a single personality trait.

Indeed the allantoin, calcium, salt and mucopolysacharrides in comfrey act as cell builders and serve to neutralise the cell-inhibiting action of the pyrrolizidine alkaloids, which in any case are in their organic state (unlike those used in laboratory studies) and are more likely to be degraded when digested in the human body.

In the experiments conducted in Japan and Austria the extracted alkaloids were isolated and injected into long-suffering laboratory animals in proportions far greater than would normally be ingested in medicinal use. The animals developed liver damage and cancerous tumours. Rats were fed comfrey root as 50 per cent of their total diet and unsurprisingly eventually developed tumours, which proves that any substance whether chemical or natural is a poison if we consume enough of it.[3] As Paracelsus observed hundreds of years ago: 'All things are poison and nothing is without poison. It is the dosage which makes the thing poisonous.' The amount these poor rats were given was the equivalent of you being asked to eat five heaped plates of comfrey leaves every day.

DOSAGE

I still use comfrey discerningly and happily in my own pharmacy. I believe you can safely use the entire plant to make a tea, but I generally use the leaves infused at a standard dose, prescribing 1 cup (240 ml) morning and evening. The tincture is best made from the whole plant and given at 15 drops three times a day.

DAMIANA

Damiana is a superb strengthening remedy for the nervous system and has an enviable reputation as an aphrodisiac in its native Mexico. The parts used are the dried leaves gathered during flowering. Specifically it acts as an anti-depressant where anxiety is complicated by issues of sexuality, including chronic infection of the nervous system, such as herpes, which affects the reproductive tract. It strengthens a woman's libido, and for women with genital herpes damiana can be effectively combined with liquorice and St John's wort as well as Siberian ginseng, which acts as an adaptogen (helping the body to adapt to new stress by stimulating its defence mechanism). Damiana also has mild laxative properties.

DOSAGE

Tea: make a standard infusion from the dried leaves and drink 1 cup (240 ml) four times a day.

Tincture: 1 teaspoon (5 ml) diluted in a cup (240 ml) of hot water three times a day. Half this dose will act as an effective anti-depressant if taken over a period of time.

DANDELION

The dandelion is familiar to almost everyone as the common, persistent weed of gardens and native to numerous habitats. The leaves, flowers and roots of dandelion can all be used medicinally and nutritionally. A remarkable herb for the liver and kidneys, it acts as a detoxifying agent. It works by promoting the flow of bile through the liver, bile ducts and gall bladder due to its bitter content, and this helps menopausal women in regulating hormonal production and clearing hepatic congestion. Wherever a congested liver cannot process cyclically produced hormones, this leads to imbalances like PMS and the growth of oestrogen-sensitive fibroids.

Dandelion also acts as a diuretic and this is why in France it is called 'piss-the-bed'. Dandelion will stimulate the elimination of toxins from the blood and tissues by working through the liver and kidneys. Its diuretic action reduces water retention throughout the body, which is helpful in relieving oedema that is often prevalent during hormonal upsets that lead to tender breasts, PMS and menstrual bloating. Dandelion will also improve pancreatic function, as well as helping to dissolve gall and kidney stones. Its diuretic action may be powerful but it does not at the same time leach potassium from the body, as do chemical diuretics.

In many cultures dandelion is much used as an addition to green salad and as a bitter tonic. It is rich in potassium, as well as iron, calcium, zinc, magnesium, beta-carotene, vitamin C, vitamin E and pectin, which acts as detoxifying agent, binding with toxins and working as a mild laxative. The dry-roasted root makes an excellent coffee substitute without the caffeine and chemicals that go with ordinary coffee. In addition, the root stimulates the production of hydrochloric acid and digestive enzymes, assisting easier elimination. Rich in phytosterols, dandelion root helps to maintain hormone balance and is particularly useful in treating chronic skin problems arising from hormonal imbalance or upset.

DOSAGE

Tea: make a standard infusion from the leaves and take 1 cup (240 ml) three times a day. Remember to take the evening dose well before going to bed, giving you plenty of time to empty your bladder. A decoction of the roasted or dried root can be made in standard measure or doubled in strength if desired. The dose should be 1 cup (240 ml) three times a day.

Tincture: 1–2 teaspoons (5–10 ml) from the fresh leaf and rhizome or root. Take 3–6 times a day for up to three weeks. In cases of very severe water retention, the fresh juice of the whole plant is more strongly diuretic than the tincture and 2 tablespoons (30 ml) of this juice can be added to other milder vegetable juices daily. Bear in mind, however, that the replacement of potassium from such fresh juice is less reliable than if given in a tincture.

CONTRAINDICATIONS

It is possible to become nauseous sucking or eating the flowers and stems which contain the fresh milky sap.

DONG QUAI

Dong Quai root is one of the most commonly used herbs in the world. It is employed extensively in China from where it originates. Other members of the Umbelliferae family to which it belongs, like fennel, are also used for their high levels of plant hormones. Dong Quai's main medicinal indications include toning the uterus and stimulating uterine contractions, while helping to regulate hormonal function. It helps with the circulation of the blood, particularly to the pelvic area, breaking up congestion and alleviating cramping while speeding tissue repair. Rich in B vitamins and vitamin E, it improves the assimilation of vitamin E and stabilises heart rhythm. Dong Quai helps to stabilise blood-sugar levels and boosts immune function through its antiviral, antibacterial and antifungal constituents. It is an excellent remedy for any menstrual irregularities and is particularly invaluable during the transition of the menopause, especially when vitamin E deficiency and circulatory problems arise.

TREATMENT OF MENOPAUSAL SYMPTOMS

- The sterols and minerals present in the herb are useful for modifying hot flushes, but if you feel hot most of the time do not use it because it will make you flush continually.
- Dong Quai moves moisture into the pelvis, hydrating the bowel and so relieving constipation as well as increasing vaginal secretions and thickening and nourishing thinned vaginal and bladder walls.
- The coumarins in Dong Quai thin the blood just like aspirin does. It reduces high blood pressure by dilating blood vessels and helps healthy circulation so preventing atherosclerosis and blood clots.
- Rich in magnesium, it helps deepen sleep disturbed by night sweats.
- It eases menopausal rheumatism.

DOSAGE

Tea: make a decoction at standard dose of the dried, cured and pressed root, thinly sliced, and drink 1 cup (240 ml) twice daily, or chew one-eighth/one-quarter of an inch (4–6 mm) of dried root 2–3 times daily.
Tincture: 10–40 drops three times daily.

CONTRAINDICATIONS

While it does help to regulate the menstrual cycle and diminish spotting and flooding caused by anaemia or hormonal imbalance, it should not be used in the menopause if you have unpredictable episodes of profuse menstrual bleeding or fibroids. This is because it relaxes the uterine muscle and excites contraction (both of which encourage flooding).

It should not be used if you have diarrhoea or bloating, and if you experience extreme breast tenderness, discontinue use.

If taking Dong Quai for an extended period of time, use it one week before the menstrual cycle, discontinue while bleeding, and resume it at the end of the cycle. Sometimes the strong flavour and action of the herb can cause gastric upset.

ECHINACEA

Echinacea is a member of the daisy family and native to North America but now cultivated internationally. Three species of the herb are used medicinally: *Echinacea angustifolia*, *Echinacea purpurea* and *Echinacea pallida*. The roots are the part of the plant that are mainly used, but the leaves and seeds are equally effective. Echinacea has a characteristic taste — even when taken in the smallest quantities, all parts of the plant should leave a metallic taste, together with a tingling and numbing sensation in the mouth. If the herb does not do this, then I am afraid you have wasted your money on poor-quality echinacea. In fact it may not even be echinacea at all!

Echinacea helps to stimulate all aspects of the immune system. It does so partly by stimulating the adrenal cortex, which explains its use in stress-related immune conditions such as hypersensitivity, allergic reactions and auto-immune disorders. In relatively high doses echinacea effectively combats viruses by blocking viral attachment to cells while stimulating production of infection-fighting white blood cells, doubling their number within days. *Echinacea angustifolia* contains an agent, polyacetylene achinalone, that can help prevent tumours.

The anti-microbial action of the herb makes it a good remedy, when combined with nasturtium, for pelvic inflammatory disease.

DOSAGE

The secret to taking echinacea effectively is to take it for ten days at a high dose. After this it tends not to work, so it is best to take it for ten days on and five days off before resuming the dose.

Tea: to be effective the tea must be a double- or triple-strength decoction. Take between 1 to 10 cups (240 ml–2.4 litres) a day depending on the level of infection. For chronic infections 3 cups (720 ml) a day will usually do; for acute infections you can safely take as many as 10 cups (2.4 litres) a day.

Tincture: for chronic infections take 15 drops three times a day. For acute infections take 1 tablespoon (15 ml) a day, which can be mixed in water or juice if you object to the fizzy aftertaste in the mouth.

FALSE UNICORN

False unicorn has a gently curved single tap root, believed to resemble a unicorn's horn, and a spike of beautiful, starlike blossoms that emerge each spring. False Unicorn root is rich in steroidal saponins which are the precursors for oestrogen. The herb can be used to normalise hormonal production and acts as a liver and uterine tonic, which is particularly helpful during the menopause when muscle tone needs to be re-established in cases of prolapse of the uterus. It also improves the secretory responses in the cyclical function of the ovaries, helping to relieve menopausal symptoms and other menstrual problems.

DOSAGE

Tea: make a standard decoction from the root and take not more than 3–4 cups (720–960 ml) a day.

Tincture: 10 drops three times a day.

FENNEL

Fennel contains phytosterols, helpful in relieving the symptoms of menopause, and is very rich in both calcium and potassium, essential nutrients for the body at any stage of life and especially during the menopause. Fennel will help to balance hormonal function, regulating the menstrual cycle and relieving menstrual pain. In addition, the herb enhances liver function, eases digestion and its diuretic properties relieve fluid retention. The essential oil can be used to treat urinary infections and is very pleasant-tasting.

DOSAGE
Tea: a decoction of the dried seeds, slightly crushed, using standard measurements. Take 1 cup (240 ml) three times a day.
Tincture: quarter to 1 teaspoon (1.5–5 ml) three times a day.

FENUGREEK

Fenugreek seed is well known for its culinary uses and as a 'green manure' in organic gardening. It also has many uses in herbal medicine, particularly for menopausal problems. The seeds of fenugreek are packed full of calcium, iron, protein, beta-carotene, lecithin, B vitamins and vitamin C — all essential nutrients for menopausal women. As well as phytosterols, the seeds contain diosgenin and other steroidal saponins in relatively large amounts, which closely resemble the body's own sex hormones. Unsurprisingly the use of fennel can promote fertility. The herb is also rich in mucilage, which makes it very soothing for the mucous membranes associated with the respiratory and digestive systems.

The phytosterols in fenugreek help correct hormonal imbalance, especially menopausal hot flushes and night sweats, together with depression associated with the menopause. It will also help thyroid function, lower blood sugar and excessive cholesterol levels, enhance liver function, and acts as a mild laxative — an added bonus as most symptoms of imbalance can usually be attributed to sluggish and congested bowel function.

DOSAGE
Tea: decoct the crushed seeds using a standard dose and take 1 cup (240 ml) three times a day.
Tincture: take 1 teaspoon (5 ml) of the tincture, made from the dried seeds and leaves, three times a day.

GARLIC

The healing properties of garlic have been revered for centuries in many cultures and I have already extolled its virtues at length in

Chapter Four. In summary, it is helpful for an extraordinarily wide range of conditions, including heart disease, cancer, AIDS, skin problems, viral, bacterial and fungal infections, diabetes, asthma, bronchitis, parasitic infections, kidney and urinary problems, liver disease and re-establishing bacterial balance in the intestines.

It is rich in nutrients, including germanium, sulphur, potassium, calcium, vitamins C and B, and beta-carotene, the precursor for vitamin A in the body. Garlic is useful throughout the menopause for its benefits to the body as a whole and because it can be used specifically to treat vaginal infections (see Chapter Five, 'Candiasis').

Apart from incorporating it into a liver flush (see Chapter Three), some of my favourite ways of incorporating raw garlic into my diet every day include slicing it thinly into fresh tomato sauce, mincing it into soya yoghurt, soya cheese or into a baked potato, adding it to olive oil to use as a salad dressing, slicing it to eat with mouthfuls of juicy pear. A whole bulb can be baked in the oven and then squeezed on to wholemeal bread. Eaten raw and in its natural state is the best way to obtain all the nutrients of garlic; garlic capsules, particularly the odour-free ones, are far less potent in their effect. To freshen the breath after eating raw garlic, chew a raw clove (that is, clove the spice), a few cardamom seeds or take a drop of aniseed oil.

DOSAGE
Up to six raw cloves daily.

CONTRAINDICATIONS
A whole clove eaten raw is very beneficial for high blood pressure, but processed garlic in the form of perles or tablets can actually aggravate the condition. It should be avoided during pregnancy as it has a very strong stimulating effect on the uterus.

GINSENG

There are three types of ginseng — Wild American, Asiatic and Siberian. The root is the part of the herb that is used.

Ginseng is well known for reducing the effects of stress. If you cannot take a break and feel exhausted and uncoordinated, take the tincture at high dose twice a day. Ginseng will nourish and strengthen the adrenal, pituitary, thyroid and hypothalamus glands. Taken by menopausal women, it will lessen fatigue by diminishing night sweats and promoting deeper restful sleep. It also reduces the intensity and frequency of hot flushes because it contains eleven hormone-like saponins, several phytosterols and hormonal building blocks such as essential fatty acids, minerals and glycosides.

Ginseng assists the functioning of the nervous system, alleviating depression and anxiety by nourishing the nerves, moderating blood-sugar swings and regulating hormones. Swings in blood-sugar levels are further assisted by ginseng's action on the metabolic process of the liver and on sugar utilisation within the muscles. In addition, ginseng aids digestion, which is beneficial in cases of digestive disorders resulting from the liver becoming overburdened by the task of dealing with the hormonal irregularities that arise during the menopause.

Ginseng normalises blood pressure and reduces cholesterol as the result of its cardiotonic properties which nourish the heart and blood vessels. (But see contraindications below.) In addition, it soothes menopausal headaches and, because it helps to regulate endocrine activity, can stem menstrual flooding. The antioxidants that ginseng contains promote general health and a longer life.

Although the benefits of taking ginseng are cumulative, you should notice an improvement in any of the abovementioned conditions within 2–3 weeks.

DOSAGE

The way ginseng is consumed in the Far East is to put a piece in the mouth and chew it and suck on it until it is all gone. For this purpose chew a piece of dried root as big as a third of your little finger daily for 6–8 weeks.

Avoid taking vitamin C supplements or food rich in vitamin C within three hours of consuming the herb because this neutralises its effect. On the other hand, taking vitamin E or a teaspoonful of flax seed or fresh wheatgerm oil magnifies its effect.

Tea: decoct a standard infusion and drink half a cup (120 ml) three times a day.

Tincture: 40 drops of the fresh root tincture 1–3 times daily.

CONTRAINDICATIONS

Be particularly cautious when purchasing commercial ginseng, which is often adulterated with totally unrelated herbs and other additives. In fact research has revealed that there may not be any ginseng root in the product at all apart from that on the label!

Because the effects of ginseng can be over-stimulating, do not use ginseng if you have a fever or if you feel jittery or have sleep difficulties. There are also documented cases of ginseng causing menstrual-like bleeding well after the menopause, and if this is the case, discontinue use. Women who feel tired but have plenty of energy that is not channelled properly may find ginseng gives them a headache. Although it certainly lowers blood pressure, it is not indicated for people with extremely high blood pressure or for those who get nose bleeds easily or have heavy menstrual bleeding. Especially avoid taking it late at night if sleeping becomes erratic and your mind is overactive. For such sensitive people the last dose should be given before mid-afternoon. Ginseng can be taken daily up to 1–2 years, but should not be taken every day for longer periods without some breaks.

GOLDENSEAL

Goldenseal is a favourite remedy in the Native American tradition and one of the most effective natural antibiotics and antivirals in the herbal kingdom. Pharmaceutical companies still use it in great quantities and because of this it has been severely over-harvested and has become an endangered species. So remember when buying it to ask only for cultivated goldenseal.

The bitter properties of the plant help liver function and digestion as well as acting as a tonic to the whole reproductive tract. It will stimulate uterine muscle, so avoid using it during pregnancy, except during labour where it may be prescribed.

DOSAGE

The tincture is more effective than the tea. For infections take 10 drops hourly if necessary, but the normal dosage would be 10 drops three times a day.

CONTRAINDICATIONS

Goldenseal should only be used for short periods of time and never longer than for six consecutive weeks because it builds up in the mucosa of the body, causing inflammation and irritation. It also depletes the digestive system of B vitamins. Stop for at least three weeks before repeating the dosage. As indicated above, it should never be used during pregnancy, nor should it be used by diabetics because it lowers blood-sugar levels.

GUELDER ROSE

Guelder rose, also known as cramp bark, is a hedgerow shrub native to Britain. High in salicylates, it is a very strong anti-spasmodic, as well as being wonderfully astringent because of its high tannin levels. The common name is well earned because of its ability to ease pain caused by tense contracted muscles and it is particularly indicated for involuntary muscle tension in the womb, lungs and stomach, although its effect extends to voluntary muscle in the legs, arms, back, shoulders and neck. Because it operates without any narcotic effect or causing mental sedation, it is particularly useful for menstrual cramps. It will also allay excessive menstrual bleeding, and is therefore helpful for menopausal women experiencing flooding periods.

DOSAGE

Tea: use double the standard decoction of the dried bark and/or berries and drink 1 cup (240 ml) three times a day.

Tincture: 1 teaspoon (5 ml) three times a day. For extreme pain I have administered 1 fl. oz (30 ml) at a time in hot water and the effect is immediate. It is perfectly safe to use up to 6 fl. oz (180 ml) per week of the tincture. However, if using this amount, it is better to take it as a glycerine tincture.

CONTRAINDICATIONS

It should not be used during pregnancy because it relaxes the uterus.

HOPS

A member of the cannabis family, this native climbing vine has affinity for damp woodland and hedgerows. The female flower and leaf bracts are the part used medicinally. The leaf bracts look like little green pine cones and are often mistaken for the flowering part. Tucked right inside the leaf bracts are the tiny fruit, containing a golden, pollen-like substance rich in lupulin, the active constituent of hops. To obtain the best results when used medicinally, the plant is most effective when used fresh or freshly tinctured, as its considerable hormonal properties are quickly lost through drying.

The sedative properties of hops are well known through their use in beer production. In fact early herbalists used to encourage beer consumption as a medical treatment for nervous stress — taken in moderation of course! In addition to their sedative properties, hops have an anti-spasmodic effect, releasing muscular tension and calming stress-induced digestive disorders. Hops have a bitter taste which enhances liver function.

They are rich in phytosterols and oestrogenic substances and these help to alleviate many menopausal symptoms. The oestrogenic properties were discovered when hops were first cultivated in large amounts for the brewing industry. Female hop pickers who worked in the fields for several weeks noticed that their menstrual cycles appeared earlier than normal, while at the same time male workers experienced a loss of libido. Hops have many other applications during the menopause other than balancing hormones, including aiding relaxation and easing digestion, as well as acting as a soothing diuretic. Thanks to the asparagin content of the plant, toxins are more easily eliminated from the bloodstream and fluid retention reduced.

Because hops are so steeped in volatile oils, they are one of the herbs traditionally used in sleep pillows. The plant's oils are released by the pressure of sleeping on the herb-filled pillow and affect the brain directly through the olfactory centre. To stimulate dreaming, add mugwort. To add fragrance, include rose petals or lavender in the sleep pillow.

DOSAGE
Tea: make a strong infusion by allowing the standard measure of the freshly dried flowers to steep for a full 30 minutes. Strain and sip 1 cup

(240 ml), cold, throughout the day.

Tincture: use 5–15 drops, made from the fresh flowers, three times a day.

CONTRAINDICATIONS

Direct-contact dermatitis can be caused by harvesting the pollen.

LADY'S MANTLE

Lady's mantle is a herb traditionally used by women throughout Europe. Its usefulness as a uterine tonic is well documented, as is its indication for heavy periods and period pain, thanks to its high tannin content. The leaves and flowering shoots are used medicinally and contain salicylic acid (giving the plant anti-inflammatory properties), saponins (bitter agents which assist liver function) and phytosterols (plant steroids which act to reduce menopausal difficulties). It is also indicated for arterial hardening and external and internal bruising.

TREATMENT OF MENOPAUSAL SYMPTOMS

- It combines well with shepherd's purse for treatment of heavy periods and fibroids.
- The fresh leaves, infused, are useful for treating cold sores and for other mucous-membrane disturbances such as vaginal itching and leukorrhoea (white vaginal discharge).
- Women in Switzerland still use poultices of lady's mantle to firm and tone breast tissue.
- It combines well with equal parts of motherwort or chaste tree as a treatment for hot flushes.

DOSAGE

Tea: to treat menopausal weight gain, use reasonable amounts of the infused leaves, at the standard measure, but steeping for 30 minutes to extract all the tannins for stronger astringent action. Take 1 cup (240 ml) morning and evening and ensure that no more than 3 oz (90 g) of the infused leaves are used for tea drinking weekly.

Tincture: half to 1 teaspoon (2.5–5 ml) three times a day.

LIQUORICE

One of the few sweet herbs, with a sweetness up to fifty times that of sugar, liquorice root adds flavour to and harmonises herbal formulations. It is rich in calcium, potassium, sodium, tannins, coumarins (which helps to thin the blood, so assisting circulation), phytosterols, saponins and glycyrrhizin (see below), and it is structurally similar to adrenal cortical hormones. Because of this, liquorice is highly beneficial in its effect on the adrenal glands and on the endocrine system as a whole. It helps the adrenal glands to function correctly, which is especially useful during the menopause since many of the symptoms associated with the menopause are similar to those of adrenal exhaustion or stress.

As we have seen (Chapter Three), the adrenal glands take over the production of oestrogen from the ovaries once the menopause begins and continue to do so up until the age of seventy and beyond. The adrenal glands also handle stress reactions in the body, both physical and mental, and unremitting stress can result in chronic fatigue and exhaustion. So it is quite possible that, by the time you begin the menopause, your adrenal glands may be a little the worse for wear and ill-equipped to cope adequately with the transition, resulting in uncomfortable menopausal symptoms.

The oestrogenic and other steroidal properties of liquorice have been used to normalise and regulate women's hormonal production for centuries. Glycyrrhizin has a similar effect to the adrenal hormone ACTH. To boost exhausted adrenal glands liquorice may be used together with herbs such as echinacea, oats, borage and Siberian ginseng, plus extra food sources of vitamin C, which is essential for maintaining optimum adrenal and hormonal function. Liquorice will also help heal intestinal ulcers, soothe and heal the respiratory system, act as a mild laxative, boost immune capabilities and enhance liver function. In addition, the herb acts as an antiviral agent and possesses anti-inflammatory properties, as well as decreasing high levels of cholesterol in the blood.

Liquorice is also helpful for treating hypoglycaemia because it reduces sugar cravings and in small amounts it is a safe sweetener even for diabetics. It decreases high testosterone levels in women with ovarian cysts and the chewed root not only reduces dental plaque and caries but lubricates and freshens a dry mouth and throat.

DOSAGE
Tea: make a decoction using half a standard dose — that is, half an ounce (15 g) to 1 pint (600 ml) of water. Drink half a cup (120 ml) morning and evening.
Tincture: half to 1 teaspoon (2.5 –5 ml) diluted in water three times a day.

CONTRAINDICATIONS
The dried root, collected in the late autumn, thoroughly cleaned, sliced thinly and dried, together with some of the leaves taken from the plant, is normally recommended by herbalists, as long as it is taken in moderate quantities for short periods of time. Large and frequent doses exacerbate high blood pressure because liquorice is a cardiac stimulant with a high proportion of sodium. It may have harmful side-effects in people who have low levels of renin (a hormone affecting blood pressure), hypokalaemia (low blood potassium), oedema, or a history of kidney or heart failure. The herb is best avoided altogether during pregnancy because of its effects on hormonal function and because it may decrease contraction of the uterus.

MILK THISTLE
Milk thistle, naturalised in Britain, has been studied and used medicinally for centuries, mainly in Europe. The seed shell yields a group of flavonoid-like compounds, excellent for restoring and maintaining liver function. Remember that the liver acts as a massive hormone-filtering system (see Chapter Three), and if it is congested or infected then almost certainly the hormonal balance of the body will be adversely affected. Hence milk thistle can be used with confidence to treat conditions such as hepatitis, cirrhosis, psoriasis and any form of toxicity. It may also be used to relieve emotional 'poisons' — anger, fear and envy — also processed by the liver.

The flavonoids present in milk thistle help protect the liver against damage from chemicals, such as pesticide residues and psycho-active drugs, and speeds up the production of new enzymes and proteins, accelerating regeneration of the liver. If you know that you are going out for a heavy night's drinking (not that I recommend this), it might be wise to have a cup (240 ml) of milk thistle decoction in advance so that the alcohol does far less damage to the liver.

DOSAGE
Tea: made a decoction of the seeds (standard measure) and take 1 cup (240 ml) morning and evening.
Tincture: 15 drops three times a day.

NASTURTIUM

The fresh flowers and leaves of nasturtium help to fight infections of the female reproductive system. It is also excellent for calming an overactive thyroid. Applied externally as an oil, it acts as a precursor for progesterone, which often proves beneficial during the menopause.

DOSAGE
Tea: make a standard infusion with the flowers and drink 1 cup (240 ml) three times a day.
Tincture: make a tincture using the leaves and flowers and take 15 drops morning and evening.
Fresh: the fresh flowers and leaves may be eaten freely in salads.

NETTLES

Nettles are probably one of the most prolific and well-known weeds in the British Isles. This is just as well as they are an unsurpassed tonic for women at any stage of life but especially during the menopause, being rich in nutrients that include beta-carotene, vitamin C, calcium, iron, potassium, magnesium, zinc and protein. Nettles are a wonderful blood rebuilder in those who are anaemic particularly as the result of menopausal flooding. They have a gentle cleansing and detoxifying action on the body. Nettles work through the liver and kidneys to oxygenate the bloodstream, clear skin problems, heal bladder infections, liver disease, water retention and arthritic conditions. They also help to combat hay fever and can improve thyroid and pancreatic functions.

Nettles are rich in choline which acts as a precursor for acetylcholine (an important neurotransmitter involved in memory and learning), helping with circulation to the brain and so dispelling mental fog. Used in their fresh state after midsummer, nettles act as a laxative.

DOSAGE

Nettles make a tasty steamed vegetable and a delicious soup. Harvest the plants before they flower (remembering to wear rubber gloves to protect your hands, although the sting goes out of the nettle once it is dried), using the aerial parts only.

Tea: make a double-strength infusion from the leaves and take 1 cup (240 ml) three times a day.

Tincture: 1–2 teaspoons (5–10 ml) in plenty of water three times a day.

Fresh Juice: take 1 tablespoon (15 ml) three times a day. The juice may be preserved for use all year round by adding 3 fl. oz (90 ml) of pure alcohol to 7 fl. oz (210 ml) of fresh juice.

CONTRAINDICATIONS

Women who have used large doses of the tincture for a long period of time sometimes complain about scratchy sensations on urination. If this is the case, simply reduce the dose or, better still, switch to herbal tea, which is preferable for long-term use.

RASPBERRY

The leaves and fruit of the raspberry have been used extensively the world over to treat a whole range of gynaecological problems, especially those that arise in pregnancy. Raspberry leaves are rich in the alkaloid fragarine which, in combination with other constituents of the plant, serves to tone and relax the pelvic and uterine muscles. The leaves are also high in tannin, which has an astringent action of tightening loose tissue along the mucous membranes. Raspberry leaves will lessen heavy menstrual bleeding, help spotting and lower high blood-sugar levels. The herb reduces breast tenderness and is used to treat uterine fibroids. Along with the ripe delicious fruits, the leaves are also abundant in nutrients essential to the menopausal woman, including iron, calcium, potassium, magnesium, zinc, pectin, B complex vitamins and vitamins C (vital for good adrenal function) and E. The minerals present in raspberries restore an imbalance of salts and act as a nutritive in cases of physical exhaustion and dehydration.

DOSAGE

Tea: standard infusion from the leaves, fresh or dried, 1 cup (240 ml) three times daily. Some women like to alleviate the taste of raspberry by adding a little mint.

Tincture: 1 teaspoon (5 ml) three times a day.

CONTRAINDICATIONS

The fragarine in the raspberries leaves strengthens the uterus but cannot promote correct uterine contraction unless a woman has a genetic background of strong pelvic muscle. Its high iron content makes it one of the favourite herbs to administer during pregnancy but it is best administered with the same quantity of another herb.

SAGE

Originally from the Mediterranean, sage is now a familiar garden plant in Britain. The leaves are used medicinally as they are very high in tannins, glycosides and saponins. It is has been used to increase fertility and is a classic remedy for hot flushes, used extensively throughout Europe for this very purpose. Taken internally, the herb works in the opposite manner to diaphoretics such as yarrow, because it prevents rather than encourages sweating. Sweating itself does not remove toxins but it does cause minerals to evaporate from the body, and such mineral loss can bring about dizziness, trembling, emotional swings and even joint pain. Not only does sage stop sweating and the resulting mineral loss but, because it is so rich in minerals itself, it makes up for previous depletion.

Sage is useful for treating a stressed immune system, being the classic remedy for inflammation of the mucous membranes (sore throats, sweating and aching). It may be used locally as an anti-inflammatory for mouth ulcers and as a carminative for indigestion. Particularly useful for treating diarrhoea, it calms the digestive tract with its astringent, anti-inflammatory and antiseptic properties.

Sage is also rich in headache-easing saponins, which encourage the free flow of blood, essential fatty acids that keep the blood vessels flexible and carotenes which nourish the liver. It contains highly disinfectant oils that concentrate in the urine discouraging the growth of harmful bacteria. For this very reason, its essential oils can accumulate in the kidneys or liver, so it is best used discriminately and not at all if you have a dry mouth or a very dry vagina.

The herb is a powerful anti-oxidant that helps to retard the onset of wrinkles and grey hair; hence the old saying — 'She who would live for aye must eat sage in May'. The leaves are best used at the beginning or just before flowering, accounting for the choice of month.

People who are very wise are known as 'sages' and sage is one of the few herbs that will cross the blood/brain barrier and contribute to mental clarity.

DOSAGE
Tea: 1–2 oz (30–60 g) of the fresh or dried leaves infused in a cup (240 ml) of boiling water for 10 minutes. Drink 1 cup (240 ml) three times a day.
Tincture: 1–2 teaspoons (5–10 ml) three times a day.

CONTRAINDICATIONS
Because it is rich in tannin it should not be used for a prolonged period of time because tannin builds up proteins and eventually reduces the absorption of B vitamins, which inhibits iron absorption. Very prolonged use of any astringent herb that contains tannin has been associated with throat and stomach cells becoming cancerous so herbs like sage that are rich in tannin are all best used only for the short term.

Sage also contains a toxic ketone as part of its essential oil complex, and if the essential oil is consumed regularly over several months this may be emmenagogic, causing womb spasms and the possibility of abortion. Sage oil is therefore not to be used by pregnant women.

SARSAPARILLA
Sarsaparilla root is a native of the Caribbean region and is famous as a

flavouring for soft drinks. Confusion sets in when you attempt to buy some as there are several species, some of which are more effective than others. Jamaican is considered the best, followed by Mexican and Honduran.

Sarsaparilla has an impressive reputation as a blood-cleansing herb. It is rich in steroidal saponins, too, enabling it to act as a gentle adrenal tonic. This is very useful for the menopausal woman as adrenal exhaustion or stress is often a contributing factor in menopausal symptoms.

DOSAGE
Tea: boil the root as a standard decoction and take half a cup (120 ml) morning and evening.
Tincture: 10–30 drops of fresh or dried root tincture taken three times a day. Sarsaparilla extracts especially well in a glycerine tincture.

CONTRAINDICATIONS
Contrary to a common misconception, the root contains no testosterone. Its steroidal saponins are metabolised in such a way that they do affect hormonal balance, although the exact mechanism defies current testing methods and still invites debate. Indeed sarsaparilla was outlawed by the orthodox medical establishment a few centuries ago, but its use as a reproductive tonic stands firm. If the herb's hormonal steroids are not needed, they are easily and readily excreted.

SASSAFRAS

Sassafras bark has been used as a blood purifier and liver cleanser for centuries. It helps to promote sweating and urination, which in turn benefits the kidneys in their function of filtering the blood. The safrole in the bark is largely insoluble in water and its properties do not emerge when made as a tea (except as a decoction) or an old-fashioned root beer.

DOSAGE
Tea: boil the dried bark as a standard decoction and drink half a cup (120 ml), hot, morning and evening.

CONTRAINDICATIONS

When safrole was isolated from the herb and injected in very high doses into laboratory animals, it was found to produce carcinogenic cells and was banned in the United States. But in the southern part of the United States, where it has been used as a decoction for generations, there is the lowest rate of cancer in the United States, nor has there ever been a recorded case of sassafras poisoning or of sassafras-related cancer.

Used medicinally, sassafras should not be taken for longer than 3–4 consecutive weeks, and should never be used during pregnancy.

SHEPHERD'S PURSE

Shepherd's purse, so named because of its purse-shaped seeds, is a common weed in gardens and fields. Dainty and rather insignificant-looking, it can often be overlooked as a medicinal agent. This is a pity as the plant has high concentrations of tannin, tyramine and other amines which help to prevent excessive bleeding, acting as a tonic for the uterus and mucous membranes. It is one of nature's strongest astringents for promoting rapid blood clotting and alleviating menstrual spotting, flooding or haemorrhaging, as well as acting as a soothing diuretic for mild bladder infections. The fresh plant extract, diluted appropriately with water, makes an excellent vaginal douche for treating discharges, inflammation of the vaginal mucosa and menopausal spotting, and it is a useful addition to hot sitz-baths in the treatment of haemorrhoids.

DOSAGE

In all instances use the fresh plant because the dried herb will degenerate after only four months and has little medicinal use at this stage. Harvest the whole plant during the seed stage and be aware that when making a tincture it will smell unpleasantly like old Brussels sprouts.

Tea: make a double-strength standard infusion and take a cup (240 ml) every hour as needed or three times a day. This can also be used as a douche or added to sitz-baths (see above). When treating haemorrhoids it is doubly effective if also taken orally.

Tincture: the taste of the tincture can be ameliorated by adding glycerine (10 per cent by volume). Ten drops to 2 teaspoons (1–10 ml) should be taken every 20 minutes or three times a day. If taking more than 2 oz (60 g) of the herb a day, please do so *only under the supervision of a qualified medical herbalist.*

SKULLCAP

The leaf of skullcap, gathered when the plant is in its early flowering stages, is used for those who suffer from PMS for a long period of time. It is also used to treat menopausal women who experience severe mood changes every month. Using the herb to treat such problems requires patience because it takes at lease three consecutive months to shift the hormonal imbalance permanently.

The herb also helps to relieve nervous exhaustion and to alleviate poor memory and concentration, particularly when the symptoms are combined with insomnia or chronic fatigue. Less strong than hops or valerian, it may be used as a sedative for sensitive people who cannot tolerate either of these herbs and has the added advantage of helping ease headaches and migraines without causing drowsiness during the day. Skullcap has an anti-allergic action and the plant itself is rich in B complex vitamins, iron, silica, calcium, potassium and magnesium. It acts as an anti-spasmodic relieving muscular cramping and, due to its bitter content, will improve liver function and help with fluid retention as it stimulates the kidneys.

DOSAGE

Tea: to help insomnia use one and a half times the standard dose and drink 1 cup (240 ml) an hour before bed and a further cupful while in bed. If night-time urination is a problem, drink smaller amounts and make sure that you go to the toilet before retiring to bed, or substitute the tea with a more concentrated tincture. For extreme agitation and pain, including that arising from menstrual cramping, the tincture is undoubtedly more effective than the tea.

Tincture: 1 teaspoon (5 ml), diluted in a little hot water, 1–4 times a day. It is perfectly acceptable to use 1 teaspoon every 10–20 minutes as needed, up to 12 doses spread over the day.

CONTRAINDICATIONS

Be sure to check meticulously your source of skullcap as it is often adulterated or confused with germander (potentially dangerous to the liver) and other herbs without the same medicinal quality.

VALERIAN

Valerian is a plant that is native to Britain and favours a damp habitat. The dried roots have a pungent smell rather like old socks or rotting mushrooms. The root is one of the most potent herbs for treating the nervous system. It is not a true sedative because it does not reduce sensitivity or motor control, but when taken by someone experiencing exhaustion and agitation it acts as if it were a sedative. It reduces reflex nervous response and activity in the psychomotor sphere, so is particularly useful for soothing an overactive mind. As well as soothing nerves, the herb relaxes the muscles, relieving menstrual cramps and settling mood swings. It is therefore particularly useful for treating menopausal woman whose symptoms interfere with sleep and therefore exacerbate the hormonal changes taking place.

Although it is a powerful herb, it can be safely given to people with fragile nervous systems. It should not be confused with valium as the two are not related in any way; the names simply sound similar. Valerian's sleep-producing and pain-relieving effects are temporary and definitely not habit-forming. In fact valerian has been shown to be remarkably safe compared to tranquillisers and anti-spasmodic drugs.

DOSAGE

Because valerian root contains volatile oils, it must be infused or steeped; never decocted or boiled. I prepare it by steeping the root overnight in cold water. Fresh root tea and tincture are much more powerful than the dried-herb preparation.

Tea: steep 2 oz (60 g) of the root in a pint (600 ml) of water overnight and drink 1–3 cups (240–720 ml) at a time as needed. Taking 500 ml at night will ease the most tenacious insomnia although you may have to persist for several consecutive nights before you notice a difference.

Tincture: 10 drops to 1 teaspoon (1–5 ml) three times a day or more often if desired. For acute pain, repeat every 15 minutes.

CONTRAINDICATIONS

Valerian can be taken when using most of the common prescription drugs, including barbiturates, but there are a few people on anti-psychotic drugs who may be sensitive to valerian and who experience unwanted side-effects. In any case, the herb should never be used to treat severe depressive states. Alcohol reacts negatively with barbiturates, so if you are taking these and trying to break your dependency on them, it would be better to use dried valerian powder in capsules rather than the alcoholic tincture.

Large amounts act on the central nervous system as a depressant in the same way that alcohol does. An excess can cause irritability and headaches as well as dullness on waking (if used at night). Very occasionally there have been reports of some people becoming headachy and anxious on a low to moderate dose of valerian. Should you experience this, use skullcap instead.

For medium- to long-term use it is safer to take valerian in a mixture with other herbs. One of my favourite combinations is equal parts of valerian, skullcap and lobelia. In addition, valerian combines well with lemon balm for a milder calming effect during the day.

WILD YAM ROOT

Wild yam root is valued the world over by practitioners of allopathic and natural medicine alike. Steroidal saponins, including diosgenin, are found in the herb in high concentrations — vital for the production of both progesterone and cortisone. Until 1970 wild yam was the pharmaceutical industry's sole source of diosgenin, used for the contraceptive pill and other steroid hormones. As a botanical medicine it is completely safe and non-toxic, there are no dangers in its long-term use and it can be applied externally as an oil or cream or taken internally as a decoction or a tincture (although the tincture is undoubtedly more effective than a decoction).

TREATMENT OF MENOPAUSAL SYMPTOMS
- Wild yam combines beautifully with chaste tree to restore hormonal imbalance and reverse menopausal symptoms.
- Its anti-spasmodic and anti-inflammatory properties are of benefit

to menopausal women experiencing cramping in the digestive tract and extremities, bloating, rheumatoid pains, migraine, constipation, menstrual cramping and nausea.

- It can stop mid-cycle spotting and regulate flooding. Twenty to 30 drops of the tincture taken two weeks before the beginning of a period can provide enough progesterone precursors to remedy flooding; 10–15 drops can halt mid-cycle spotting.

- A low dose of wild yam will relieve chronic menstrual headaches — 10 drops of the tincture three times a day; 30 drops six times a day will ease acute ones. In this instance a tincture will act more effectively when added to hot water.

- Homemade wild yam cream applied to the vulva and vagina will stop burning and itching but it is not curative. Discontinuing the treatment will lead to recurrence.

- Used as a liver tonic, wild yam activates and stimulates liver activity. The high concentration of steroidal saponins present in the herb provide the building blocks needed by the liver needed to synthesise sex hormones. If both the liver and the reproductive system are responsible for hormonal imbalance, use wild yam.

- Combined with black cohosh, wild yam is an effective pain-relieving remedy for aching joints or full-blown rheumatoid arthritis.

DOSAGE
The encapsulated powder can cause minor intestinal gas in some people. It is best to make the tincture from the fresh or dried root — 1 teaspoon (5 ml) three times daily.

YARROW
Yarrow is a member of the daisy family and is found growing in gardens, hedgerows, meadows and woodlands. The flowers and other aerial parts are used medicinally. Due to its phytosterol content it helps to correct hormonal imbalance, and stems excessive bleeding thanks to the high levels of tannin present. Its bitter content stimulates the liver and the volatile oil present in it improves digestive function. Yarrow has antiseptic properties and is useful in stimulating a sluggish

metabolism, helping to normalise irregular menstrual cycles during the menopause. Taken as a cold tea, it is helpful in reducing hot flushes and night sweats. Taken hot, it can be used to shrink fibroids and encourages the elimination of toxins through the skin and kidneys, balancing blood pressure and relieving pelvic and uterine congestion.

Combined with hawthorn and lime blossom, yarrow reduces high blood pressure and, combined with shepherd's purse, it stops haemorrhaging.

DOSAGE

Tea: make a standard infusion from the aerial parts and take 2 cups (480 ml) or more as desired three times a day.

Tincture: half to 1 teaspoon (2.5–5 ml) diluted in 1 cup (240 ml) of water three times a day.

CONTRAINDICATIONS

Yarrow is an emmenagogue (a substance that stimulates normal menstrual function) and should therefore not be used in pregnancy. Nor should it be used to treat anyone who is sensitive to light.

YELLOW DOCK

Yellow dock, also known as curly dock, grows in many habitats. It is a powerful herb with excellent blood-oxygenating properties as a result of the 40 per cent iron compounds that it contains. It is thus particularly useful during the menopause when iron deficiency can result in fatigue, exhaustion and irritability. If anaemia is the result of excessive menstrual bleeding, the toning effect that yellow dock has on the liver makes it a useful addition to a liver tonic for correcting hormonal imbalance. The iron content of yellow dock does not cause constipation, unlike its synthetic counterpart. The herb is useful for treating excessive menstrual bleeding, irregular periods and uterine fibroids, and it promotes the elimination of metabolic toxins through the bowel when other eliminative organs such as the skin, lungs and kidneys are over-stressed. Its astringent and purifying effects encourage healthy blood flow to the sweat and digestive glands. Yellow dock is an excellent tonic for the body as a whole.

DOSAGE

Tea: do not harvest the roots until the plant is at least 2.5 ft (75 cm) high and the seeds have dropped. The older the plant, the larger the root. Make a standard decoction from the root and take 1 cup (240 ml) three times a day.

Tincture: take 1–2 teaspoons (5–10 ml) daily. The tincture is best taken before meals if you are not absorbing your nutrients properly, and while taking it avoid anything containing caffeine and tannin as these will impede its proper absorption.

ENDNOTES

INTRODUCTION

1. Ellen Cantarow, 'Moving the Mountain', *Women Working for Social Change*, New York: Feminist Press 1980.

CHAPTER ONE

1. M. Tarlan and N. A. Smallheiser, 'Personality patterns in patients with malignant tumours of the breast and cervix', *Psychosomatic Medicine* 13 (1951), 117.
2. Leslie Kenton, *Passage to Power*, London: Vermilion 1996.
3. Paavo Airola, *Every Woman's Body*, Phoenix, Arizona: Health Plus Publishers 1979, 506.
4. Louise Hayes, *You Can Heal Your Life*, London: Airlift Books 1988, 5.
5. From an essay by Ann Wright in Ann Voda, Myra Dinnerstein and Charles R. O'Donnell, eds, *Changing Perspectives in Menopause*, Austin: University of Texas Press 1982.

CHAPTER TWO

1. Frances McCrea, 'The politics of menopause: the discovery of a deficiency disease', *Social Problems* 31 (1), 111–23.
2. Sandra Coney, *The Menopause Industry*, London: The Women's Press 1995, 48.
3. *New England Journal of Medicine* (14 October 1993).
4. Jan Vandenbroucke, 'Postmenopausal oestrogen and cardio protection', *The Lancet* 337 (6 April 1991), 833–4.
5. Ibid.
6. *Journal of the American Medical Association* (26 May 1993).

7. Dr Susan Bewley and Dr Thomas Bewley, *The Lancet* (1 February 1992).

8. *Obstetrics and Gynaecology* (February 1992).

9. *New England Journal of Medicine* 332/24 (1995), 1589–3.

10. *British Medical Journal* (17 February 1990).

11. *American Journal of Epidemiology* (May 1995).

12. F. Grodstein et al., 'Postmenopausal hormone use and choleaystectomy in a large prospective study', *Obstetrics and Gynaecology*, 83 (January 1994), 5–11.

13. *Clinical Therapeutics* (September–October 1990).

14. David Jones, 'HRT … the bitter pill that is hard to swallow', *Daily Mail* (16 January 1995).

15. L. Avioli, 'Osteoporosis: a growing natural health problem', *Female Patient* 17 (September 1997), 84.

16. Susan S. Weed, *Menopausal Years*, New York: Ash Tree Publishing 1992.

17. John Robbins, *Diet for a New America*, Walpole, N.H.: Stillpoint Publishing 1987 — see especially pp. 189–96; see also Leslie Kenton, *Passage to Power*,115.

18. Quoted in Leslie Kenton, *Passage to Power*, 115.

19. Ibid., 266.

CHAPTER THREE

1. Dr Christiane Northrup, *Women's Bodies, Women's Wisdom*, London: Piatkus 1995.

2. S. N. Blair et al., 'Physical fitness and all cause mortality: a prospective study of healthy men and women', Journal of the American Medical Association 262/17 (3 November 1989).

3. G. C. Pitts et al., 'Factors affecting work output in hot environments', *American Journal of Physiology* (1944).

4. 'A. M. exercisers stay with it', *Aviation Medical Bulletin* (December 1990).

5. David Nieman, *Bottom Line* 12/21 (15 November 1991).

6. James R. White, *Bottom Line* 12/12 (30 June 1991).

7. A. Leaky, 'Can This Man Help You to Live to 140?', *Los Angeles Magazine* (April 1983).

8. Harvey Diamond, *You Can Prevent Breast Cancer*, San Diego: Promotion Publishing, n.d.

Chapter Four

1. Barbara Griggs, *The Food Factor*, Harmondsworth: Penguin 1988, 99.
2. William Duffey, *Sugar Blues*, New York: Warner Books 1975.
3. T. Hiryama, 'Epidemiology of breast cancer with special reference to the role of diet', *Preventive Medicine* 7 (1978).
4. Dr Christiane Northrup, *Women's Bodies, Women's Wisdom*.
5. John Robbins, *Diet for a New America*, 166.
6. George K. Davies, 'Effect of a Nightshade on Livestock', in *Childers' Diet to Stop Arthritis: The Nightshades and Ill Health*, Somerville, N.J.: Horticultural Publications 1987.
7. One of numerous studies quoted by John Robbins, *Diet for a New America*, 291–7, including A. Parke, 'Rheumatoid arthritis and food', *British Medical Journal* 282 (1981), 2027.
8. Quoted in Nathaniel Mead, 'The Champion Diet', *East-West Journal* 10/9 (September 1990).
9. Dr William C. Roberts, *Vegetarian Times* (February 1991).
10. Annemarie Colbin, *Food and Healing*, New York: Ballantine 1986, 166.
11. Dr Johanna Budwig has written numerous books (in German) on the subject, all published by Hyperion Verlag (address: 7800 Freiburg im Breisgau, Germany).
12. Udo Erasmus, *Fats and Oils*, Vancouver: Alive 1986 — see especially p. 294.

Chapter Five

1. Dr Christiane Northrup, *Women's Bodies, Women's Wisdom*, London: Piatkus, 1995.
2. A. G. Hauley, 'The late urological complications of total hysterectomy', *British Journal of Urology* 41 (1969), 602–4.
3. Pauline Bart, *Depression in Middle-Aged Women: Some Sociocultural Factors*, UCLA Dissertations (December 1967).

4. Caroline Myss quoted in Dr Christiane Northrup, *Women's Bodies, Women's Wisdom*, 163.

5. Ibid., 422.

CHAPTER SIX

1. Agnes Fyfe, *Moon and Plant*, 2nd ed., Stuttgart (German translation): Verlag Freies Geistesleben 1975.

CHAPTER SEVEN

1. Susan S. Weed, *Menopausal Years*, 105.

2. Rosemary Gladstar, *Herbal Healing for Women*, London: Bantam 1994, 237.

3. Ibid., 238.

SELECT BIBLIOGRAPHY

Boston Women's Health Collective, *Our Bodies, Our Selves*, New York: Simon & Schuster 1973.

Cabot, Dr Sandra, *The Menopause Handbook*, London: Boxtree 1996.

Campion, Kitty, *Holistic Herbal for Mother and Baby* and *Holistic Family Herbal* London: Bloomsbury 1996 and 1997.

Colbin, Annemarie, *Food and Healing*, New York: Ballantine 1986.

Coney, Sandra, *The Menopause Industry*, London: The Women's Press 1995.

Diamond, Harvey, *You Can Prevent Breast Cancer*, San Diego: Promotion Publishing n.d.

Gladstar, Rosemary, *Herbal Healing for Women*, London: Bantam 1994.

Glenville, Marilyn, *Natural Alternatives to HRT*, London: Kyle Cathie 1997.

Hall, Dorothy, *What's Wrong with You?*, South Melbourne: Thomas Nelson Australia 1984.

Kenton, Leslie, *Passage to Power*, London: Vermilion 1996.

McQuade Crawford, Amanda, *The Herbal Menopause Book*, Freedom, California: The Crossing Press 1996.

Northrup, Dr Christiane, *Women's Bodies, Women's Wisdom*, London: Piatkus 1995.

Patent, Arnold M., *You Can Have It All*, Dublin: Gill & Macmillan 1995.

Rogers, Carol, *The Women's Guide to Herbal Medicine*, London: Hamish Hamilton 1995.

Weed, Susan S., *Menopausal Years*, New York: Ash Tree Publishing 1992.

Resources Directory

ASSOCIATIONS

Action on Smoking and Health (ASH)
16 Fitzhardinge Street, London W1H 9PL
Tel. 0171 224 0743/Fax 0171 224 0471

Alcoholics Anonymous
Head Office, 11 Redcliffe Gardens, London, SW10 9BQ
Tel. 0171 352 9779

Other addresses include:

Alcoholics Anonymous
61 Great Dover Street, London SE1 4YF
Tel. 0171 403 0888
For the families of alcoholics.

Alcoholics Anonymous
109 South Circular Road, Dublin 8, Ireland
Tel. 01453 8998

British Anti Vivisection Association
PO Box 82, Kingswood, Bristol BS15 1YF
Tel./Fax 0117 909 5048

The British Association for Counselling
1 Regent Place, Rugby CV21 2PJ
Tel. 01788 550899

THE BRITISH SOCIETY FOR NUTRITIONAL MEDICINE
5 Somerhill Road, Hove, East Sussex, BN3 1RP
This society is interested in the effects of food on health.

THE EATING DISORDERS ASSOCIATION
Sackville Place, 44 Magdalen Street, Norwich NR3 1JU
Tel. 01603 621414

MYALGIC ENCEPHALOMYELITIS
The Moss, Third Avenue, Stanford-le-Hope, Essex SS17 8EL
Tel. 01375 642466
An organisation that helps sufferers from ME.

THE NATIONAL ENDOMETRIOSIS SOCIETY
50 Westminster Palace Garden, Artillery Row, London SW1P 1RL
Tel. 0171 222 2776

NATIONAL PURE WATER ASSOCIATION
Bank Farm, Aston Pigott, Westbury, Shrewsbury ST5 9HH
Tel. 01784 383445
This organisation is interested in the quality of water and sends out
regular newsletters.

THE SCHOOL OF MEDITATION
158 Holland Park Avenue, London W11 4UH
Tel. 0171 603 6116

THE SOCIETY OF ALEXANDER TECHNIQUE TEACHERS
20 London House, 266 Fulham Road, London SW10 9EL
Tel. 0171 282 0828

THE SOIL ASSOCIATION
86–88 Colston Street, Bristol BF1 5BB
Tel. 0117 290661

VEGAN INFORMATION CENTRE FOR IRELAND
c/o Mrs C. Gunn-King, 'Braidiyle', 120 Knockan Road, Ballydoghan
Td, near Broughshane, Ballymena, Northern Ireland BT43 7LL

THE VEGAN SOCIETY
7 Battle Road, St Leonards on Sea, East Sussex TN37 7AA
Tel. 01424 427393

THE VEGETARIAN SOCIETY
Parkdale, Dunham Road, Altrincham, Cheshire WA14 4QJ
Tel. 0161 928 0793

VIVA
12 Queens Square, Brighton, East Sussex, BN1 3FD
Tel. 01273 777688
Promotes vegan and vegetarian lifestyles, and sells an excellent
videotape, *A Diet for All Reasons*, by Dr Michael Clapper. Enclose an
SAE for information.

THE WOMEN'S HEALTH INFORMATION CENTRE
52 Featherstone Street, London EC17 8RJ
Tel. 0171 251 6580

WORLD SOCIETY FOR THE PROTECTION OF ANIMALS
2 Langley Lane, London SW8 1TJ
Tel. 0171 793 0540

BACH FLOWER REMEDIES

Available from homeopathic chemists and healthfood stores
throughout the country as well as from:

DR EDWARD BACH CENTRE
Mount Vernon, Sotwell, Wallingford, Oxfordshire OX10 0PZ
Tel. 01491 834678

DIAGNOSTIC TESTS

BIOLAB
The Stonehouse, 9 Weymouth Street, London W1M 3FF
Tel. 0171 636 5959
Tests for *Candida albicans*, parasites and blood disorders.

JOHN MORLEY
140 Harley Street, London NW1 1AH
Tel. 0171 487 2617
John Morley is an excellent vega tester.

SWANFLEET ORGANICS
Swanfleet Centre, 93 Fortress Road, London NW5 1AG

YORK NUTRITIONAL LABORATORY
Tudor House, Lysander Close, Clifton Moor, York YO3 4XB
Tel. 01904 690640
Blood tests for allergies.

ESSENTIAL OILS

BUTTERBUR & SAGE
7 Tessa Road, Reading RG1 8HH
Tel. 0118 950 5100
I have not encountered essential oils commercially available made to the extremely high standards this company employs. Most experienced aromatherapists tend to agree with me.

DANIELE RYMAN'S ESSENTIAL OILS
Can be purchased through mail order by writing to her at Marguerite Maury Clinic, Park Lane Hotel, Piccadilly, London W1Y 8BX. Tel. 0171 753 6708.

HERBAL SUPPLIERS
(See also 'Superfoods'.)

BALDWIN'S

173 Walworth Road, London, SE17 1RW

Tel. 0171 703 5550

Both Neal's Yard (see below) and Baldwin's supply small quantities of herbs by post.

BIOCARE LIMITED

54 Northfield Road, Kings Norton, Birmingham B30 1JH

Tel. 0121 433 3727

This company is run by a team of very experienced chemists and its unique formulations are extremely innovatory and of a very high standard. Biocare's products are available direct from the company and through herbal practitioners.

BIOFORCE UK LIMITED

2 Brewster Place, Irvine, Ayrshire, Scotland KA11 5DD

Tel. 01294 277344/Fax 01294 277922

I have dealt with this company now for many years and greatly admire the fact that, uniquely among herbal manufacturers, they use only freshly harvested herbs in their tinctures. The herbs are cultivated in a remote north-eastern corner of Switzerland between 800 to 1500 ft (250–600 metres) above sea level which encourages the condensation of the healing properties. This company is also particularly strict about harvesting protocols. For example, *Echinacea purpurea* is harvested when it reaches 3–4 ft (0.9–1.2 metres) in height when 50 per cent of the flowers are in bloom and 50 per cent in bud. Harvesting takes place after midday.

While many professional herbalists in practice, including myself, are particularly keen to harvest their own herbs freshly whenever possible, most commercially available herbal tinctures are not manufactured to Bioforce's particularly high standard. All Bioforce's products are readily available in healthfood shops.

BLACKMORES LIMITED

Unit 7, Poyle Tech Centre, Willow Road, Poyle, Colnbrook, Buckinghamshire SL3 0PD

This is a long-established Australian company who use organic herbs only, grown, harvested and processed to very high standards. What I particularly like about them is that they donate part of their turnover to environmental causes all over the world and are acutely aware of the strain on certain herbal resources worldwide, choosing instead to use alternatives in any new formulae rather than put a strain on any existing dwindling crops. They also have a very strict cruelty-free policy.

THE HERBAL APOTHECARY
103 The High Street, Syston, Leicester LE7 1BQ
Tel. 0116 602690
Also suppliers of powdered herbs and gelatine capsules. Please note: before ordering capsules specify if you require vegetarian ones in bulk, i.e. not less than one thousand at a time.

MARIGOLD HEALTH FOODS LIMITED
Unit 10, St Pancras Commercial Centre, London NW1 OBY
Tel. 0171 267 7368
This company sells superb nutritional yeast flakes under the brand name Engevita.

D. NAPIER & SONS
18 Bristol Place, Edinburgh, Scotland EH1 1EZ
Tel. 0131 225 5542

NEAL'S YARD APOTHECARY
2 Neal's Yard, Covent Garden, London WC2 9DP
Tel. 0171 371 7662

A. NELSON & COMPANY LIMITED
5 Endeavour Way, Wimbledon, London SW19 9UE
Tel. 0181 946 8527
Makes a superb range of herbal ointments and creams. I particularly like this company because, like Bioforce, they use as many fresh base herbs as they can. Scientific testing using chromatography proves that fresh herb preparations contain more of the active constituents and are

more stable compared to their counterparts manufactured from dried herbs.

THE NUTRI CENTRE
7 Park Cresent, London, W1N 3HE
Tel. 0171 436 5122/Fax 0171 436 5171
This efficiently mail orders almost every natural-health product you can think of, including a very wide range of books on natural health published throughout the world. This company, which is part of the Hale Clinic, offers the widest range of everything pertaining to natural health I have encountered anywhere in this country.

POTTERS
Leyland Mill Lane, Wigan, Lancashire WN1 2SB
Tel. 01942 34761
This company makes an excellent range of herbal syrups for coughs and colds, as well as herbal tonics.

PHYTO PRODUCTS LIMITED
3 Kings Mill Way, Heritage Lane, Mansfield, Notts NG18 5ER
Tel. 01623 644334
Sells fresh plant juices.

SANDRO CAFOLA
Design by Nature
Creltyard, Co. Carlow, Ireland
Supplier of seeds and herbs for planting.

SAVANT DISTRIBUTION LIMITED
7 Wayland Croft, Adel, Leeds LS16 8LA
Tel. 0113 230 1993
Supplier of nutritional oils, including Udo's oil.

SOLGAR VITAMINS LIMITED
Solgar House, Chiltern Centre, Asheridge Road, Chesham, Buckinghamshire HP5 2PY

This company supplies Earth Source, a good combination of many of the superfoods, together with single herbs and combination formulae which are grown and processed to an extremely high standard and mainly packed in vegetarian capsules.

XYNERGY HEALTH PRODUCTS
Lower Elsted, Midhurst, West Sussex GU29 0JT
Tel. 01730 813642
Suppliers of biogenic aloe vera juice which is organically grown and prepared in a unique way that does not denature or destroy its delicate enzymes and vital biogenic stimulators. I know of no comparable aloe vera juice on the market.

HOME KITS AND NATURAL PRODUCTS

COLGATE MEDICAL LIMITED
1 Fairacres Estate, Dedworth Road, Windsor, Berkshire SL4 4LE
Tel. 01753 860378
Supplier of Femina Cones (for testing and strengthening of pelvic-floor muscles).

COMMUNITY FOODS LIMITED
Micross, Brent Terrace, London NW2 1LT
Tel. 0181 208 2966
Supplier of natural sanitary towels.

CRYSTAL SPRING
Hentmore, Leighton Buzzard, Bedfordshire L47 0GH
Tel. 01296 662074
Supplier of natural deodorants.

CYTOPLAN
205 West Malvern Road, West Malvern, Worcestershire UR14 4BB
Tel. 01684 577777
Supplier of enema kits.

EDGAR CAYCE CENTRE
13 Prospect Terrace, New Kyo, Stanley, Co. Durham DH9 7TF
Tel. 01207 237696
Sells cold-pressed castor oil and pure woollen flannel poultices.

KITTY CAMPION
25 Curzon Street, Basford, Newcastle-under-Lyme, Staffordshire
ST5 0PD
Tel. 01782 711592/Fax 01782 713274
Supplier of tea tree pessaries, skin brushes, douche and enema kits and most of the composite herbal formulae mentioned in this book. (See also 'Practitioners', 'Residential Care and Workshops', 'Superfoods'.)

MARIGOLD HEALTH FOODS LIMITED
(See 'Herbal Suppliers' for address.)
Suppliers of the House of Mistry's natural soap to healthfood outlets.

THE NUTRI CENTRE
(See 'Herbal Suppliers'.)

SAVANT DISTRIBUTION LIMITED
(See 'Herbal Suppliers' for address.)
Supplier of the Green Power juicer.

VITA NATURA
PO Box 67F, Chessington, Surrey KT9 1YL
Supplier of an aloe vera cleaner for vegetables.

WHOLISTIC RESEARCH COMPANY
Brighthaven, Robin's Lane, Lolworth, Cambridge CB3 8HH
Tel. 01954 781074
Supplier of wheatgrass juice presses and reverse-osmosis water filters as well as enema/douche kits, juicers, slant boards, rebounders and natural-awareness fertility kits.

PRACTITIONERS

COLONIC IRRIGATION

Some colonic therapists in this country, including Kitty Campion (see below), are willing to offer Dr Bernard Jensen's Deep Tissue Cleansing programme, but some of the supplementation in it has been altered as it is both inorganic and chemical, and herbal substitutes have been used. Ask her for details.

KITTY CAMPION

(See 'Home Kits and Natural Products' for address.)
Kitty is the treasurer of the European Herbal Practitioners Association, an umbrella group of six different herbal schools and their associations throughout Europe. For details of your nearest practitioner, send her an SAE.

MANUAL LYMPHATIC DRAINAGE ASSOCIATION

8 Wittenham Lane, Dorchester on Thames, Oxon OX10 7JW
Tel. 01865 340385

NATURAL MEDICINE SOCIETY

Edith Lewis House, Back Lane, Ilkeston, Derby DE7 8EJ

RESIDENTIAL CARE AND WORKSHOPS

KITTY CAMPION

(See 'Home Kits and Natural Products' for address.)
Kitty runs residential natural healing workshops in the UK throughout the year. She also teaches these abroad.

THE PARK ATTWOOD THERAPEUTIC CLINIC

Trimpley, Bewdley, Worcestershire DY12 1RE
Tel. 01299 861444
Based on Rudolph Steiner's theories of anthraposophical medicine.

Ten Day Residential Meditational Teaching and Retreat
The Vipassana Trust, Dhamma Dipa, Harewood End, Hereford
HR2 8JS
Tel. 01989 730234

Tyringham Naturopathic Clinic
Newport Pagnell, Bucks MK16 9ER
Tel. 01908 610450
An excellent residential naturopathic clinic offering hydrotherapy, acupuncture, osteopathy, physiotherapy, massage, yoga and supervised fasts as well as light diets.

SUPERFOODS

Earthrise
All Seasons Healthcare, Southsea, Hants PO15 1PL
Tel. 01705 755660
Supplier of chlorella, spirulina, barley and wheat grasses.

Higher Nature Limited
The Nutrition Centre, Burwash Common, East Sussex TN19 7LX
Tel. 01435 882880
All Higher Nature's formulations come in vegetarian capsules and the company supplies flax seed oil in bottled form.

Kitty Campion
(See 'Home Kits and Natural Products' for address.)
Supplier of Nature's Superfoods, which contain most of the ingredients mentioned in Chapter Four.

Lamberts Healthcare Limited
1 Lamberts Road, Tunbridge Wells, Kent TN2 3EQ
Tel. 01892 546488
Lamberts make good-quality flax seed, evening primrose and borage seed oil. They also supply the Ultra Detox formulation.

SOLGAR VITAMINS LIMITED
(See 'Herbal Suppliers' for address.)
Supplier of Earth Source, a good combination of many of the superfoods.

XYNERGY HEALTH PRODUCTS
(See 'Herbal Suppliers' for address.)
This company imports extremely high-quality spirulina from the clean waters around New Zealand, so I particularly condone the purity and the excellence of their product.

INDEX OF HERBS

INDEX